⁘ *Day by Day*

Day by Day

Reflections on the Themes of the Torah from Literature, Philosophy, and Religious Thought

Edited by Chaim Stern

BEACON PRESS · BOSTON

Beacon Press
25 Beacon Street
Boston, Massachusetts 02108-2892
www.beacon.org

Beacon Press books
are published under the auspices of
the Unitarian Universalist Association of Congregations.

Printed in the United States of America

03 02 01 00 99 98 8 7 6 5 4 3 2 1

This book is printed on recycled acid-free paper that contains at least 20 percent postconsumer waste and meets the uncoated paper ANSI/NISO specifications for permanence as revised in 1992.

Text design by Scott-Martin Kosofsky at The Philidor Company, Boston

Library of Congress Cataloging-in-Publication Data
Day by day : reflections on the themes of the Torah from literature, philosophy, and religious thought / edited by Chaim Stern.
p. cm.
ISBN: 0–8070–2804–5 (cloth)
1. Bible. O.T. Pentateuch—Meditations. 2. Jewish devotional calendars. I. Stern, Chaim.
BS1225.4.D339 1998
222'. 106—DC21 98–7811

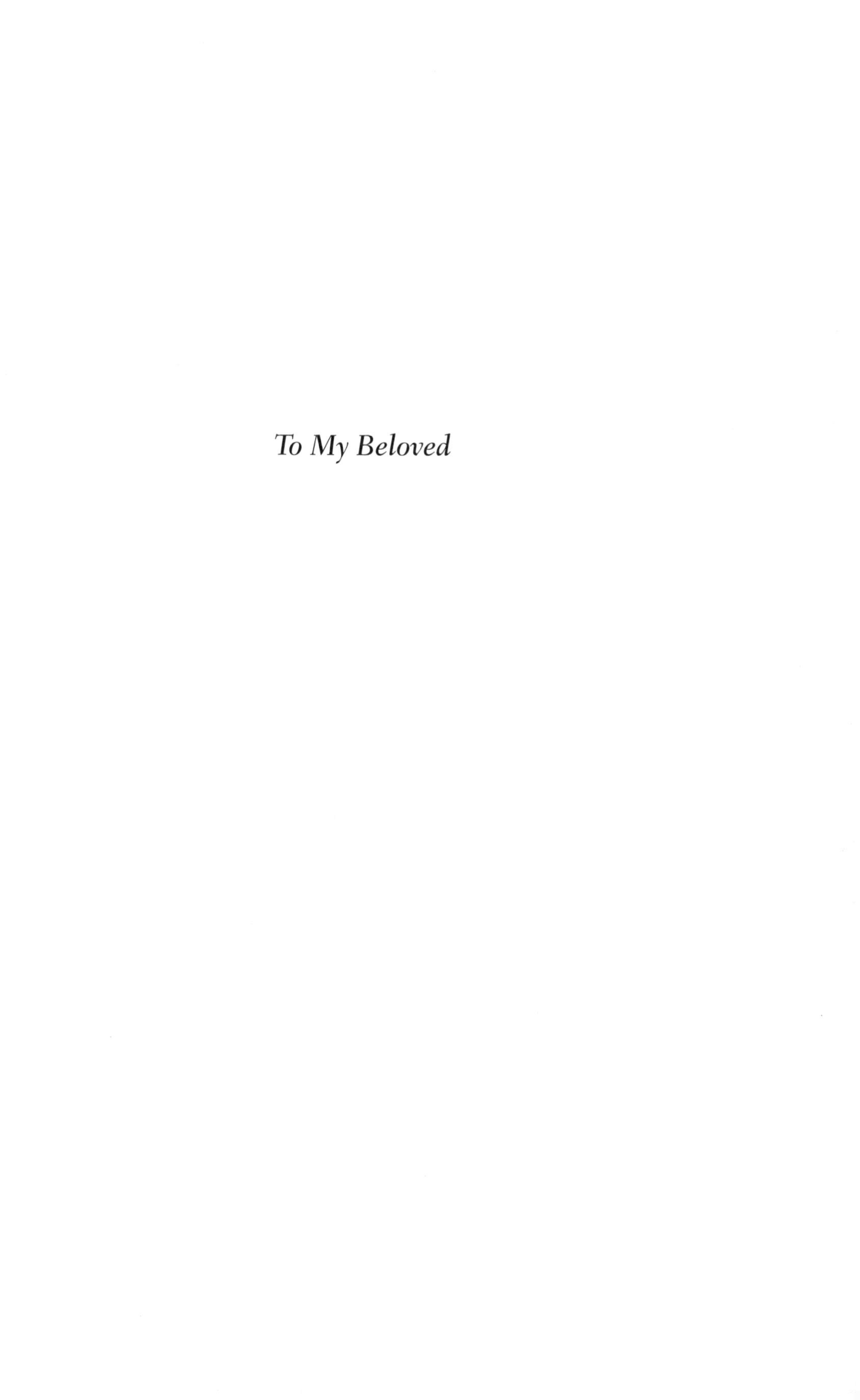

To My Beloved

∴ Contents

Preface

We live in a time of widespread hunger and homelessness, a time in which famine has taken and continues to take millions of lives, and in which malnutrition stunts the lives of many others. Many good people, aware of the plight of their neighbors, do what they can to nourish and shelter them.

And since we do not live by bread alone, there is widespread hunger and homelessness of the spirit; many are famished for lack of direction, a loss of any sense of meaning or "place." This book offers nourishment and shelter for the spirit.

Beginning with the Jewish tradition, *Day by Day* brings together voices from many of the world's cultures, from diverse times and places, and makes them available to people of any and every background. The voices are men's and women's, Western and Eastern, ancient and modern. All have been chosen because they have something to offer—a teaching, a moment of inspiration or insight, a provocation to further thought or self-examination, a signpost toward growth and understanding.

How this book is put together

In the Jewish tradition, the weeks of the year are arranged according to a cycle of readings from the Torah. The year begins at the "creation" of the world in Genesis and concludes at the end of the book of Deuteronomy, the fifth and final book of the Torah. This book follows that pattern. Each week offers a major theme, taken from the week's Torah reading. The week begins with a quotation from the Torah and a brief preface on the week's theme. On Sunday, the first day of the week, and on each subsequent day, there is a meditation, followed by other readings. The unattributed passages beginning each day of the week are mine. This book allows readers to connect, in very personal, varied, and flexible ways, to some of the central themes of the Torah.

⁂

How to use this book

This book can be used in a variety of ways.

You can read one day's passages at a time throughout the year, following the cycle of weekly readings from the Torah. In that case, start on the Sunday of that week, so that you complete the week's theme on the appropriate Shabbat. Or you might prefer to seek enlightenment by choosing a particular theme each week anywhere in the book. Or you might simply browse and see where your hidden need takes you.

The book can be used by a group of people in a classroom or study group, or by a group of people who come together weekly or occasionally in quest of spiritual and intellectual sustenance. It might be best if the group members knew in advance what would be discussed; on the other hand, others might benefit equally from greater spontaneity.

However you use this book, may you find in it some of the joy of discovery, of challenge, and of comfort, that I found in making it.

⁂

Some people I want to thank

Three people read an early version of this book and made critical comments and suggestions that improved it. They are Rabbi H. Leonard Poller, Rabbi Donna Berman, and Cantor Edward Graham. Rabbi John D. Rayner, in London, with whom I edited the new prayer book of the Liberal Movement of Great Britain, gave me more help than he knows. That book, *Siddur Lev Chadash,* shares some of its form and content with this one. And Seymour Rossel helped this book come out into the light, and Mel Wolfson (Mosheh ben Nachman) was unfailingly helpful in his meticulous reading of the text. Elliot Stevens and Bonny

Fetterman came along like the cavalry at a dark moment in the winding road toward publication. Finally, there are the people of the Chug Shabbat of Temple Beth El of Northern Westchester. For a year we wrestled with the contents of this book. They strengthened it.

—Chaim Stern

1 *Creation*

The Week of B'reishit
Genesis 1:1–6:8

This week's portion, *B'reishit* (Genesis 1), begins the book of Genesis with an epic poem about the creation of the universe; it starts with familiar words: *In the beginning God created heaven and earth. . . . God said, "Let there be light," and there was light* (1:1), and when all has been created, we learn that *God found it very good* (1:31). Our Sidra invites us to reflect on the miracle of creation, on the wondrous nature of all being: how precious it is, how gratefully we need to accept the gift of creation, we who are part of the creation and creators ourselves!

Sunday

Forms of Prayer

God of dawn and dusk, open my eyes to the beauty of the world and its goodness. Your peace brings all life together: through the love of mother and child, the loyalty of friends, and the companionship of animal and human. As I awaken to the world You have made, I know this harmony again and Your presence in it. With all creation I respond with praise, and give thanks to Your name. Amen.

Midrash

Before creating this world,
God made world after world and discarded each of them, saying: This does not please me.
At last God created this one and said:
—This one is good!
God then made Adam and showed him all the world.
God said: Look at this beautiful world! Take good care of it; do not abuse or destroy it, for I am done with making worlds. If you ruin this one, there will be none to follow it.

Tao / cs

The earth is not yours to remake.
A sacred vessel, it breaks at your touch.
You lose it even as you reach for it:
Let it be. Look:
Some things go forward, some are left behind.
Some things are hot, some are cold.
Some things are strong, some are weak.
Some things are born, some things die:
All things are only for a time.
The wise do not overreach,
The wise do not overspend,
The wise do not overrate themselves.

Chasidic The Lekhivitzer Rebbe said: The Torah begins with the word בראשית, *b'reishit*, which can be understood to say, God created the world "for the sake of the beginning." All the Creator asks is that you make a beginning in the right direction.

Monday

Gates of Prayer Heaven and earth, O God, are the work of Your hands. The roaring seas and the life within them issue forth from Your creative will. The mysteries of life and death, of growth and decay, alike display the miracle of Your creative power. The universe is one vast wonder proclaiming Your wisdom and singing Your greatness.

Chasidic The Baal Shem Tov used to teach: Believe that each day the world is created anew, and that you yourself are born anew each morning. Then your faith will grow, and every day you will find yourself newly eager to serve God.

Chasidic Rabbi Bunam said: God created "a beginning." The universe is always incomplete, always beginning. Unlike a vessel that one works at and finishes, putting it aside, it requires continuous labor and unceasing renewal by creative forces. Let these forces pause one second, and the universe would revert to primal chaos.

The Bratzlaver Rebbe said: Always say, *The world was created for my sake.* Never say, *What does all this have to do with me?* And do your share to add some improvement, to supply something that is missing, and leave the world a little better for your sojourn in it.

Chasidic

⁘

Tuesday

Praise the Eternal One, O my soul!
O God, how very great You are!
Arrayed in glory and majesty,
You wrap Yourself in light as with a garment,
You stretch out the heavens like a curtain.
The clouds are Your chariot;
You ride on the wings of the wind.
How manifold are Your works, Eternal One!
In wisdom You have made them all;
The earth is full of Your creations.
I will sing to the Eternal One all my days;
I will sing praises to my God as long as I live.

From *Psalm 104*

I need the trees that bear fruit, I need the barren trees.

Midrash

Every April God rewrites the Book of Genesis.

William Blake

But the first vernal days are younger. Spring steals in shyly, a tall, naked child in her pale gold hair, amidst us the un-innocent, skeptics in wool mufflers, prudes in gumshoes and Grundies with head-colds. Very secretly the old field cedars sow the wind with the freight of their ancient pollen. A grackle in the willow croaks and sings in the uncertain, ragged voice of a boy. The marshes brim, and walking is a muddy business. Oaks still are barren and secretive. On the lilac tree only the twin buds suggest her coming maturity and flowering. But there in the pond float the inky masses of those frog's eggs, visibly life in all its rawness, its elemental shape and purpose. Now is the moment when the secret of life could be discovered, yet no one finds it.

Donald Culross Peattie

Wednesday

From *Psalm 148*

Halleluyah! Praise the Eternal One.
Praise God from the heavens,
praise God in the heights.
Give praise, all God's angels,
give praise, all God's hosts.
Give praise, sun and moon;
give praise, you shining stars.
Give praise, you highest heavens,
and you waters above the heavens.
Let them praise the name of the Eternal One,
at whose command they were created,
who established them to abide forever,
by a decree that does not change.

J. E. Boodin

There is the laughter which is born out of the pure joy of living, the spontaneous expression of health and energy—the sweet laughter of the child. This is a gift of God. There is the warm laughter of the kindly soul which heartens the discouraged, gives health to the sick and comfort to the dying. . . . There is, above all, the laughter that comes from the eternal joy of creation, the joy of making the world new, the joy of expressing the inner riches of the soul—laughter that triumphs over pain and hardship in the passion for an enduring ideal, the joy of bringing the light of happiness, of truth and beauty into a dark world. This is divine laughter par excellence.

Pablo Casals

There are times when I feel like a boy. As long as you are able to admire and to love, you are young. And there is so much to admire and to love. . . . Look at the sea, the sky, trees, flowers! A single tree—what a miracle it is! What a fantastic, wonderful creation this world is, with such diversity. That is the law of nature—diversity.

Thursday

From *Psalm 148*

Praise God from the earth:
crocodiles, creatures of the deep,
Fire and hail, snow and mist,
storm winds that obey the divine command;
Mountains and hills,
fruit trees and cedars,
Animals and cattle,
creatures that creep and birds on the wing.
Let them praise the Eternal One,
whose name is exalted,
whose majesty spans heaven and earth.

Joseph Braddock

Now I have no fear—my mind is at peace.
See the rain that falls straight and gentle on flowers,
On golding oaks, on greying willows, on wet leaves . . .
If I could give you riches it were these . . .
Oh! now the garden is all music under rain,
Waiting a shout, a live fanfare when the sun comes out.
My peace combines with joy, and is all bliss.
Today how bright earth shines in the garment of God.

Anonymous

I wonder if
anything is impossible
to a God
who can make
evergreen trees with black trunks
cast blue shadows
on white snow.

Austin O'Malley

To create a little flower is the labour of ages.

Friday

⁘

Gates of Prayer / cs

How can I know You? Where can I find You? You are as close to me as breathing, yet You are farther than the farthermost star. You are as mysterious as the vast solitudes of night, yet as familiar to me as the light of the sun. Your goodness passes before my eyes continually, in the wonder and beauty of this world.

> *By Your word the heavens were made,*
> *and all their host by the breath of Your mouth.*

You have given me the power to hear the world's music, as the winds play their song upon the leaves of the wood.

Midrash

The goal of creation is redemption.

Chasidic

The Neshkizer Rebbe said: To every one of us creation comes as a new thing, again and again, and so we are bound to acknowledge the Creator again and again.

Albert Friedlander

Va-y'hi erev, va-y'hi voker:
and it was evening, and it was morning:
the next day of Creation.
O God, let us be worthy of it.

⁘ Shabbat

You made me in Your image, a creature able to walk in Your footsteps; You made me a creator, a dreaming child in a universe filled with wonder. Let me look with grateful eyes upon the world, to see Your creation with new eyes, and draw new pictures in the sand, visible dreams of an invisible love.

ON NOT UNDERSTANDING, WHICH IS ZEN

James Kirkup

Out of all the world
take this forest.
Out of all the forest
take this tree.
Out of all the tree
take this branch.
Out of all the branch
take this leaf.
And on this leaf
that is like no other
observe this drop of rain
that is like no other.
And on this single drop
observe the reflection
of leaves and branches,
of the entire tree,
of the forest
of all the world—
Then only
will you see
the stars beyond
the light of day.

נח

2 *The Yetzer*

The Week of Noach
Genesis 6:9–11:32

The Sidra called *Noach* (Genesis 6) is named for Noah, who—in the face of catastrophe—becomes the bearer of the hopes of human and animal life. This catastrophe (the Flood) is our own doing, for "the earth became corrupt before God; the earth was filled with violence." Noah builds an ark, the rains fall, and the earth is devastated. When the waters subside, God thinks: *Never again will I bring doom upon the world on account of what people do, for the inclination (YETZER) of the human heart is wicked from youth onward* (8:21).

Such is our inclination—but we can transcend that inclination, transforming its energy into a power for good.

Sunday

Gates of Prayer

Guard my tongue from evil and my lips from deceitful speech. Purify my heart that there be in it no malice, but a prayer for the good of all. Lead me in the ways of righteousness, that I may hurt no one; and help me to bring the blessing of love to others. Open my heart to do Your will. Strengthen my desire to obey Your commandments. May my thoughts and my prayers be acceptable to You, O God, my Rock and my Redeemer.

Chasidic

I run about the world keeping my hand closed. Nobody knows what is in it. I go up to everyone and ask: *What do you suppose I have in my hand?* And every person thinks: *What I most want must be hidden there.* So everyone runs after me. But when at last I open my hand, it is empty. And that is what the Yetzer is—a "nothing" after which we run.

It is the favorite stratagem of our passions to sham a retreat, and to turn sharp round upon us at the moment we have made up our minds that the day is our own. *George Eliot*

There are only two kinds of folk: the righteous who believe themselves sinners; the rest, sinners, who believe themselves righteous. *Blaise Pascal*

Rabbi Michal said: When the Yetzer tries to tempt us to sin, it tempts us to become all too righteous. *Chasidic*

⁘

Monday

Guard me from despising others for their weaknesses, and, whatever my faults and weaknesses may be, let me not come to despise myself. Instead, encourage me to try harder to see the good in others, that I may come to see that there is strength and goodness in everyone—including me!

Rabbi Simeon ben Elazar said: An iron bar in a smithy—as long as it is in the fire you may mold it into any implement you like; so with the Yetzer. *Period of Mishnah*

Rabbi Pinchas of Koretz entered the House of Study, and his disciples fell into a profound silence. He asked: "What were you talking about just now?" "We were saying how afraid we were that the Yetzer will pursue us." "Don't worry," said he. "You haven't reached that point yet. Right now, you are still pursuing it." *Chasidic*

Rabbi Abraham said: I have learned a new way of acting from the wars of Frederick king of Prussia. There is no need to attack the enemy by a direct approach. You can retreat, marshal your forces, and circle around and strike from the rear. So do not strike straight at evil but pull back and draw upon the sources of divine power, then circle around evil, bend it, and transform it into its opposite. *Chasidic*

Marquis de Vauvenargues Our actions are neither so good nor so evil as our impulses.

Chasidic A Chasid complained to the Seer of Lublin that he was tormented by evil desire and had become despondent over it. The rabbi said to him: Guard yourself from becoming despondent above all else, for it is worse and more harmful than sin. When the Yetzer awakens desires in us, it is not concerned with plunging us into sin, but with plunging us into despair by way of our sinning.

Tuesday

⁘

If I am neither as bad as I am at my worst nor as good as I am at my best, I am in this like everyone I know. Keep this knowledge before me, O my soul, and teach me how to forgive failings—my own and those of others.

Friedrich Nietzsche Whoever battles with monsters had better see to it that it does not turn him into a monster. And if you gaze long into an abyss, the abyss will gaze back into you.

Blaise Pascal What a monster, what a chaos, what a contradiction, what a prodigy! Judge of all things, imbecile worm of the earth; depository of truth, a sink of uncertainty and error; the pride and refuse of the universe!

Talmud Rav Judah bar Rav Illai expounded: In the time to come the Holy One will bring the Yetzer and slaughter it in the presence of the righteous and the wicked. It will appear to the righteous as a tall mountain; to the wicked it will look like a thread. Both will weep. The righteous will say: "How could we have conquered so mighty a mountain?" The wicked will say: "How could we have failed to overcome this thin thread?" The Holy One, too, will be astonished, as it is said (Zechariah 8:6): *Thus said the God of all being: If it will seem a wonder to the remnant of this people . . . so will it seem a wonder to Me.*

Look how much we thus expel of sin, so much we expel of virtue: for the matter of them both is the same; remove that, and we remove them both alike.

John Milton

⁘

Wednesday

What I need is to live a whole life, daring but not driven, caring and not careless. Teach me not to be afraid of myself, yet not to be so confident that I don't look before I take my next step. Teach me to listen to my inner voice, but to remember that others, too, have voices.

The sages once took counsel and said: The time is ripe for our prayers to be answered. Let us ask that the Yetzer be delivered into our hands.

They prayed with fervor and met with success: the Yetzer was given over to them. Along with their captive came the warning: If you kill your captive you will kill your world.

Taking note of this, they merely kept the Yetzer under restraint. After three days they sent messengers out to all the Land of Israel. These came back and told them: *Not a single new-laid egg anywhere, those three days.* The sages released their captive.

Talmud

Every vice you destroy has a corresponding virtue, which perishes along with it.

Anatole France

When you look over your own vices, winking at them, as it were, with sore eyes, why are you with regard to those of your friends as sharp-sighted as an eagle . . . ?

Horace

⁘

I think of the many ways in which I cannot help but go wrong! Should I then do as little as possible? In that way, I will certainly go wrong!

Chasidic The Baal Shem Tov said: Satan's chief joy is to convince me that an evil deed is a Mitzvah. For when I am weak and commit an offense, knowing that it is wrong, I will probably repent of it. But if I believe it to be a good deed, does it stand to reason I will repent of it?

Talmud At first the Yetzer is like the thread of a spider's web;
in the end it is as thick as wagon-rope.

Period of Mishnah The power of the Yetzer is overwhelming, and few of any generation escape from its evil effects. The only way to mold it is through the words of Torah, which are like fire.

Joseph ben Judah Aknin Those few are the only ones who are truly free, who are not slaves to but masters of their passions.

John Donne

I am a little world made cunningly
Of Elements, and an Angellike sprite,
But black sinne hath betraid to endlesse night
My worlds both parts, and (oh) both parts must die.

I am a glutton at times, though not necessarily for food and drink. I binge on other things, including resentment. When that happens, keep me from thinking that I need to give up my appetites, when what I really need to learn is how to keep my balance.

Rabbi Samuel bar Nachman said in the name of Rabbi Jonathan: Here the Yetzer seduces you, there the Yetzer betrays you. *Talmud*

The Yetzer yearns only for the forbidden. *Talmud*

Rabbi Haggai was ill one Yom Kippur day, and Rabbi Mana paid him a visit.

I am terribly thirsty, Rabbi Haggai told him.

Since you are sick, you may drink, said his visitor.

Rabbi Mana left and returned later in the day. He asked Rabbi Haggai: Are you still thirsty?

Rabbi Haggai answered: My thirst went away the minute you gave me permission to drink!

We are conscious of an animal in us, which awakens in proportion as our higher nature slumbers. It is reptile and sensual, and perhaps cannot be wholly expelled; like the worms which, even in life and health, occupy our bodies. Possibly we may withdraw from it, but never change its nature. I fear that it may enjoy a certain health of its own; that we may be well, yet not pure. . . . Who knows what sort of life would result if we had attained to purity? . . . Yet the spirit can for a time pervade and control every member and function of the body, and transmute what in form is the grossest sensuality into purity and devotion. *Unknown*

Keep me from sinning out of embarrassment: doing things because others are doing them, and saying "yes" when I really want to say "no"—only because it might be awkward. Teach me to learn how to go a straight, simple way.

Augustine of Hippo

Here, then, O God, is the memory still vivid in my mind. I would not have committed that theft alone: my pleasure in it was not what I stole but that I stole: yet I would not have enjoyed doing it, I would not have done it, alone. O friendship unfriendly, unanalysable attraction for the mind, greediness to do damage for the mere sport and jest of it, desire for another's loss with no gain to oneself or vengeance to be satisfied! Someone cries, "Come on, let's do it!"—and we would be ashamed to be ashamed!

Yiddish proverb

We fall not because we are weak
but because we think we are strong.

Tao/cs

Colors blind,
Sounds deafen,
Flavors dull the palate.
Desires madden the heart,
Ambitions stun the mind.
Between the inner and the outer eye,
The wise know which to choose.

Chasidic

Turn aside from evil and do good (Psalm 34:15). The Gerer Rebbe said: If you find it difficult to follow this advice, try doing good first, and the evil will automatically depart from you.

3 *Our Way*

The Week of Lech L'cha
Genesis 12:1–17:27

In the Sidra *Lech L'cha* ("Go forth") (Genesis 12), Abraham and Sarah and their household are told: *Go forth from your native land and from your father's house to the land that I will show you* (12:1). Thus their great adventure begins, and above all it is an inner journey, symbolized by the establishment of a covenant between Abraham and God. The Sidra sums it up with the words: *Walk along before Me and be pure of heart.* (17:1).

We begin a journey at birth, whose destination we discover as we go along. In our journey we learn, as did Abraham and Sarah, that wonders and trials abound along the way.

Sunday

Give me a quiet heart, and help me to hear the still, small voice that speaks within me. It calls me to come closer to You and to grow in Your likeness. It teaches me to do my work faithfully, even when no one's eye is upon me, so that I may come to the end of each day feeling that I used its gifts wisely and faced its trials bravely. It counsels me to judge others less harshly and to love them more freely. It persuades me to see the divinity in everyone I meet.

Mishnah

Rabbi [Judah the Prince] said:
What is a right path to choose?
One noble in itself,
he answered,
and noble in effect.

Know what is beyond— what above:
an eye that sees,
an ear that hears,
a hand that writes.

Mishnah

Know this, and you will be free:
Where do you come from?
Where are you going?
To whom do you give an account?

Talmud

I shall walk before the Eternal in the land of the living. (Psalm 116:9) That is to say: I shall walk before the Holy One not only in the privacy of my home, but amidst the crowd, even in the public square.

Monday

As I walk toward an unseen end, I grow anxious and fearful. And when I call to mind the good companions who once shared my journey, the pain of their loss returns. I feel like crying. Yet in a strange way they seem to help me move along my way, and we walk together.

Mishnah

Rabbi Yochanan ben Zakkai said to them:
What is a right path?
Rabbi Eliezer said: A good eye.
Rabbi Joshua said: A good friend.
Rabbi Yosé said: A good neighbor.
Rabbi Simeon said: Foresight.
Rabbi Elazar said: A good heart.
He said to them:
I prefer the words of Elazar ben Arach,
for his words include all of yours.

Mencius

The path of duty lies in what is near:
why seek for it in what is remote?

Even when a virtue is second nature to you, do not be overconfident and say, "It can never leave me." There is always the possibility that it will. Therefore, never neglect an opportunity to do good, and thus to strengthen yourself in that habit. *Maimonides*

⁘

Tuesday

Along my way, I stumble and fall. There are times when I feel as though all the signposts haved been taken down. Help me to feel that wherever I go, You are with me. Then when I fall, I will get up; when I go astray, I will not forever be lost.

A man was on a journey that took him through a forest. There he lost his way. After several days of wandering, he encountered another. To this one he appealed: Can you show me the way out of this forest? The other replied: I too have lost my way. Each path I have taken has been wrong. But at least I know what paths not to take. Let us search for the way out together. *Chasidic*

In the middle of the journey of our life
I came to myself in a dark wood
where the straight way was lost.
Dante Alighieri

There is a way that seems right,
yet its end is the way to death.
Who heed instruction are on the path to life;
who reject reproof lose their way.
Proverbs

The man ran down the slip at the Staten Island ferry and flung himself into space, across the patch of water, landing on the boat with a terrific crash. He picked himself up, breathing hard, dusting off his trousers. "I made it!" *Anonymous*

"So what was your hurry?" asked a passenger. "We're coming *in*."

⁘

You have always been with us; before we call, You are there; before we ask, Your answer comes. This is true for all of us, Your children, with whom You made a covenant long ago. You called us to walk in Your ways. We saw a sign high above us. Today, as I lift up my eyes, show me a rainbow, a sign that we are still together.

The Dhammapada

Our way looks right to each of us,
but what of the truth?
That is weighed beyond our sight.
Heaven prefers righteousness and justice to sacrifice.

Sufi

A one-legged dragon said to the centipede: How do you manage all those legs? It is all I can do to manage one!
—To tell you the truth, replied the centipede, I do not manage them at all.

Tao

Unawareness of one's feet is the
mark of shoes that fit.
Unawareness of one's waist is the
mark of a belt that fits.
Unawareness of right and wrong is the
mark of a mind at ease.

Midrash

May your heart carry your feet.

Yesterday I asked for a sign; now teach me to see it in what happens when I am my best self, quiet within, just and loving without. Perhaps then I will see that rainbow, or others will see it on my face.

Tao / cs

Be useful and feel well used,
Be hospitable and feel at home,
Trust and you will earn trust.

Mencius

If you would live greatly,
never think to make your words sincere,
your actions resolute:
Simply speak and do what is right.

Chasidic

In expounding the Torah, Rabbi Yitzchak Meir of Ger came to these words of Jacob to his servant (Genesis 32:18): *When Esau my brother meets you and asks you, saying: Whose are you, and where are you going, and who are these before you?* He said to his disciples: Note how much Esau's questions resemble the saying of our sages: *Know this, and you will be free: Where do you come from? Where you are going? To whom do you give an account?* Note it well, for when you reflect on these three things you need much self-examination, lest it be Esau asking within you. For Esau too can ask these questions, and bring heaviness into the heart.

Do not neglect your own task in order to take up a task for which someone else is responsible, however great that other task may be. Once you have discerned your own task, attend to it.

⁘

The covenant You made long ago with Your children is one I can renew. You offer it to me without conditions. Help me always to be faithful to its terms: You will be You, and I will be me.

Chasidic

Rabbi Yaakov Yitzchak of Pzhysha, known as the Yehudi ("Jew"), once told his disciple Rabbi Bunam to go on a journey. Bunam did not ask any questions but left the town with a number of other Chasidim and just followed the highway. Toward noon they came to a village and stopped at an inn. The innkeeper was so pleased to have such devout guests that he invited them to have dinner with him. Rabbi Bunam sat down in the main room, while the others went in and asked all sorts of questions about the meat that was to be served them: whether the animal was unblemished, what the butcher was like, and just how carefully the meat had been salted. At that a man in rags spoke up. He had been sitting behind the stove and still had his staff in his hand. Oh you Chasidim! he cried. You make a big to-do about what you put in your mouths being clean, but you don't worry half as much about the purity of what comes out of your mouths!

And before Rabbi Bunam could reply, the wayfarer vanished: it had been Elijah the prophet. Then the rabbi understood why his teacher had sent him on this journey.

Mishnah

Heaven joins the feast
when Torah is in the mouth
and heart of the invited guests.
For Wisdom calls us, saying:
Come, eat of my bread
and drink of my wine.
Leave folly and live;
walk in the way of understanding.

✦

Today I turn to You—but how can I not? Wherever I turn, know it or not, I turn to You! You bind me to You with invisible cords—my words, my thoughts, my hopes, my fears, my spirit's yearnings, my loyalties—these all find in You their center, even when I am not mindful of it. And since this is Shabbat, the day You called a sign between us, a reminder that You create the world anew each and every moment, help me to be aware that You are the One who forms me, and that even when I feel lost, I can turn, and find You within me!

Happy is the people that know the joyful shout; they walk, O God, in the light of Your presence. (Psalm 89:16) The Baal Shem Tov said: When the people depend not on heroes but themselves know "the joyful shout," then they will walk in "the light of Your presence." *Chasidic*

Simeon the Righteous was one of the [last] members of the Great Assembly. He would say: *Mishnah*

The world stands on three things:
On the Torah,
On worship,
On deeds of loving kindness.

Rabban Simeon ben Gamaliel said: *Mishnah*

The world sustains itself by three things:
By truth,
by justice,
and by peace.

ויירא

4 *God*

The Week of Vayeira
Genesis 18:1–22:24

In the Sidra *Vayeira* (Genesis 18), God discloses the divine intention to destroy Sodom and Gomorrah, knowing that Abraham will attempt to save these cities from destruction. God says: *Shall I hide from Abraham what I am about to do? Yet I have acknowledged him, so that he may teach his children and those who come after him to keep the way of the Eternal, doing what is right and just* (18:19). Such stories challenge our understanding of God. This is especially true of the last tale, in which Abraham, in obedience to God's will, is about to put his son Isaac to the knife as a sacrifice and is restrained only at the last moment.

Sunday

cs / Gates of Prayer

God enthroned by Israel's praise,
God my hope,
for You alone my soul waits in silence.
By day extend Your steadfast love,
and at night I shall sing to You:
a prayer to the God of my life.
Praised be the Eternal One
who day by day upholds me,
the God who is my Help.

Midrash Rabbi Simeon ben Yochai said: *You are My witnesses, says the Eternal, and I am God* (Isaiah 43:10). When you are My witnesses, I am God; but when you are not My witnesses, I am, as it were, not God.

Three things conspire together in my eyes
To bring the remembrance of You ever before me:
The starry heavens,
The broad green earth,
The depths of my heart.

Solomon ibn Gabirol

Two things fill the mind with ever new and increasing admiration and awe, the oftener and the more steadily we reflect on them: the starry heavens above and the moral law within.

Immanuel Kant

God is a scientist, not a magician.

Albert Einstein

It is terrible to watch a man who has the incomprehensible in his grasp, does not know what to do with it, and sits playing with a toy called God.

Leo Tolstoy

⁘

Monday

Reason's last step is the recognition
that there are an infinite number of things
that are beyond it.

Blaise Pascal

The universe is here, and among other things it has produced us. It contains among other things . . . beings capable of love and unselfish sacrifice, capable of appreciating beauty and creating it, and finding everywhere beauty and order. In fact, . . . the facts of disorder, suffering and evil are difficulties for us only because there is something in us which can stand, as it were, apart from them and say they ought not to be. The problem of evil is only a problem because of the existence of good. The problem of disorder is only a problem when we know what order is. . . . I always find it incredible that order and beauty and heroism come about by accident, and that the mindless movings of innumerable electrons and the rest going on for long enough could, in fact, produce among other things beings who could know them and criticize the electrons and each other.

T. R. Milford

Claude G. Montefiore

Hard as the world is to explain *with* God,
it is harder yet without God.

Michael Drayton

Think not it was these colors, red and white,
Laid but on flesh that could affect me so,
But something else, which thought holds under lock
And hath no key of words to open it.
They are the smallest pieces of the mind
That pass the narrow organ of the voice;
The great remain behind in that vast orb
Of the apprehension, and are never born.

Tuesday

cs / Gates of Prayer

I know You, yet I cannot name You.
I say the word "God,"
scarcely knowing what I mean:
how can I know You?
I say "God of Abraham, God of Isaac,
  and God of Jacob,
God of Sarah, God of Rebekah, God of Leah,
  and God of Rachel":
What did You mean to them?
What might You mean to me?
Yet here I am; help me:
I cannot name You; help me to love You.

Chasidic

If you divide your life between God and the world, through giving the world "what belongs to it" to save for God "what belongs to God," you are denying God the service the Holy One demands: to hallow the everyday in the world and the soul.

Midrash

God is compassionate like a father,
and comforts like a mother.

The heart has its reasons
that reason knows nothing of.

Blaise Pascal

One does not serve God with the spirit only, but with the whole of one's nature, without any subtractions.

Martin Buber

Let the heart of all rejoice who seek the Eternal (I Chronicles 16:10). The Apelier Rebbe said: When I seek a particular object, I don't feel glad until I find it. But when I seek the Eternal, my heart rejoices from the very act of seeking.

Chasidic

⁘

Wednesday

Something is very gently,
invisibly, silently,
pulling at me—a thread
or net of threads
finer than cobweb and as
elastic. I haven't tried
the strength of it. No barbed hook
pierced and tore me. Was it
not long ago this thread
began to draw me? Or
way back? Was I
born with its knot about my
neck, a bridle? Not fear
but a stirring
of wonder makes me
catch my breath when I feel
the tug of it when I thought
it had loosened itself and gone.

Denise Levertov

Canst thou by searching find out God?

Job 11:7

Do not speak of God much. After a very little conversation on the highest nature, thoughts desert us and we run into formalism.

Ralph Waldo Emerson

Uri Zvi Greenberg

God, You taunt me: "Flee if you can!"
But I can't flee.
For when I turn away from You, angry and heartsick,
With a vow on my lips like a burning coal:
"I will not see You again"—
I can't do it.
And I turn back
And knock on Your door,
Tortured with longing.
As though You had sent me a love-letter.

Havelock Ellis

God is an unutterable Sigh in the human heart, said the old German mystic. And therewith said the last word.

Thursday

Martin Buber

Many true believers know how to talk to God but not about God.

cs / Gates of Prayer

Source of all being, I turn to You as did those who came before me. They beheld You in the heavens; they felt You in their hearts; they sought You in their lives.

Now their quest is mine. Help me, O God, to see the wonder of being. Give me the courage to search for truth. Teach me the path to a better life.

Bachya ibn Pakuda

We must not take the divine attributes literally; they are metaphors. Any representation of God forming itself in our minds applies to something other than God.

Sandra M. Schneiders

Metaphors for God drawn from human experience can easily be literalized. While we are immediately aware that the personal God is not really a rock or a mother eagle, it is easy enough to imagine that God is really a king or a father.

Alfred North Whitehead

God is in the world, or nowhere, creating continually in us and around us. This creative principle is everywhere, in animate and so-called inanimate matter, in the ether, water, earth, human hearts. . . . In so far as . . . [we] partake of this creative process . . . [do] we partake of the divine, of God.

> The more we understand individual things,
> the more we understand God.

Baruch Spinoza

Traditionally we think of God as being "above." In childhood we got the impression that God is up in the sky somewhere. . . . I would have you think of God as underneath, like the foundation of a skyscraper, or the concrete foundations of a giant bridge. We do not have to reach for love, courage, tolerance, faith; they are foundation qualities.

Eilferd E. Peterson

⁘

Friday

> God be in my head,
> And in my understanding;
> God be in my eyes,
> And in my looking;
> God be in my mouth,
> And in my speaking;
> God be in my heart,
> And in my thinking;
> God be at my end,
> And in my departing.

Sarum Missal

Abbayé taught: What is *Kiddush ha-Shem*, the sanctification of the Divine Name? It is conduct that leads people to love the name of Heaven.

Talmud

> Now from the world the light of God is gone,
> And we in darkness move and are afraid,
> Some blaming heaven for the evil done,
> And some each other for the part they played.
> And all their woes on God are strictly laid,
> For being absent from these earthly ills,

Robert Nathan

Who set the trees to be the noontide shade,
And placed the stars in beauty of the hills.
Turn not away and cry that all is lost;
It is not so, the world is in God's hands
As once it was when Egypt's mighty host
Rode to the sea and vanished in the sands.
For still the heart, by love and pity wrung,
Finds the same God as when the world was young.

James Russell Lowell

God is in all that liberates and lifts,
In all that humbles, sweetens, and consoles.

Shabbat

Gates of Prayer

True prayer is the opening of our hearts Godward, and the answer is a flow of light and influence from God.

Prayer means a consciousness full of God's presence and of our relation with the Divine.

Chasidic

Rabbi Baruch's grandson Yechiel was once playing hide-and-seek with another boy. He hid himself well and waited for his playmate to find him. When, after a long wait, he came out of his hiding-place, the other was nowhere to be seen. It seemed his friend had not looked for him at all!

That made him cry and, crying, he ran to his grandfather and complained of his friend. Then tears brimmed in Rabbi Baruch's eyes, and he said: God says the same thing: *I hide, but no one comes looking for Me.*

Gregory Vlastos

If one is not clear about God, one will always tend to shy away toward something more accessible, like one's own conscious states. To talk about commitment brings one face to face with the question of God, so that one cannot dodge it. . . . God is that within and beyond the universe which expresses the greatest good which now is and ever can be: the direction of life against death, the direction of unity against discord, the direction of creation and increasing growth against destruction and decay. God is the power of good in all its various forms: in the order and structure of inorganic matter, in the process of growth and sensitivity in the realm of life, in the conditions of intelligence, co-operation, appreciation and creative love on the human level.

5 *Acceptance*

The Week of Chayei Sarah
Genesis 23:1–25:18

The Sidra *Chayei Sarah* (Genesis 23), meaning "The Life of Sarah," begins with her death, and describes Abraham's purchase of a burial ground for his wife. This done, he dispatches his servant to find a wife for Isaac. The servant finds Rebekah, and she agrees to go with him to Canaan to marry Isaac. We read: *And Isaac brought her into the tent of his mother Sarah; he took Rebekah, and she became his wife and he loved her. Thus did Isaac take comfort after [the death of] his mother* (25:67).

There is a time to mourn, and a time to accept; a time to rage against the fading of the light, and a time to kindle another light.

Sunday

⁘

cs / Gates of Prayer

In my great need for light I look to You. Holy One, help me to feel Your presence and to find the courage to affirm You, even when the shadows fall upon me. When my own weakness and the storms of life hide You from my sight, teach me that You are near to me at all times. Give me trust, give me peace, and give me light. May my heart find its rest in You.

Ephraim Rosenzweig

How suddenly it comes, this last today;
Tomorrow seems so far away when we are young,
Then it is here;
The end of now.
There was a time when, if I could, I would have forced
 the door to yesterday,
To live again the joys of early love,

To feel once more the thrust of time into tomorrow's
  endlessness.
But I am older now, and know that there is a last today,
And that the sun will not more rise
To wash with light my clouded eyes.
Tomorrow . . . ? Who knows where I shall be?
Perhaps in some eternity
Where all time gone and still to be are one.
How beautiful is death . . .
How gratefully I go. . . .

⁛

Monday

When the storm is loud and the night dark, I look to You; when the soul is sad, and the heart oppressed, I look to You; let me see the light of Your love, and by that light let me go on, and on, and on.

Chasidic

Rabbi Nachum of Stepinesht once said this:

When my brother David Moshe opens the Book of Psalms and begins to praise, God calls down to him: "David Moshe, My son, I am putting the whole world into your hands. Now do with it just as you like." O, if only God would give me the world, I'd know well enough what to do with it! But David Moshe is so faithful a servant that when he gives the world back, it is exactly as it was when he received it.

Leigh Hunt

A Grecian philosopher being asked why he wept for the death of his son, since the sorrow was in vain, replied, "I weep on that account." And his answer became his wisdom. It is only for sophists to contend that we, whose eyes contain the fountains of tears, need never give way to them. It would be unwise not to do so on some occasions. . . .

Where we feel that tears would relieve us, it is false philosophy to deny ourselves at least that first refreshment; and it is always false consolation to tell people that because they cannot help a thing, they are not to mind it. The true way is, to let them grapple with the unavoidable sorrow, and try to win it into gentleness by a reasonable yielding. . . . The end is an acquittal from the harsher bonds of affliction, from the tying down of the spirit to one melancholy idea.

Wallace Stegner

I have always said that the way to deal with the pain of others is by sympathy, which in first-year Greek they taught me meant "suffering with," and that the way to deal with one's own pain is to put one foot after the other.

Tuesday

⁘

In my weakness, bring out the strength You have given me; in my fear, quicken the faith You have lodged within me; in my despair, renew my hope that there is a rock on which to stand.

Morris Joseph

Something precious is taken from us, and we think of it as something we have lost, instead of something we have had. We remember only how empty our lives are now, we forget how full and rich they were before. . . . Let us count the past, happy days not as loss, but as gain. We have had them; and, now that they are ended, let us turn the loss to glorious gain—the gain that comes with new courage, with nobler tasks, with a wider outlook on life and duty. . . .

Sidney Harris

We learn, slowly but undeniably, that nothing belongs to us, completely, finally. The job is ended, the children grow up and move away, even the money (when there is money) buys little that we want. For what we want cannot be bought. And it is then, if ever, that we learn to make our peace with destiny; to accept the fact that our dreams have been half-realized, or unrealized; that we did not do what we set out to do; that our goals have receded as we approached them. There may be a sadness in this prospect, but also a serenity. Illusions lose their power to disturb us; we value life by what it has given us, not by the promise of tomorrow. For only by accepting Time can we, in a measure, learn to conquer it.

Whether I flie with angels, fall with dust,
Thy hands made both, and I am there:
Thy power and love, my love and trust
Make one place ev'rywhere.

George Herbert

❖

Wednesday

The consoling words of friends and family are well-meant, but something within me remains unhealed. Is it time I need? The sense that life does not begin or end with me and my pain? Or the understanding that life and death are not two but one? Perhaps it is all of them. Give me then time, and perspective, and understanding.

A king once owned a large, beautiful diamond of which he was proud, for it had no equal. One day, the diamond accidentally sustained a deep scratch. The king called in the most skilled artisans and offered them a great reward if they could remove the imperfection from his treasured jewel. But none could repair the blemish.

After some time a lapidary came to the king and promised to make the diamond even more beautiful than it had been before the mishap. The king was impressed by his confidence and entrusted the stone to his care. And the man kept his word.

With his art he engraved a rosebud around the imperfection and he used the scratch to make the stem.

Dubner Maggid

Spend your brief moment according to nature's law, and serenely greet the journey's end as an olive falls when it is ripe, blessing the branch that bore it, and giving thanks to the tree that gave it life.

Marcus Aurelius

Remind yourself that . . . what you love is not your own, it is given you for the present, not irrevocably nor forever, but even as a fig or bunch of grapes at the appointed time of the year.

Epictetus

Help me to plant a flower in the scarred earth; grant me the grace to live through my own sorrow and not give it to another. And what I cannot change, let me endure, until, unnoticed, it passes from my view.

Midrash On a Sabbath afternoon, while he was at the House of Study, the two sons of Rabbi Meir died. Their mother laid them on a bed and covered them.

Upon his return home after the evening prayer, Meir asked for his sons. They have gone to the House of Study, his wife Beruriah told him. I was just there, said Meir, but I did not see them. She simply said: It is time [to end the Sabbath with] Havdalah.

Meir took the wine and proclaimed the Havdalah. Then he said: Where are the boys? No doubt, said she, they will be home soon; meantime, eat your evening meal. He ate and gave thanks.

Afterward, Beruriah began: Rabbi, I must ask you a question. Some time ago, several jewels were given me for safekeeping. Now their owner has come and wants them back. What should I do?

Meir was taken aback: You know the law as well as I. What you hold in trust you must return on demand!

In spite of the law, she answered, I would have kept them, had you not said this.

Beruriah then took Meir by the hand and led him to the room where his boys lay covered by a sheet.

He began to weep. Then he screamed: My sons! My teachers! They brightened my face with their Torah!

Beruriah said: Rabbi, I have returned the jewels to their owner, just as you told me to.

Meir then said: *God gives; God takes; praised be the name of God.* (Job 1:21)

A woman lost her son and came to the Master for comfort. *Anonymous*

She poured out her grief as he listened patiently.

Then he said to her: My dear, I cannot wipe away your tears. I can only show you how to make them holy.

⁘

Friday

When hope seems foolish; when day grows dark; when life has lost its point: Be with me, be. . . .

Danny Siegel

O God,
You are a consolation to Your creatures,
for in moments of forgetting
we but call to mind Your care,
and we are comforted.
When we hope no more,
a pattern in the snow
reminds us of Your lovingkindness.
Your dawns give us confidence,
and sleep is a friend.
Our sorrows dissipate
in the presence of an infant's smile,
and the wise words of the old
revive our will-to-wish.
Your hints are everywhere,
Your signals in the most remote of places.
You are here,
and we lack words to say
"Mah Tov!"
How good our breath,
our rushing energies,
our silences of love.

George Eliot

For the first sharp pangs there is no comfort. Whatever goodness may surround us, darkness and silence still hang about our pain. But, slowly, the clinging companionship with the dead is linked with our living affections and duties, and we begin to feel our sorrow as a solemn initiation, preparing us for that sense of loving, pitying fellowship with the fullest human lot, which, I must think, no one who has tasted it will deny to be the chief blessedness of our life.

Shabbat

⁘

We are told not to mourn on Shabbat. O Source of light, surprise my heart and touch it with peace! Is there peace in remembered joy, remembered love? Give me the peace of questions transposed into thankfulness, wordless songs, recovered hope.

Chasidic

The Kobriner Rebbe said: When you suffer tribulation, do not say, *This is evil*—God sends no evil. Say, rather, *This is a bitter experience.* Think of it as though it were a bitter medicine prescribed by a physician in order to cure a patient.

Rainer Maria Rilke

The leaves fall, fall as from afar.
They fall with slow and lingering descent.
And in the nights the heavy earth, too, falls,
From out the Stars into the Solitude.
Thus all must fall. This hand of mine must fall,
And lo! the other one—it is the law.
But there is One who holds this falling
infinitely softly in His hands,
in Her hands.

Michel de Montaigne

Life's profit consists not in its duration but in its use. Some have lived long, yet their life has been short. While you have time, employ it, for life is measured not in years but your perception that you have lived long enough. While you were on the way to your destination, did you think you would never arrive? Every journey comes to an end. And if having company is a solace, think: does not the whole world walk the same path?

6 *Growing Old*

The Week of Tol'dot
Genesis 25:19–28:9

Tol'dot (Genesis 25) is the Sidra of Isaac, Rebekah, and their twin sons, who from the womb are destined to be rivals. The core of the Sidra is its conclusion, when Isaac, grown old, says, as a prelude to blessing Esau: *I am old now, and do not know how soon I may die* (27:2). But it is Jacob who will stand in Esau's place, to be blessed.

The young find it hard to imagine being old. But when in fact we do grow old, we will have done well if we are content with having known each stage of life as good in itself, without having demanded that time stand still for us, only for us.

Sunday

Anonymous

You know better than I know myself that I am growing older, and will some day be old. Keep me from the fatal habit of thinking I must say something on every subject and on every occasion. Release me from craving to straighten out everybody's affairs. Make me thoughtful but not moody, helpful but not bossy. Keep my mind from the recital of endless details; give me wings to get to the point. Seal my lips on my aches and pains. Teach me the glorious lesson that occasionally I may be mistaken. Give me the ability to see good things in unexpected places, and talents in unexpected people. And give me, O God, the grace to tell them.

Martin Buber

The older we get, the greater becomes our inclination to give thanks, especially heavenwards. We feel more strongly than we could possibly have felt before that life is a free gift, and [we] receive every unqualifiedly good hour . . . as an unexpected gift.

But we also feel, again and again, an urge to thank our brothers and sisters, even if they have not done anything special for us. For what, then, do I thank you? For really meeting me when we met; for opening your eyes, and not mistaking me for someone else; for opening your ears, and listening carefully to what I had to say to you; indeed, for opening up to me what I really want to address—your securely locked heart.

James A. Garfield

If wrinkles must be written upon our brows, let them not be written upon the heart. The spirit should not grow old.

Monday

✣

Robert Frost

Happiness makes up in height what it lacks in length.

What will I remember at end of day—the joy of walking the road, or the turnings I didn't take? The happiness I had, or what I might have had?

Leah Goldberg

The road is so beautiful, says the lad.
The road is so hard, says the youth.
The road is so long, says the man.
The old man sits on the roadside to rest.
Sunset colors his beard a reddish gold.
Grass gleams with evening dew.
A late bird sings unbidden. . . .
Will you remember how long the road was,
  and how beautiful?

Edna St. Vincent Millay

What lips my lips have kissed, and where, and why,
I have forgotten, and what arms have lain
Under my head till morning; but the rain
Is full of ghosts tonight, that tap and sigh
Upon the glass and listen for reply;
And in my heart there stirs a quiet pain
For unremembered lads that not again

Will turn to me at midnight with a cry.
Thus in the winter stands the lonely tree,
Nor knows what birds have vanished one by one,
Yet knows its boughs more silent than before:
I cannot say what loves have come and gone;
I only know that summer sang in me
A little while, that in me sings no more.

⁘

Tuesday

Forms of Prayer

Let me not separate myself from the true strength of my community: the experience and wisdom of old people, the hopes of the young, and the examples of care and courage that sustain me. Give me an open heart and an open mind to welcome those who need me, and to receive Your presence in my daily life.

And keep my lips from saying how wonderful it would be always to be young. Remind me how I wanted to be older, once, and remind me, too, that I must go, and make room for the kids.

Chasidic

The Bratzlaver said: The prosperity of a country depends on its treatment of the aged.

Samuel Ullman

Youth is not a time of life—it is a state of mind. It is not a matter of ripe cheeks, red lips, and supple knees; it is a temper of the will, a quality of the imagination, a vigor of the emotions; it is a freshness of the deep spring of life.

Mishnah

Hillel says:
Do not be sure of yourself until the day you die.
Do not judge your friends until you are in their place.
And do not say, "When I have time I will study"—
you may never have the time.

Lisa Alther

Just as you began to feel that you could make good use of time, there was no time left to you.

Cicero The great affairs of life are not performed by physical strength, or activity, or nimbleness of body, but by deliberation, character, expression of opinion. Of these old age is not only not deprived, but, as a rule, has them in a greater degree.

Wednesday

I was young, and in many ways foolish; older now, O God, may I not be foolish in the same ways.

Chasidic The Lizensker Rebbe said: We often see an old man who has spent his life in excesses, imitating in his declining years the works of the pious. He eats sparingly; he rises early to pray and to recite psalms. By performing acts which simulate piety he imagines he has become a pious man. But he forgets that his abstinence from food and sleep is due chiefly to his weakened desires. He becomes so self-satisfied that he "forgives himself his own sins," and as a result he dies without true repentance. God preserve us from such a fate!

Samuel Ullman Whether seventy or sixteen, there is in every being's heart the love of wonder, the sweet amazement at the stars and the star-like things and thoughts, the . . . challenge of events, the unfailing childlike appetite for what [is] next, and the joy and the game of life.

You are as young as your faith, as old as your doubt; as young as your self-confidence, as old as your despair.

Seneca Let us see to it . . . that our lives, like jewels of great price, be noteworthy not because of their width, but because of their weight. Let us measure them by their performance, not their duration.

Rabindranath Tagore

The butterfly counts
not months
but moments,
and has time enough.

✣

Thursday

Though I would not be foolish in Your sight, O God, help me to see that there may be times when I must be foolish in the sight of others and follow the singular wisdom of my own soul.

Chasidic

As the Baal Shem Tov lay dying, the townspeople came to him as they always did at this time of the year, and he spoke words of Torah to them. After this he said to the disciples standing around him, "I am not concerned for myself. I am well aware that I am going out through one door and going in through another." And he added, "Now I know what I was created for."

George Santayana

Old places and old persons in their turn, when spirit dwells in them, have an intrinsic vitality of which youth is incapable; precisely the balance and wisdom that come from long perspectives and broad foundations.

The Dhammapada

You are like a yellow leaf and the angel of death is not far off. You stand at the exit: where are your provisions for the journey?

✣

Friday

All my life I struggle, even when things seem easy; and, especially then, it may happen that my eye opens to the miracles that have kept me alive, that have let me grow older, and that give me hope that there is eldering left for me to do.

William Butler Yeats

When you are old and grey and full of sleep,
And nodding by the fire, take down this book,
And slowly read, and dream of the soft look
Your eyes had once, and of their shadows deep;
How many loved your moments of glad grace,
And loved your beauty with love false or true,
But one man loved the pilgrim soul in you,
And loved the sorrows of your changing face.

And bending down beside the glowing bars,
Murmur, a little sadly, how Love fled
And paced upon the mountains overhead
And hid his face amid a crowd of stars.

Cicero The course of life is fixed, and nature admits of its being run but in one way, and only once; and to each part of our life there is something specially seasonable; so that the feebleness of children, as well as the high spirit of youth, the soberness of maturer years, and the ripe wisdom of old age—all have a certain natural advantage which should be secured in its proper season.

Midrash You cannot say to the Angel of Death:
I wish to arrange my affairs before I die.

Shabbat

On Shabbat I think of the young, and pray that I have come to know something that they will want to learn. I hope to become an old bottle from which someone may yet drink and be satisfied. Don't let me rest until I have learned enough to be a teacher whom those that will follow me can trust.

Talmud When Rabbi Yochanan heard that Rabbi Eliezer was mortally ill, he went to see him for the last time.

Eliezer lay in his bed; the room was dark. Some words passed between them, and then, as Yochanan lifted his arm in a gesture, a shaft of light caught it, and his bare skin illuminated the room. Eliezer began to weep, and Yochanan said to him: Why are you weeping, Eliezer? Do you regret your life? Or do you think that even such as you failed to learn enough Torah in his lifetime?

True enough, old friend. While I had strength and time I should have learned more.

Do not let yourself grieve, Eliezer. We have learned: "A little more, a little less—no matter, so long as the heart is turned to

Heaven." This seemed little comfort, for Eliezer continued to weep.

Yochanan went on: Do you weep because of the years you were poor? If so, what need had you for two tables?

Into the silence broken only by the soft sound of tears, Yochanan ventured yet again: Do you perhaps mourn the sons you never had? If that: I mourn the sons I did have. Look now: here is the tooth of my tenth!

Now Eliezer raised himself up and gave answer: Let me tell you the reason for my tears: *I weep for your beauty, that must fade into dust!*

Old friend, cried Yochanan, oh, my dear old friend, for that you well may weep.

And the two old men shed tears together.

7 *Mystery*

The Week of Vayeitzei
Genesis 28:10–32:3

The Sidra *Vayeitzei* (Genesis 28) relates the wondrous tale of "Jacob's Ladder"—his dream of angels ascending and descending from earth to heaven, and God standing above him with the assurance of a safe return to the home and land that he has fled. Jacob responds with awe to his dream: *And Jacob awoke . . . and said: Surely, God is present in this place, and as for me, I did not know it! He was awestruck, and said: How awesome is this place! This is none other than the house of God; this is the gate of heaven!* (28:10,16). Mystery of mysteries—the traffic between heaven and earth!

Sunday

Mechtilde von Magdeburg

Of all that God has shown me
I can speak just the smallest word.
Not more than a honey bee
Takes on her foot
From an overspilling jar.

cs

Take this small word of mine, O Infinite, whose word created worlds. Take it into the mystery of Your being, the splendor of Your word.

Abraham J. Heschel

How do we seek to apprehend the world? Intelligence inquires into the nature of reality, and, since it cannot work without its tools, takes those phenomena that appear to fit its categories as answers to its inquiry. Yet, when trying to hold an interview with reality face to face, without the aid of either words or concepts, we realize that what is intelligible to our mind is but a thin surface of the profoundly undisclosed, a ripple of inveterate silence that remains immune to curiosity and inquisitiveness like distant foliage in the dusk.

The fairest thing we can experience is the mysterious. It is the fundamental emotion which stands at the cradle of true art and true science. One who knows it not, who can no longer wonder, no longer feel amazement, is as good as dead, a snuffed out candle. It was the experience of mystery that engendered religion.

Albert Einstein

⁘

Monday

You made me in Your image, yet I am a mystery to myself. To myself—but not to You who made me. Who am I?

A single simple song to you:
you are the silence & I the song
you you you the song are,
and I, I am the silence
I/you/we are the
blue burst of dawn / and the darkening dusk

cs

Because we live through most of the day, we fasten our wonderment on night. Because most of the great poets have been men, it is women that have been thought to be the mystery. But Adam is not less a riddle than Eve.

Shmaryahu Levin

There is only one thing valuable in art:
the thing you cannot explain.

Georges Braque

A genuine faith must recognize the fact that it is through a dark glass that we see; though by faith we do penetrate sufficiently to the heart of the mystery not to be overwhelmed by it. A genuine faith resolves the mystery of life by the mystery of God. It recognizes that no aspect of life or existence explains itself, even after all known causes and consequences have been traced. All known existence points beyond itself. To realize that it points

Reinhold Niebuhr

beyond itself to God is to assert that the mystery of life does not dissolve life into meaninglessness. Faith in God is faith in some ultimate unity of life, in some final comprehensive purpose which holds all the various, and frequently contradictory, realms of coherence and meaning together.

Tuesday

⁘

There is a mystery within me, and try as I may, I cannot come to the end of it. It teaches me reverence for the unfathomable wonder at my core. Hidden One, You alone know the secret within the secret within me, for are You not that secret?

Chasidic / cs

Even in the lowliest of human beings there dwells a soul, a sacred mystery, the garment of the living God. This garment we must keep spotless and return it without blemish. How? Through purity of heart, clarity of mind, and love for all creatures.

Upanishad

Bring me a fruit from that tree.
Here it is, venerable Sir.
Cut it open.
It is cut open, venerable Sir.
What do you see in it?
Very small seeds, venerable Sir.
Cut open one of them.
It is cut open, venerable Sir.
What do you see in it?
Nothing, venerable Sir.
Then he said:
That hidden thing which you cannot see,
O gentle youth,
from that hidden thing
has this mighty tree grown.

We dance round in a ring and suppose,
But the Secret sits in the middle and knows.

Robert Frost

In wonder all philosophy began; in wonder it ends. . . . But the first wonder is the offspring of ignorance: the last is the parent of adoration.

Samuel Taylor Coleridge

⁛

Wednesday

A mystery surrounds my being. What comes before it and what lies after it are hidden from me. My life is short, and Your universe is vast. But in the darkness is Your presence, and in the mystery, Your love. I put my trust in You, as did those who came before me. Be praised, Eternal God of time and space: You are what is hidden from my sight.

Forms of Prayer / cs

To pray is to take notice of the wonder, to regain a sense of the mystery that animates all beings—the divine margin in all attainments. Prayer is our humble answer to the inconceivable surprise of living. It is all we can offer for the mystery in which we live.

Abraham J. Heschel

Is not a flower a mystery no flower can explain? Is not God the growing, the pattern that has no end and is never quite the same? Is not God in the heart that sees it and weeps for beauty? Why, then, God, this mystery: that the bombs fall and the sprays kill and the flames rise and the children go up in smoke? Why is there still a flower to remind us of You? Why does the sun still burn to give us life? How do we still turn to You? Why cannot we help but turn to You, but why, why do we turn to You so late? And when we do, where are You?

cs

As I look back on the part of the mystery which is my own life, my own fable, what I am most aware of is that we receive more than we can ever give; we receive it from the past, on which we draw with every breath, but also—and this is a point of faith—from the Source of the mystery itself, by the means which religious people call grace.

Edwin Muir

Thursday

◆◆◆◆

What is my life, what my destiny? Where do I come from and where am I going? Coming and going, such questions surround me. I thank You, Source of my being, for the great question - mark that is my life.

cs Two ways of unknowing: To know one does not know, and not to know one does not know. Two mysteries: One may know that one walks among mysteries, and one may not know this. We seek only when we know we do not know; we are filled with awe only when we know how profound is the mystery of our being.

Henry Vaughan

There is in God (some say)
A deep, but dazzling darkness. . . .

Morris West Wherever I turn . . . I am confronted with mystery. I believe in the Godly harmony which is the result of the eternal creative act. . . . But I do not always hear the harmony. I must wrestle with the cacophony and apparent discord of the score, knowing that I shall not hear the grand resolution until the day I die and, hopefully, am united with God. . . .

Paul Tillich The question of being is not the question of any special being, its existence and nature, but it is the question of what it means to be. It is the simplest, most profound, and absolutely inexhaustible question—the question of what it means to say that something is. This word "is" hides the riddle of all riddles, the mystery that there is anything at all.

Friday

◆◆◆◆

So many things are strange. I gaze at a hyacinth and have no words for what I see. I look into the eyes of a dog and wonder: Looking at me, what do you see? In the presence of one whose life has just departed, I encounter the mystery of personality:

Where has it gone? I study the face of a newborn infant, and think: Where did you come from, life? To all these, are You the answer I seek?

All religious reality begins with what Biblical religion calls the "fear of God." It comes when our existence between birth and death becomes incomprehensible . . . , when all security is shattered through the mystery. This is not the relative mystery of that which is inaccessible only to the present state of human knowledge and is hence in principle discoverable. It is the essential mystery, the inscrutableness of which belongs to its very nature; it is the unknowable. *Martin Buber*

One aspect of religious experience is the wondering, the marveling, the becoming aware of life and one's own existence, and of the puzzling problem of one's relatedness to the world. Existence . . . is not taken for granted but felt as a problem, is not an answer but a question. Socrates' statement that wonder is the beginning of all wisdom is true not only for wisdom but for religious experience. One who has never been bewildered, who has never looked upon life and his (or her) own existence as phenomena which require answers and yet, paradoxically, for which the only answers are new questions, can hardly understand what religious experience is. *Erich Fromm*

Stupidity consists in wanting to reach conclusions. We are a thread, and we want to know the whole cloth. *Gustave Flaubert*

Every lock has its key. But what if one has no key—a thief, for example? What do thieves do? They break the lock. So every mystery in the world has its answer, its key. But what if one does not know it? God loves those who break open the lock—who break their hearts for God. *Chasidic*

Shabbat

On Shabbat You come out of hiding, or so it sometimes seems; for on Shabbat my questions seem to fade, and it is enough to say: It is. You are who You are. I am what I am, "fearfully and wonderfully made"—and so are all things great and small. It is enough. Be praised, Eternal One, Source of creation and its wonders.

Sir Arthur Eddington

It is by looking into our own nature that we first discover the failure of the physical universe to be co-extensive with our experience of reality. The "something to which truth matters" must surely have a place in reality whatever definition of reality we may adopt. In our own nature, or through the contact of our consciousness with a nature transcending ours, there are other things that claim the same kind of recognition—a sense of beauty, of morality, and finally at the root of all spiritual religion an experience which we describe as the presence of God. In suggesting that these things constitute a spiritual world I am not trying to substantialise them or objectivise them—to make them out other than we find them to be in our experience of them. But I would say that when from the human heart, perplexed by the mystery of existence, the cry goes up, "What is it all about?" it is no true answer to look only at that part of experience which comes to us through certain sensory organs and reply: "It is about atoms and chaos; it is about a universe of fiery globes rolling on to impending doom; it is about tensors and non-commutative algebra." Rather it is about a spirit in which truth has its shrine, with potentialities of self-fulfillment in its response to beauty and right. Shall I not also add that even as light and colour and sound come into our minds at the prompting of a world beyond, so these other stirrings of consciousness come from something which, whether we describe it as beyond or deep within ourselves, is greater than our own personality?

8 *Human Being*

The Week of Vayishlach
Genesis 32:4–36:43

In the Sidra *Vayishlach* (Genesis 32), Jacob is on the way back from his long exile; hearing that his brother Esau is coming to meet him, he is greatly afraid. In the night before that encounter, he finds himself in a struggle with a mysterious stranger. Himself? Another man? God? We know this: The outcome of that struggle is a blessing, signified by a new name, Israel, meaning *one who wrestles with God*. Jacob's new understanding of himself leads him to say: *I have seen God face to face, and yet I am alive* (32:31).

Let us suppose that we are each strangers to ourselves, and must struggle to discover who we are, what makes us who we are, what it is to be a "human being."

Sunday

In this moment of silence a still, small voice speaks within me; it speaks of what it means to be made in the likeness of the Divine. It says: Come to the end of each day feeling that you have used its gifts wisely and faced its trials bravely. Be tender and understanding toward the members of your family. Do your work faithfully, even when no one's eye is upon you. Try to judge others with compassion, and to love them as yourself.

How do I know what it means to be made in "the likeness of the Divine?" As I learn to see the divinity in every person, so I become ever more conscious of my own dignity as a child of God.

Talmud Creation began with a single being: to teach you that to destroy a single life is to destroy an entire world; and to sustain one human being is to sustain an entire world. . . .Therefore let every human being say: For my sake the world was created.

Mishnah He [Rabbi Akiba] would say:

Beloved is humankind, created in the image of God.

Love greater still made us aware that we were created in the image of God, as it is said (Genesis 9:6), *God made humankind in the divine image.*

Chasidic Rabbi Noah of Lekhivitz said: We are called "a small world." If we are small in our own eyes, we are indeed "a world," but if we are "a world" in our own eyes, we are small indeed.

Monday

From *Psalm 8*

Eternal One, our God, how glorious is Your name
in all the earth!
You have stamped Your glory upon the heavens!
When I look at the heavens, the work of Your fingers;
the moon and the stars that You have established,
What are we, that You are mindful of us,
we human beings, that You care for us?
Yet You have made us little lower than the angels,
and crowned us with glory and honor!
You have appointed us to look after all that
You have made,
You have placed all creation in our care:
Sheep and cattle, all of them; beasts and birds and fish,
and all who travel the ocean's paths.
Eternal One, our God, how glorious is Your
name in all the earth!

Chasidic The virtue of angels is that they cannot deteriorate, and their flaw is that they cannot improve. The flaw of human beings is that they can deteriorate, and their virtue is that they can improve.

The room of the Great Maggid Dov Baer adjoined that in which his disciples slept. Sometimes he went to them at night, a light in his hand, and looked into their sleeping faces. Once he bent down to the low bench by the stove on which young Shneur Zalman lay under a threadbare, three-cornered cover. He looked at him for a long time and then said to himself: Miracle of miracles, that so great a God lives in so frail a dwelling.

Chasidic

What is the ultimate truth about ourselves? Various answers suggest themselves. We are bits of stellar matter gone wrong. We are physical machinery-puppets that strut and laugh and die. But there is one inescapable answer. We are that which asks the question. Whatever else there may be in our nature, responsibility to truth is one of its attributes. . . . In our own nature, or through the contact of our consciousness with a nature transcending ours, there are things that claim the same kind of recognition—a sense of beauty, or morality, and finally . . . an experience which we describe as the presence of God.

Sir Arthur Eddington

⁘

Tuesday

The stars of heaven, awesome in their majesty,
are not more wonderful
than the one who charts their courses.
The elements, arrayed in perfection,
are not marvels greater
than the mind that beholds them.
This miracle, matter, begets a wonder:
the body thinks, insight comes from flesh;
the soul is born of dust to build towers of hope,
opening within us doors of lamentation and love.
For You have made us little less than divine,
and crowned us with glory and honor!

cs / Gates of Prayer

Chasidic The Koretzer Rebbe said: Within us are all the worlds, and we can therefore be in contact with them all. Within us are all the qualities, good and evil, but they are unborn, and we have the power to beget them. We can transform evil qualities into good, and good into evil. By studying Torah and performing commandments we give birth to the angelic within us.

Ernest Becker This is the paradox: we are out of nature and hopelessly in it; we are dual, up in the stars and yet housed in a heart-pumping, breath-grasping body that once belonged to a fish and still carries the gill-marks to prove it. . . . We are literally split in two: we have an awareness of our own splendid uniqueness in that we stick out of nature with a towering majesty, and yet we go back into the ground a few feet in order blindly and dumbly to rot and disappear forever.

Wednesday

⁘

William James

The deepest thing in our nature
is this . . . region of the heart
in which we dwell alone
with our willingnesses and unwillingnesses,
our faiths and fears.

Mishnah

Despise no one,
Regard nothing as impossible:
You will find no one whose hour does not come,
And not a thing without its place.

Jonathan Brierly God sleeps in the stone, breathes in the plant, moves in the animals, and wakes to consciousness in human beings.

Blaise Pascal When the universe has crushed us we—humankind—will still be nobler than that which kills us, because we know that we are dying, and of its victory the universe knows nothing.

Anonymous Taking the size of his body into account, man emits more sperm than any other animal.

Between the laughing and the weeping philosopher there is no opposition: the same facts that make one laugh make one weep. No whole-hearted man, no sane art, can be limited to either mood. *Unknown*

We want to be great and we see ourselves small. We want to be happy and we see ourselves miserable. We want to be perfect and we see ourselves full of imperfections. . . . Truly it is an evil to be full of faults, but it is a still greater evil to be full of them and to be unwilling to recognize them, since that is to add the further fault of a voluntary illusion. *Unknown*

⁘

Thursday

A certain day became a presence to me;
there it was, confronting me—a sky, air, light:
a being. And before it started to descend
from the height of noon, it leaned over
and struck my shoulder as if with
the flat of a sword, granting me
honor and a task. The day's blow
rang out, metallic—or was it I, a bell awakened,
and what I heard was my whole self
saying and singing what it knew: *I can.*

Denise Levertov

If I try to be like someone else, who will be like me? *Yiddish Proverb*

Human nature is not a machine to be built after a model, and set to do exactly the work prescribed for it, but a tree, which requires to grow and develop itself on all sides, according to the tendency of the inward forces which make it a living thing. *John Stuart Mill*

The Koretzer Rebbe said: In the Creation Story we are told that humankind was created last, and it was for the following reason: if we are worthy, we find all nature at our service; if we are unworthy, we find all nature arrayed against us. *Chasidic*

Chasidic A man said to Mendel of Kotzk:
This one is greater than that one.
He replied:
Why make comparisons?
If I am I because I am I, and you are you because you are you,
then I am truly I and you are truly you.
But if I am I only because you are you, and if you are you only because I am I,
then I am not I, and you are not you.

Friday

And now we praise the weaver:
weaving the word, this life,
weaving it;
weaving, weaving, weaving & weaving;
shearing/spinning
shearing and spinning it
forth and back,
shearing, spinning, weaving
O & dyeing the vivid hues in the colors of Why
& mending the fraying fabric with the threads of Because.

Midrash One righteous human being is equal to the whole world, as it is said (Proverbs 10:25), *The righteous is the foundation of the world.*

W. MacNeile Dixon The astonishing thing about the human being is not so much . . . intellect or bodily structure, profoundly mysterious as they are. The astonishing and least comprehensible thing about us is our range of vision; our gaze into the infinite distance; our lonely passion for ideas and ideals . . . for which . . . we will stand till we die, the profound conviction we entertain that if nothing is worth dying for nothing is worth living for.

Unknown I only know myself as a human entity; the scene, so to speak, of thoughts and affections; and am sensible of a certain doubleness by which I can stand as remote from myself as from another. However intense my experience, I am conscious of the presence and criticism of a part of me, which, as it were, is not a part of me, but spectator, sharing no experience, but taking note of it, and that is no more I than it is you.

If a man lives in slime—and there is slime always at the core of the soul—it is nevertheless this briefly animated dust that beholds stars, writes symphonies, and imagines God.

Unknown

⁘

Shabbat

Stephen Spender

I think continually of those who were truly great.
Who, from the womb, remembered the soul's history
Through endless corridors of light where the hours are suns,
Endless and singing. Whose lovely ambition
Was that their lips, still touched with fire,
Should tell of the spirit clothed head to foot in song.
And who hoarded from the spring branches
The desires falling across their bodies like blossoms.
What is precious is never to forget
The delight of the blood drawn from ageless springs
Breaking through rocks in worlds before our earth;
Never to deny its pleasure in the simple morning light,
Nor its grave evening demand for love;
Never to allow the traffic to smother
With noise and fog the flowering of the spirit.
Near the snow, near the sun, in the highest fields
See how these names are fêted by the waving grass,
And by the streamers of white cloud,
And whispers of wind in the listening sky;
The names of those who in their lives fought for life,
Who wore at their hearts the fire's centre.
Born of the sun they traveled a short while towards the sun,
And left the vivid air signed with their honour.

Midrash *Love your neighbor as yourself* (Leviticus 19:18). Rabbi Akiba said: This is the great principle of the Torah. Ben Azzai said: Here is an even greater principle: *This is the book of the generations of Adam. . . . God made them in the divine image* (Genesis 5:1), for then you cannot say, Since I despise myself I can despise another as well; since I curse myself, let the other be accursed as well. Rabbi Tanchuma said: [Ben Azzai is right, for] if you do thus, know that the one you are despising is made in the divine image.

9 *Connections*

The Week of Vayeishev
Genesis 37:1–40:23

The Sidra *Vayeishev* (Genesis 37) begins the story of Joseph and his brothers, a story about connections, or relationships. Young Joseph is the favored son of Jacob, and he dreams he will be lord over his kin. His brothers are jealous and vengeful; they plot his doom. *I am looking for my brothers,* says Joseph at an early point in the tale. (37:16). It is a remark that echoes throughout the tale, for when he finds them, they sell him to a group of traders passing by on the way to Egypt. But this is only the beginning of the complex tale that unfolds as Joseph and his brothers mature.

Sunday

Looking inward, I see that there is in me a yearning to use my gifts for the well-being of those around me.

Renew my vision, O God; give meaning to my life and substance to my hopes; help me understand those about me and fill me with the desire to serve them. Let me remember that I depend on them as they depend on me; quicken my heart and hand to reach for them, and teach me to make my words of prayer fruitful by deeds of loving-kindness.

A sage taught before Rabbi Nachman bar Yitzchak:
Shame your friend in public,
and you have shed blood.
Well said! remarked Rabbi Nachman,
for his complexion was ruddy, and now it is pale!

Talmud

Mencius If people suddenly see a child about to fall in a well, they will all without exception experience a feeling of alarm and distress. They will feel so not in order to gain the favor of the child's parents, nor to seek the praise of their neighbors and friends, nor from a fear of being thought to have been unmoved by such a thing.

Unknown

If there is sincerity in the heart,
There will be beauty in the character.
If there is beauty in the character,
There will be harmony in the home.
If there is harmony in the home,
There will be order in the nation.
When there is order in the nation,
There will be peace in the world.

Monday

❖

There are times when I look too long at those around me, and try too hard to serve them; let me look to my own needs, too; and then, it may be, I will be better able to serve myself and others!

Mishnah

Hillel said:
If I am not for myself, who will be for me?
And if I am only for myself, what am I?
And if not now, when?

Chasidic Rabbi Michal said: If I am not for myself, *that is, if I work not for myself alone, but continually participate in the congregation,* who will be for me? In that case, whatever any member of the congregation does in my place counts just as though I had done it myself. But if I am only for myself, *if I do not participate with others, if I do not join with them,* what am I?

Chasidic Rabbi Yitzchak, a grandson of Rabbi Nachum of Tchernobyl, told: In a small town, not far from Tchernobyl, several Chasidim of my grandfather's were seated together at the conclusion of the Sabbath. They were all honest and devoted men, and at this meal they were considering the state of their souls. So humble were they, and so God-fearing, that they thought they were great sinners and agreed that there was no hope for them, except for their devotion to the great Tzaddik Rabbi Nachum, who could uplift and redeem them. Then they decided that they must immediately go to their teacher. They started out right after the meal and together they went to Tchernobyl. But at the end of that same Sabbath my grandfather was sitting in his house and considering the state of his soul. In his humility and fear of God it seemed to him that he was a great sinner, and that he had only one hope: that those Chasidim, so earnest in the service of God, were so deeply devoted to him that they would comfort him now. He longed for themtheir comfort and went to the door and gazed in the direction of their town. When he had stood for a while, he saw them coming.

In this instant two arcs fused into a ring.

Tuesday

So often I say that the men and women about me are my brothers and sisters; now teach me to mean it. Help me, God, to look and see, to reach out and touch, not only to hear what I am saying but also to listen to the voices and souls of those around me.

Chasidic

The Radviller Rebbe said: The commandment to love our neighbors as ourselves does not imply that if you buy yourself a garment you must buy one also for another person. The Torah does not contain a command that only the wealthy are able to observe. What we can do, rich and poor alike, is to participate in our neighbor's joys or griefs. If we hear that someone else is prospering, we must rejoice as if we ourselves had benefited. If another person is in distress, we must come and help, just as if we ourselves were in trouble and praying for help from others. The Talmud tells that Jerusalem was destroyed because of hatred that had no cause (Yoma 9); people were apparently happy at the misfortunes of their companions. We are all children of the God who feels compassion for the pain of every one of us.

Harry Emerson Fosdick

To pass from a mirror-mind to a mind with windows is an essential element in the development of real personality.

Ralph Waldo Emerson

When I have attempted to join myself to others by services, it proved an intellectual trick—no more. They eat your service like apples, and leave you out. But love them, and they feel you, and delight in you all the time.

Wednesday

⁘

Is it love or need that predominates in me? Ah, let me act at least as much from love as from the urgent needs that so often seem to control me!

Midrash

Whosoever shall be called by the name of the Eternal One shall be delivered (Joel 3:5). But how is it possible to be called by the name of the Holy One? As the All Present is called compassionate and gracious, so must you be compassionate and gracious, and as God is called loving, so must you be loving.

Joseph Joubert

The wish to be independent of all people, and not to be under obligation to anyone, is the sure sign of a soul without tenderness.

Theodor Reik

To connect one's life in thoughts and deeds with others is the only way to make it worth living.

Thursday

⁘

Friend, I need to be real; help me peel away the artifices I have devised to keep from getting near you, and melt the walls I have built to prevent you from truly reaching me.

Chasidic

The Koretzer Rebbe said: Sometimes you may not understand what you are studying; then you discuss it with a comrade, and it suddenly becomes clear. Two souls have come together, and it gives birth to new understanding, and to new wisdom.

It is more shameful to distrust one's friends than to be deceived by them. *François de La Rochefoucauld*

A friend whom you have been enjoying during your whole life, you ought not to be displeased with in a moment. A stone is many years in becoming a ruby; take care that you do not destroy it in an instant against another stone. *Saadi*

If you think you can find in yourself the means to get along without others, you are much mistaken; but if you think that others cannot do without you, you are mistaken all the more. *François de La Rochefoucauld*

⁘

Friday

Some days I suddenly feel a lightness in me; I find myself smiling at someone, I seem to be at home in the world, and everyone seems somehow part of the family. O bring this to life in me on other days!

The Baal Shem Tov said: There are two ways to serve God. One is to separate yourself from people and from the world's affairs, and to devote yourself wholly to a study of religious books. This is the safe way. The other way is to mingle with people, to engage in the affairs of the world, and, at the same time, to try to be an example of godliness. This way has its dangers, but it is far the more worthy. *Chasidic*

Life is too brief
Between the budding and the falling leaf,
Between the seed time and the golden sheaf,
For hate and spite.
We have no time for malice and for greed:
Therefore, with love make beautiful the deed;
Fast speeds the night.

W. M. Vories

To do unto others as you would have them do unto you is well; but to do unto them as they would themselves be done by is better. *Comtesse Diane*

Zohar When all the members of the human body suffer through an illness, one member must be treated in order to heal the whole body. So it is with the human race: its members are to each other like members of the human body.

Shabbat

✦

Forms of Prayer Eternal God, I thank You for the precious gift of the Sabbath, and for the rest it brings to me. I thank You for the opportunities it gives me to come closer to those I love and to those who worship with me; for this chance of reading my own heart, of estimating more accurately how I stand toward You, and toward my own soul. On this day of calm and holiness I see my life more clearly. My judgment of it comes nearer to Yours. The things I thought big now seem pitifully small; and what I thought was worthless or unimportant now seems filled with significance and meaning. O God, bless this clearer insight, this truer judgment. Give me the strength and integrity to go forward in joy, with this light which illuminates my being, into the coming week.

Unknown "Sire," announced the servant to the King, "the saint Narottam has never deigned to enter your royal temple. He is singing God's praises under the trees by the open road. The temple is empty of worshippers. They flock round him like bees round the white lotus, leaving the golden jar of honey unheeded."

The King, vexed at heart, went to the spot where Narottam sat on the grass. He asked him, "Father, why leave my temple of the golden dome and sit on the dust outside to preach God's love?"

"Because God is not in your temple," said Narottam.

The King frowned and said, "Do you know, twenty millions of gold went into the making of that marvel of art, and it was consecrated to God with costly rites?"

"Yes, I know it," answered Narottam. "It was in that year when thousands of your people whose houses had been burned stood vainly asking for help at your door. And God said, 'The poor creature who can give no shelter to his brothers and sisters would build my house! I will take my place with the shelterless under the trees by the road.' That golden bubble is empty of all but pride."

The King cried in anger, "Leave my land!"

"Yes, banish me where you have banished my God."

מקץ

10 *Dream and Aspiration*

The Week of Mikeitz
Genesis 41:1–44:17

The Sidra *Mikeitz* (Genesis 41) continues the story of Joseph, and dreams figure in Joseph's rise. Joseph is called in to interpret Pharaoh's dreams. Pharaoh says to Joseph: *I have heard this about you: you have but to hear a dream to interpret it* (41:15). Pharaoh, struck by Joseph's brilliant understanding, gives him control over Egypt: he is to be second only to Pharaoh. The boy who once dreamed of glory, gains it by understanding the dreams of others.

We may disparage others by calling them impractical dreamers. But to have the courage to dream of a fairer day—and then to work at making dreams real—is not to be impractical, but to be a benefactor.

Sunday

cs / Forms of Prayer

Hallow my dreams, Holy One. May the gleams of Your light, the visions of Your truth, that bless me here, abide with me when I go out into the world, keeping me steadfast in loyalty to You and Your commandments.

Louis Binstock

Failures are made only by those who fail to dare, not by those who dare to fail.

John Andrew Holmes

Never tell a young person that something cannot be done. God may have been waiting for centuries for somebody ignorant enough of the impossible to do that very thing.

If age is strictly honest with youth, it has to tell it things that are not altogether good for youth to take to heart. The experience of the years is largely made up of vanished dreams, deluded hopes and frustrated ambitions. But it is the very dreams, hopes and ambitions of youth that accomplish so many things that age in its wisdom knows to be impossible. Where would the world be if wisdom ruled youth and power rested in age?

Thomas A. Woodlock

Give thanks, O heart, for the high souls,
That point us to the deathless goals:
Brave souls that took the perilous trail
And felt the vision could not fail.

Edwin Markham

⁘

Monday

I thank You for possibilities, for the promise life holds for those who dare to dream. Yet there are times when I grow afraid and forget what it means to dream. In such times of fallow thought and stunted feeling, help me to see again Your creative power, to hear again Your commanding voice. Renew my sense of life's wonder, my confidence in what lies ahead for the adventurous spirit, my faith in the power of my dreams.

cs / Siddur Lev Chadash

God said to Moses: *Take off your sandals from your feet, for the place on which you stand is holy ground* (Exodus 3:5).

The Hafetz Hayyim said: We all need to rise higher in goodness. Never say, I will be able to lift myself up, but at another time, in a different place. No, *the place on which you stand is holy ground,* it is available. Take off the unclean, and strive to rise up.

Chasidic

Aim at the sun, and you may not reach it; but your arrow will fly higher than if aimed at an object on a level with yourself.

John Hawes

Pray that your loneliness may spur you into finding something to live for, great enough to die for.

Dag Hammarskjöld

Marilynne Robinson

The force behind the movement of time is a mourning that will not be comforted. That is why the first event is known to have been an expulsion, and the last is hoped to be a reconciliation and return. So memory pulls us forward, so prophecy is only brilliant memory—there will be a garden where all of us as one child will sleep in our mother Eve, hooped in her ribs and staved by her spine.

Tuesday

When the darkness is too dark for me, give me light, and renew my hope, my dream, my faith that the gloom will not last, that despair will not be the final word. And give me the courage to believe in my dreams.

Philip M. Raskin

I will not change one golden dream for all your dreams of gold.

Phillips Brooks

It is not for us to pray for tasks equal to our powers, but for powers equal to our tasks, to go forward with a great desire forever beating at the door of our hearts as we travel towards our distant goal.

Helen Keller

One can never consent to creep
when one feels an impulse to soar.

C. V. Wedgwood

Discontent and disorder were signs of energy and hope, not of despair.

Wednesday

There is a vision of justice and righteousness in my heritage; a dream of peace and well-being in my tradition: Help me, God, to be among those who maintain the vision and work to make real the dream.

Anonymous

Every act of ours begins with a dream and ends with one.

"Hope" is the thing with feathers—
That perches in the soul—
And sings the tune without the words—
And never stops—at all.

Emily Dickinson

The greatest achievement was at first and for a time a dream. The oak sleeps in the acorn; the bird waits in the egg; and in the highest vision of the soul a waking angel stirs. Dreams are the seedlings of realities.

James Allen

⁘

Thursday

Give me a purpose that will outlast my own days, one that will live in the days of those who come after me: my children, it may be; my friends and comrades along life's path; and others, whom I may never meet, but whose souls resonate to the same dreams as mine.

Aryeh ben Pinhas took his little granddaughter into the synagogue. They walked down its center aisle hand in hand. They walked up the steps of the Bimah, and stood in front of the Holy Ark. The grandfather opened the doors of the Ark, to show her the Scrolls of the Torah, clad in their velvet mantles. The little girl looked at them raptly, and then exclaimed: "I want to go still higher!"

The grandfather bent down and kissed her, and said: "May you always want to go higher."

Chasidic

We are never at home, we are always beyond. Fear, desire, hope, project us toward the future and steal from us the feeling and consideration of what is, to busy us with what will be, even when we shall no longer be.

Michel de Montaigne

It matters not how small the beginning may seem to be: what is once done well is done for ever.

Henry David Thoreau

I was not looking for my dreams to interpret my life, but for my life to interpret my dreams.

Susan Sontag

Friday

∴

Give me time enough to see something of my hopes and ideals come true; and give me the will to make the effort myself to accomplish some part of my highest aim.

Chasidic

You shall not go up by steps upon My altar (Exodus 20:26).

The Gerer Rebbe said: If you ascend a roof by a ladder you can count the rungs already taken and those yet to climb. But if there are no "steps"—only a smooth ramp? Don't serve God by "steps," as though you could estimate how far you have gone and therefore might suppose you've earned the right to slow down. You'll know whether you have reached the "end" only when you reach the end.

Phillips Brooks

We are haunted by an ideal life, and it is because we have within us the beginning and the possibility of it.

Louise Imogen Guiney

No pleasure or success in life quite meets the capacity of our hearts. We take in our good things with enthusiasm, and think ourselves happy and satisfied; but afterward, when the froth and foam have subsided, we discover that the goblet is not more than half-filled with the golden liquid that was poured into it.

Helen Keller

I long to accomplish a great and noble task, but it is my chief duty to accomplish humble tasks as though they were great and noble. The world is moved along, not only by the mighty shoves of its heroes, but also by the aggregate of the tiny pushes of each honest worker.

Shabbat

∴

I know what it is to lose confidence: what it is to doubt myself—who I am and whether my life has meaning. On this day, especially, I look to You for rest from my doubts and fears. Give me, if only for this brief moment, peace of soul, the assurance that Your presence, Your purpose, Your strength, will uphold me always, and give meaning to my fleeting days.

God, give us dreams to match our nights
And let us awake to hope and light
And to the memory of stars that will return
When it grows dark again.

Albert Friedlander

Rage for the world as it is
but for what it may be
more love now than last year.

Muriel Rukeyser

Hope is a strange invention—
A Patent of the Heart—
In unremitting action
Yet never wearing out.

Emily Dickinson

If you have built castles in the air, your work need not be lost; that is where they should be. Now put the foundations under them.

Henry David Thoreau

11 *Our Journey Through Life*

The Week of Vayigash
Genesis 44:18–47:27

In the Sidra *Vayigash* (Genesis 44), Joseph reveals himself to his brothers and bids them bring their father Jacob to Egypt, and at long last, after many a journey, the family is reunited. Looking back on all that transpired among them, Joseph says to his brothers: *God sent me ahead of you to assure your survival in the land and to keep you alive, for a great deliverance* (45:7). We do not know how our life's journey will turn out.

Jacob sets out with *all that was his*—all his possessions. "All" includes our spiritual possessions; when we spend them with ardor we enrich ourselves no less than we do our companions of the road.

⁘

Sunday

cs / Liberal Jewish Prayer Book

You have called me into life, setting me in the midst of purposes I cannot measure or understand. Yet I thank You for the good I know, for the life I have, and for the gifts that—in sickness and in health—have been my daily portion: the beauty of earth and sky, the visions that have stirred me from my ease and quickened my endeavors, the demands of truth and justice that move me to acts of goodness, and the contemplation of Your eternal presence, which fills me with hope that what is good and lovely cannot perish. For all this, I give thanks.

Talmud

Act while you can:
while you have the time,

the means,
the strength.

To youth . . . it should be carefully inculcated, that to enter the road of life without caution or reserve, in expectation of general fidelity and justice, is to launch on the wide ocean without the instruments of steerage, and to hope that every wind will be prosperous and that every coast will afford a harbour.

Samuel Johnson

It seems to me we can never give up longing and wishing while we are thoroughly alive. There are certain things we feel to be beautiful and good, and we must hunger after them.

George Eliot

Rabbi Uri of Strelisk once said to the Chasidim who had come together in Strelisk: You journey to me [to cling to me], and where do I journey? I journey and journey continually to that place where I can cling to God.

Chasidic

⁘

Monday

I am not alone on the journey. My loved ones are with me; the teachers of my youth are a real presence in me. O that I may such a presence be for those who come after me: a voice bravely urging them onward, assuring them that the reward is worth their toil.

Noah walked with God (Genesis 6:9). Rabbi Judah said: This is like the case of a king who had two sons, one grown, the other young. The young one had to walk with him, while the grown one could walk before him.

So with Abraham, whose strength was great, God says (Genesis 17:1), *Walk before Me and be whole-hearted.* But of Noah, whose strength was minute, it is said (Genesis 6:9), *Noah walked with God.*

Midrash

In order to reap the full possibilities of youth we must not tie them too rigidly to the theories of an older generation. Their value lies in being a voice, not an echo.

Willett L. Hardin

Ignazio Silone Everyone of us is given the gift of life, and what a strange gift it is. If it is preserved jealously and selfishly it impoverishes and saddens, but if it is spent for others it enriches and beautifies.

Madeleine L'Engle The great thing about getting older is that you don't lose all the other ages you've been.

✣

Tuesday

Tasks great and small await me; patiently they wait for me to arrive with enough strength of mind to undertake them, whether or not I have the strength to complete them.

Chasidic The Hafetz Hayyim said: Jacob dreamed of a ladder standing on the ground and reaching to heaven. This means: We never stand still. We either ascend, or we descend.

Chasidic A woman came to Rabbi Israel of Kosnitz and told him tearfully that she had been married for twelve years and still had not borne a son. What are you willing to do about it? he asked her. She did not know what to say.

The Tzaddik told her, my mother was aging and still without child. Then she heard that the holy Baal Shem was stopping over in Apt in the course of a journey. She hurried to his inn and begged him to pray for her. What are you willing to do about it? he asked her. My husband is a poor bookbinder, she replied, but I do have one fine thing that I shall give to the rabbi.

She went home as fast as she could and fetched her good cape, which was stowed away in a chest. But when she returned to the inn with it, she heard that the Baal Shem had already left for Mezbizh. She immediately set out after him and, since she had no money, she walked from town to town with her cape until she came to Mezbizh.

The Baal Shem took the cape and hung it on the wall. It is well, he said. My mother walked all the way back, from town to town, until she reached Apt. One year later, I was born.

I too, cried the woman, will bring you a good cape of mine so that I may get a child.

That won't work, said the Tzaddik. You heard the story. My mother had no story to go by.

✣

Wednesday

I know that at the end of my time all that I accomplish will seem small. This is my prayer: Give me work till my life shall end, and life till my work is done.

Two came to a crossroads. One chose an uneven road, and the other a straight even road. The first encountered many obstacles but at last reached the city. The other had a much smoother journey at first, but near the end of the journey found the path blocked and had to return.

Chasidic

Cato the Elder began to study Greek when he was about eighty. When asked why he was beginning so large a task at such an advanced age, he replied that "it was the youngest age he had left"—and went on studying.

Michel de Montaigne

The truly wise must be as intelligent and expert in the use of natural pleasures as in all the other functions of life. So the Sages live, gently yielding to the laws of our human lot, to Venus and to Bacchus. Relaxation and versatility, it seems to me, go best with a strong and noble mind, and do it singular honor. There is nothing more notable in Socrates than that he found time, when he was an old man, to learn music and dancing, and thought it time well spent.

Michel de Montaigne

It's not how old you are but how you are old.

Marie Dressler

All around him people were growing old, but he grew up.

Anonymous

Thursday

⁘

I go astray so often, and I need You to find me: I need Your love, Your smile, Your grace. I need to feel at home in this world, at home enough to find my way when I am lost.

Chasidic We were created to lift up the heavens.

Chasidic The Koretzer said: A man who lived in Cracow dreamed several times that there was a treasure near a mill awaiting his arrival to dig it up. He left his house early in the morning, and dug diligently, but could find nothing. When the miller came, he asked him why he was digging near the mill. The man explained and the miller cried out: Why, I dreamed that there is a treasure in the courtyard of a certain man in Cracow, and he named the man who was digging. The man promptly returned home and uncovered the treasure in his own yard.

Benjamin Franklin When we launch our little fleet of barks into the ocean, bound to different ports, we hope for each a prosperous voyage; but contrary winds, hidden shoals, storms, and enemies, come in for a share in the disposition of events; and though these occasion a mixture of disappointment, yet, considering the risk where we can make no insurance, we should consider ourselves happy if some return with success.

Chasidic Rabbi Pinchas said: In the book *The Duties of the Heart,* we read that if we conduct our life as we should we see with eyes that are no eyes, hear with ears that are no ears. And that is just how it is! For often, when people come to ask my advice, I hear them give themselves the answers to their questions.

Friday

⁘

Service of the Heart

When evil darkens the world, give me light.
When despair numbs my soul, give me hope.
When I stumble and fall, lift me up.

When doubt assails me, give me trust.
When nothing seems sure, give me faith.
When ideals fade, renew my vision.
When I lose my way, be my Guide,
That I may find peace in Your presence,
And purpose in doing Your will.

Rabbi Hirsch Rimanover said: Some Tzaddikim serve God in the old way: they walk the beaten path (the state road). Others at times adopt a different way: they walk on the side road. Still others pursue their own way, and reach their destination first.

Chasidic

It is an absolute perfection and virtually divine to know how to enjoy our being rightfully. We seek other conditions because we do not understand the use of our own, and go outside of ourselves because we do not know what it is like inside. Yet there is no use our mounting on stilts, for on stilts we must still walk on our own legs. And on the loftiest throne in the world we are still sitting on our own rump.

Ralph Waldo Emerson

To be really great in little things, to be truly noble and heroic in the insipid details of everyday life, is a virtue so rare as to be worthy of canonization.

Harriet Beecher Stowe

Faith in divine Providence is the faith that nothing can prevent us from fulfilling the ultimate meaning of our existence. Providence does not mean a divine planning by which everything is predetermined, as in an efficient machine. Rather, Providence means that there is a creative and saving possibility implied in every situation, which cannot be destroyed by any event. Providence means that the daemonic and destructive forces within ourselves and our world can never have an unbreakable grasp upon us, and that the bond which connects us with the fulfilling love can never be disrupted.

Paul Tillich

⁘

cs / Gates of Prayer

You are with me in my prayer and my love, in my doubt and my fear, in my longing to feel Your presence and do Your will. You are the still, clear voice within me.

Yet there are times when doubt troubles me, when anxiety makes me tremble and pain clouds the mind. Then I look inward in search of You.

And may I find courage there, and insight, and endurance; discovering again that which gives meaning and purpose to my journey—You, the Answer to my prayer.

Thomas Merton

I do not see the road ahead of me, I cannot know for certain where it will end. Nor do I really know myself, and the fact that I think I am following your will does not mean I am actually doing so. But I believe the desire to please you does in fact please you. And I hope I have that desire in all that I am doing. I hope that I will never do anything apart from that desire. And I know that if I do this you will lead me by the right road, though I may know nothing about it. Therefore, I will trust you always, though I may seem to be lost and in the shadow of death. I will not fear, for you are ever with me, and you will never leave me to face my perils alone.

Mary Renault

How can people trust the harvest, unless they see it sown?

Ralph Waldo Emerson

We ask for long life, but 'tis deep life or grand moments that signify. Let the measure of time be spiritual not mechanical.

ויחי

12 *Conflict and Reconciliation*

The Week of Va-y'chi
Genesis 47:28–50:26

The Sidra *Va-y'chi* (Genesis 50) concludes Genesis on a note of reconciliation. It narrates the death of Jacob and his burial in the cave of Machpelah. After his father's death, Joseph's brothers are fearful that he will finally punish them for selling him into slavery, but Joseph assures them of his forgiveness, saying: *Have no fear, for am I in place of God? Though you intended me harm, God intended it for good, in order to accomplish what is now the case, to keep alive a numerous people. Thus did he comfort them and speak straight to their hearts* (50:19–20).

Sunday

For the times when I could have made peace with my neighbor but picked a quarrel, forgive me; and forgive me, too, for the times when I could have accepted with grace an offering of friendship or reconciliation but did not choose to listen. At times, in my willfulness, I may have closed my heart to the possibility of a healing word: Today—and tomorrow—let my heart be open.

Mishnah

Hillel said:
Be a disciple of Aaron,
loving peace and pursuing peace,
loving all people
and drawing them near to the Torah.

Period of Mishnah

What was Aaron's way of reconciling people who had quarrelled? To each he would go and say, "Your friend feels terrible over your quarrel, and wants only to accept the blame for this dispute." Thus, when the two met, they would embrace and make peace. He would do the same thing when there was a dispute between husband and wife. For this reason, when Aaron died, it says (Numbers 20:29), *All the house of Israel wept for him.* Everyone wept for him, because he was the great peacemaker. When Moses died, what does it say (Deuteronomy 34:8)? *The sons of Israel wept for Moses.* Only the men, to whom he had taught Torah, wept for him.

Monday

⁘

May I be among those who are hard to provoke and easy to appease. May I be a friend of peace at home and at work, and everywhere I go. When I am angry let me reflect whether my anger is proportionate to its cause and appropriate in its expression. May I strive at all times to keep from adding to the world's woes.

Yiddish proverb

Keep saying long enough that you're right
and you'll end up in the wrong.

Chasidic

Moshe Leib's father bitterly opposed the Chasidic way. When Moshe Leib left home to study with Shmelke of Nikolsburg, he flew into a rage. He cut a rod and kept it in his room against his son's return. Every so often he would cut a new rod for this purpose. Time passed and many rods were exchanged. One day, a servant cleaning house took the rod up to the attic.

Soon afterward, Moshe Leib went home for a visit. When he saw his father jump up at the sight of him and start on a furious search, he went straight up to the attic, fetched the rod, and laid it down in front of the old man. Gazing into the grave and loving face of his son, the father was won over.

In a controversy, the instant we feel anger we have already ceased striving for the truth, and have begun striving for ourselves.

Thomas Carlyle

Two things, well considered, would prevent many quarrels: first to have it well ascertained whether we are not disputing about terms rather than things; and secondly, to examine whether that on which we differ is worth contending about.

Caleb C. Colton

Tuesday

Keep me from stubborn insistence on always having my way, even when my cause is doubtful, and the truth is unclear. Keep me, however, from conceding to wrong and from accepting violence as a way to resolve disputes. O help me to walk serenely and with good conscience, to accept that I am not the only one with integrity. May I seek the good, even when it seems not to my own advantage.

—Is there controversy that bears fruit?
One engaged in for the sake of Heaven.

Mishnah

A clash of doctrines is not a disaster—it is an opportunity.

Alfred North Whitehead

For to be desperate is to discover strength.
We die of comfort and by conflict live.

May Sarton

The aim of argument, or of discussion, should not be victory, but progress.

Joseph Joubert

Rabbi Abraham Yaakov of Sadagora was asked: According to our sages in Pirké Avot, *There is not a thing that has not its place.* So humanity, too, has its own place. Why then do people sometimes feel so crowded? He replied: Because each wants to occupy the place of the other.

Chasidic

Wednesday

God, make the door of my heart wide enough to receive all whom I may meet this day. And make it too narrow to allow entrance to envy, pride, and strife.

Talmud

Rav Beroka of Bei Chozai often came to the market of Bei Lapat. There, from time to time, he would encounter Elijah the Prophet.

At one of their meetings, he said to Elijah: Is there anyone in this market who has earned Paradise?

Elijah's answer was: No.

For a time, there was a silence between them. Then two men came along.

When he saw them, Elijah said: These two will enter Paradise.

Rav Beroka went to them and said: Who are you and what are your deeds?

They answered: We are jesters.

And your deeds: what are they?

When people are dejected we make them laugh. When people quarrel we find a way to help them make peace.

W. F. Faber

No one was ever corrected by a sarcasm—crushed, perhaps, if the sarcasm was clever enough, but drawn nearer to God, never.

May Sarton

It was completely fruitless to quarrel with the world, whereas the quarrel with oneself was occasionally fruitful, and always . . . interesting.

Thursday

Help me to enter into the mind of the one who stands before me, and keep me alive to the feelings of each one present. Let no word or act—mine or theirs—divide me from my kin. Give us all, instead, a quick eye for little kindnesses, that we may be ready in doing them and gracious in receiving them.

Hezekiah said: Great is peace, for concerning all the [other] Mitzvot it is written: *If you find your enemy's ox that has strayed* (Exodus 23:4), *If you should see your foe's donkey* (Exodus 23:5), *If you should happen upon a bird's nest* (Deuteronomy 22:6)—that is, only if the Mitzvah comes to hand are you called upon to do it; but what is said about peace? *Seek peace and pursue it* (Psalm 34:15)—seek it where you are and pursue it elsewhere.

Midrash

It takes in reality only one to make a quarrel. It is useless for the sheep to pass resolutions in favour of vegetarianism, while the wolf remains of a different opinion.

William Ralph Inge

Return evil for good, and evil will not depart from your house (Proverbs 17:13). Rabbi Judah said in the name of Rav: And beyond this: if you return evil for evil, evil will not depart from your house.

Midrash

Friday

Increase the good in me.
Show me how best to nurture what is of value.
What is good? To befriend you.
What is of value? Really to hear what you are,
  really to see who you are.
And when you weep, let me dry your tears.

The First Temple was destroyed by [reason of] three things: idolatry, immorality, and bloodshed. But in the time of the Second Temple people were devoted to Torah, Mitzvot, and deeds of loving-kindness. What then destroyed it? Causeless hatred.

Talmud

When one subdues others by force,
they do not submit in heart.
They submit because their strength is not adequate to resist.
When one subdues others by virtue,
in their hearts' core they are pleased, and sincerely submit. . . .

Mencius

Sir Thomas Browne

In all disputes, so much as there is of passion, so much there is nothing to the purpose; for then reason, like a bad hound, spends upon a false scent, and forsakes the question first started.

⁘

Shabbat

God, I give thanks for this Sabbath day and for Your peace within me that will bring me a quiet spirit in the company of friends and family. I thank You for the joys that lighten all my days. If, in the rush of other days, I have failed to hear Your voice, and if in their blinding glare I did not recognize Your presence, please open my eyes today to the peace that is within me.

Talmud

Abba said in the name of Rabbi Samuel:

One year the School of Shammai and the School of Hillel were at odds. Another year. A third. Each held to its way. A Voice from Beyond then proclaimed: *The words of both are the words of the living God, but the School of Hillel's way is the one to follow.*

Why? Though both followed the living God, the School of Hillel's way was gentle, conciliatory; they would teach their own view and that of their opponents, and give priority to the School of Shammai—[thus we learn that] the Holy One exalts those who humble themselves, and humbles those who exalt themselves.

Alfred North Whitehead

In formal logic, a contradiction is the signal of a defeat; but in the evolution of real knowledge it marks the first step in progress towards a victory. This is one great reason for the utmost toleration of variety of opinion.

13 *The Divine Presence*

The Week of Sh'mot
Exodus 1:1–6:1

In *Sh'mot* (Exodus 3), the first Sidra of Exodus, the people of Israel are slaves in Egypt. Moses is a shepherd who takes his sheep into the wilderness. There he turns aside to see a wonder—and encounters God! *He gazed, and there was a bush all aflame, yet the bush was not consumed* (3:2). A Voice calls out: *Take your sandals off your feet, for the place on which you stand is holy ground* (3:5). God has appeared to Moses to send him on a mission: Tell Pharaoh to let My people go, tell Israel the time of liberation is at hand.

Just as the flame does not harm the bush, so God's nearness is not a threat but a reassurance.

Sunday

You are near as the very air I breathe and the light around me; yet my thought's uttermost reach falls short of You, and I often feel that You are hidden from me. I long to reach You, but cannot. I seek the light and warmth of Your presence, as a plant turns to the sun, but my heart is chilled. O make my desire for You so strong that it will hold in itself the power of fulfillment! Let Your light penetrate my dull vision, to reveal to me the glory and joy of Your eternal presence.

Service of the Heart / cs

A man asked the Baal Shem Tov: Why do I sometimes feel that God is absent or too far away to reach, however hard I try?

He answered: When you set out to teach your little children

Chasidic

to walk, didn't you stand in front of them and, as they walked toward you, held your two hands on either side of them to keep them from falling? Then, when they came near, didn't you move away a little, holding your hands farther apart? After a while, your children learned to walk on their own, didn't they?

Chasidic

As the atmosphere envelops the earth, so does God, and there is no place devoid of the Divine Presence. As the Midrash says (Sh'mot Rabbah 2:9), "Why did God choose to appear [to Moses] in a thornbush? To teach us that there is no place devoid of the Divine Radiance, not even a thornbush."

Monday

cs / Gates of Prayer

God of my mothers and fathers, lead me in Your way, and teach me to see each new day as a token of Your love. Open my eyes to Your presence in my daily life, that again and again, I may find myself eager to serve You. Strengthen in me the voice of conscience, prompt me to deeds of goodness, and turn my thoughts toward kindness: then shall I be confident of Your love and of the goodwill of all who behold me.

Midrash

Where is God?

Behold, I will stand before you there on the rock at Horeb (Exodus 17:6). The Holy One said to Moses: In every place where you find a trace of human footsteps, there I am before you.

William Wordsworth

And I have felt
A presence that disturbs me with a joy
Of elevated thoughts; a sense sublime
Of something far more deeply interfused,
Whose dwelling is the light of setting suns,
And the round ocean and the living air,
And the blue sky, and in the mind of man;
A motion, and a spirit, that impels
All thinking things, all objects of all thought,
And rolls through all things.

When we are alone on a starlit night; when by chance we see the migrating birds in autumn descending on a grove of junipers to rest and eat; when we see children in a moment when they are really children; when we know love in our own hearts; or when, like the Japanese poet Basho we hear an old frog land in a quiet pond with a solitary splash—at such times the awakening, the turning inside out of all values, the "newness," the emptiness and the purity of vision that make themselves evident, provide a glimpse of the cosmic dance.

Thomas Merton

⁘

Tuesday

Fill me with Your spirit. Let me so open my heart to You that I become aware of Your indwelling presence.

I ask this gift in humility, trusting to Your grace in the knowledge that the hungry heart seeking You may find You within itself. Holy One, give me tranquillity of spirit, and with it, the will to work for righteousness with all my might. So will Your grace and power lead me to blessing.

cs / Israel I. Mattuck

Rabbi Meir was accustomed to say:
The Holy One calls to us, saying:
With heart and soul strive to know My ways
and I will be with you.
Approach My Torah's doors with zeal
and I will open them for you.
Keep My Torah in your heart
and reverence for Me before Your eyes,
and I will teach you.
Keep your tongue from all sin,
purify and hallow yourself against wrongdoing,
and I will stay near to you.

Talmud / cs

The Holy One mirrors your laughter and your weeping, your scowl and your smile. As You are with God, so is God with you.

Chaim ben Isaac

Ralph Waldo Emerson

If the stars should appear one night in a thousand, how would men believe and adore; and preserve for many generations the remembrance of the City of God which had been shown! But every night come out these envoys of beauty, and light the universe with their admonishing smile. (Ralph Waldo Emerson)

Wednesday

⁘

cs / Gates of Prayer

Days pass and years vanish, and I walk sightless among miracles. Eternal God, fill my eyes with seeing and my mind with knowing; let there be moments when the lightning of Your Presence illuminates the darkness in which I walk. Help me to see, wherever I gaze, a world aflame with the wonder of Your presence. And I, clay touched by God, will reach out for holiness, and exclaim in wonder: Surely God is in this place—and I did not know it!

Abraham ibn Ezra

I see You in the starry field,
I see You in the harvest's yield,
In every breath, in every sound,
An echo of Your name is found.
The blade of grass, the simple flower,
Bear witness to Your matchless power.

Elizabeth Barrett Browning

Earth's crammed with heaven,
And every common bush afire with God!
But only he who sees, takes off his shoes.

Sir Thomas Browne

Life is a pure flame, and we live by an invisible sun within us.

Unknown

Your enjoyment of the world is never right, till every morning you awake in Heaven. . . . You never enjoy the world aright, till the Sea itself floweth in your veins, till you are clothed with the heavens, and crowned with the stars. . . . Till you can sing and rejoice and delight in God, as misers do in gold, and Kings in sceptres, you never enjoy the world. . . .

I thank You, Holy One, for the times when I become conscious of Your presence, and place before You my desires, my hopes, and my gratitude. This consciousness, this inner certainty of Your presence, is my greatest blessing. God, bless me with the sense that You are here, a smiling presence embracing me when I wake and when I sleep, when I go out and when I come in. I thank You for the intimations of Your presence that uphold me this day.

cs / Forms of Prayer

God said to Moses, and God says to us (Exodus 3): *Remove your shoes from your feet*—meaning, remove the shell of habit that encloses you, that keeps you from your immediate experience, and you will recognize that the place on which you happen to be standing at this moment is holy ground. For there is no rung of being on which we cannot find the holiness of God everywhere and at all times.

Chasidic

I hear and behold God in every object, yet understand
God not in the least,
Nor do I understand who there can be more wonderful
than myself.
Why should I wish to see God better than this day?
I see something of God each hour of the twenty-four, and
each moment then,
In the faces of men and women I see God, and in my own
face in the glass,
I find letters from God dropped in the street—and every
one is signed by God's name,
And I leave them where they are, for I know that others
will punctually come forever and ever.

Walt Whitman

Friday

⁘

Ishpriya O Holy One, I ran through the fields and gathered flowers of a thousand colors—
And now I pour them out at Your feet.
Their beauty and their brightness shout for joy in Your presence.
You created the flowers of the field and made each one far more lovely
than all that human skill could design.
Accept my joy along with theirs,
this field of blossoms at Your feet.
Holy One,
as the wind blows through these flowers
till they dance in the ecstasy of creation,
send Your Spirit to blow through my being
till I too bloom and dance with the fullness of Your life.

Judah Halevi I have sought Your nearness, called You with all my heart,
And on the way toward You, I find You have come to meet me!
Who can deny they have seen You?
The heavens and all their host voiceless declare Your glory.

Sir Arthur Eddington In the case of our human friends we take their existence for granted, not caring whether it is proven or not. Our relationship is such that we could read philosophical arguments designed to prove the non-existence of each other, and perhaps even be convinced by them—and then laugh together over so odd a conclusion. I think it is something of the same kind of security we should seek in our relationship with God. The most flawless proof of the existence of God is no substitute for it; and if we have that relationship the most convincing disproof is turned harmlessly aside. If I may say it with reverence, the soul and God laugh together over so odd a conclusion.

Chasidic Rabbi Rafael of Bershad, the favorite disciple of Rabbi Pinchas, told: On the first day of Chanukah, I complained to my teacher that in adversity it is very difficult to retain perfect faith that God provides for every human being. It actually seems as if God were hiding from such an unhappy being. How to strengthen this faith?

Rabbi Pinchas replied: It ceases to be a hiding, if you know it is hiding.

⁘

Shabbat

O God, where can I find You? Your glory fills the world.
Behold, I find You in the mind free to sail by its own star,
In words that spring from the depth of truth,
Where the scientist toils to unravel Your world's secrets,
Where the artist makes beauty in Your world,
Where men and women struggle for freedom in Your world,
Among the lonely and poor, the lowly and lost,
Wherever noble deeds are done.
Behold, I find You
In the merry shouts of children at play,
In the mother's lullaby, as she rocks her baby to sleep,
In the sleep that falls on an infant's eyes,
And in the smile that plays on sleeping lips,
And in the child as she grows to embrace a world of wonders,
A world of sun and light, of food and drink, laughter,
And dream, and the mystery of love.
Behold, I find You
In the life that dances in my blood,
In death knocking on the doors of life,
And in birth, as the generations ever renew themselves.
O God, where can I find You? Your glory fills the world!
I find You here where I am, O God. I find You here.

Rabindranath Tagore / cs

Along the mountain path
The scent of plum-blossoms—
And on a sudden the rising sun!

Basho

God never appears to you in person but in action.

Mohandas K. Gandhi

וארא

14 *Freedom*

The Week of Va'eira
Exodus 6:2–9:35

The second Sidra of the book of Exodus is *Va'eira*. God has heard the groans of the people of Israel, their suffering and their pain, and is determined to set them free. *I will free you from the labors of the Egyptians and deliver you from their bondage. I will redeem you with an outstretched arm and with great acts of judgment* (6:6).

The Sidra describes the struggle for freedom, distilling it to a conflict between Moses and Pharaoh, in which God gradually raises the level of Egypt's suffering as the result of Pharaoh's stubborn refusal to let Israel go: *The Eternal One said to Moses: Go to Pharaoh and say to him, Thus says the Eternal One—Let My people go, that they may serve Me!* (7:26).

Sunday

"Why?" is of all questions the deepest, the most profound. And so the right to ask is the primary means to the liberation of mind and soul. The ability to question is a precious gift that parents must nurture within their children.

John Stuart Mill

This, then, is the appropriate region of human liberty. It comprises, first, the inward domain of consciousness; demanding liberty of conscience, in the most comprehensive sense; liberty of thought and feeling; absolute freedom of opinion and sentiment on all subjects, practical or speculative, scientific, moral or theological. The liberty of expressing and publishing opinions may seem to fall under a different principle, since it belongs to that part of the conduct of an individual which concerns other people; but, being almost of as much importance as the liberty of thought itself, and resting in great part on the same reasons, is practically inseparable from it. Secondly, the principle requires liberty of tastes and pursuits; of framing the plan of our life to suit our own character; of doing as we like, subject to such consequences as may follow: without impediment from our fellow creatures, so long as what we do does not harm them, even though they should think our conduct foolish, perverse, or wrong. Thirdly, from this liberty of each individual follows the liberty, within the same limits, of combination among individuals, for any purpose not involving harm to others: the persons combining being supposed to be of full age, and not forced or deceived.

No society in which these liberties are not, on the whole, respected, is free, whatever may be its form of government; and never is completely free in which they do not exist absolute and unqualified.

⁘

Monday

You made me free, free to choose between good and evil, between generosity and selfishness; often I feel this freedom as a burden, a weight heavy to bear. Help me to see it as a privilege, one granted to those You made in Your image.

You envy my comfort and you don't notice my cage. *Midrash*

Grace Paley

I lived my childhood in a world so dense with Jews that I thought we were the great imposing majority and kindness had to be extended to the others because, as my mother said, everyone wants to live like a person. In school I met my friend Adele, who together with her mother and father were not Jewish. Despite this, they often seemed to be in a good mood. There was the janitor in charge of coal and my father, unusually smart, spoke Italian to him. They talked about Italian literature, because the janitor was equally smart. Down the hill under the Southern Boulevard El, families lived, people in lovely shades of light and darkest brown. My mother and sister explained that they were treated unkindly; they had in fact been slaves in another part of the country in another time.

Like us? I said.

Like us, my father said year after year at Seders when he told the story in a rush of Hebrew, stopping occasionally to respect my grandmother's pained face, or to raise his wineglass to please the grownups. In this way I began to understand, in my own time and place, that we had been slaves in Egypt and brought out of bondage for some reason. One of the reasons, clearly, was to tell the story again and again—that we had been strangers and slaves in Egypt and therefore knew what we were talking about when we cried out against pain and oppression. In fact, we were obligated by knowledge to do so.

Tuesday

⁘

Am I free? The lines within which I exercise my freedom are narrow, my nature is limited. I live between the twin poles of necessity and freedom; my task: to find my bearings.

Israel I. Mattuck

The Exodus is about a quest for freedom—the freedom to worship God. Yet in worshipping God we take on a responsibility. Indeed, Freedom and Responsibility are intimately related. Freedom is a necessary condition of responsibility; and the assumption of responsibility gives worth and meaning to freedom.

Learned Hand

The spirit of liberty is the spirit which is not too sure that it is right; the spirit of liberty is the spirit which seeks to understand the minds of other men and women; the spirit of liberty is the spirit which weighs their interests alongside its own without bias.

Edmund Burke

The liberty, the only liberty, I mean is a liberty connected with order; that not only exists along with order and virtue, but which cannot exist at all without them. It inheres in good and steady government, and in its substance and vital principle.

The freedom we should seek is not the right to oppress others, but the right to live as we choose and think as we choose where our doing so does not prevent others from doing likewise.

Bertrand Russell

⁘

Wednesday

The liberties I cherish for myself, may I wish for all. Teach me to be sensible, to see that I cannot be free by myself, for my life is part of a greater life—the life of humanity, formed to be free.

What constitutes the bulwark of our own liberty and independence? It is not our frowning battlements, our bristling sea coasts, our army and our navy. These are not our reliance against tyranny. All of these may be turned against us without making us weaker for the struggle. Our reliance is the love of liberty which God has planted in us. Our defense is in the spirit which prizes liberty as the heritage of all men, in all lands everywhere. Destroy this spirit and you have planted the seeds of despotism at your own doors. Familiarize yourselves with the chains of bondage and you prepare your own limbs to wear them. Accustomed to trample on the rights of others, you have lost the genius of your independence and become the fit subjects of the first cunning tyrant who rises among you.

Abraham Lincoln

But if the slave declares: "I love my master. . . . I do not wish to be freed," his master shall take him before God. He shall be brought to the door or the doorpost, and his master shall pierce his ear with an awl; then he shall remain his slave for life (Exodus 21:56).

Rabbi Yochanan ben Zakkai drew the following lesson: Why, of all the parts of the body, is the ear chosen for the ceremony signifying perpetual servitude? The Holy One said: *For to Me the people of Israel are servants* (Leviticus 25:55)—and not servants of servants! This man heard God call him to freedom, and yet he went and sought out a master: let his ear be pierced!

Period of Mishnah

Remember that to change your opinion and to follow the one who corrects your error is as consistent with freedom as it is to persist in your error.

Marcus Aurelius

⁘

In Your service, O God, is freedom, the freedom to serve my brothers and sisters, the freedom to grow in knowledge and skill, to live with others, permitted to be myself as they are themselves.

cs Every one of us contains all four children of the Haggadah: we are the one unable to ask, the simple child, the wicked one, and the wise child. Sometimes we don't even know there is a question: we are then the one who does not know enough to ask; yet again we are the child who asks an innocent question and is satisfied by a "simple" answer: we don't think to look beneath the surface. And within us, as well, is the "wicked" child, alienated, estranged, wondering why we are part of all this, wanting to go on a different path. But we are wise, too, sometimes: wise enough to ask, not once but repeatedly, humbly but passionately seeking truth invisible to the naked eye, well aware that answers beget questions, but feeling, too, the privilege that belongs to a community that values the liberty of the seeker.

Rabindranath Tagore I have on my table a violin string. It is free to move in any direction I like. If I twist one end, it responds; it is free. But it is not free to sing. So I take it and fix it into my violin. I bind it, and when it is bound, it is free for the first time to sing.

Mark Twain It is by the goodness of God that in our country we have these three unspeakably precious things: freedom of speech, freedom of conscience, and the prudence never to practice either of them.

Lillian Smith The unpardonable sin for every human being is to have more knowledge than understanding, more power than love; to know more about the earth than about the people who live in it; to invent quick means of travel to faraway places when one cannot grope one's way within one's own heart. For freedom is a dreadful thing unless it goes hand in hand with responsibility.

Others may call me free, but I know how bound I am: I am hungry for your word: feed me; thirsty to know my life's meaning: give me to drink; painful ignorance wounds me day after day: heal me; with imperfect love I cannot always make myself known: give wings to my heart. Then I shall know I am free.

Chasidic

Rabbi Bunam said: At the Seder we eat the Matzah first and the Bitter Herbs next, though the reverse order would seem more appropriate, since we first suffered and later went free. There is a reason for this. As long as they had no hope of redemption, they did not feel the real bitterness of their lot. But as soon as Moses spoke to them of freedom, they awoke to the bitterness of their slavery.

Lynn Harold Hough

The escape from the Ten Commandments through violating them has never kept its promise of giving a new freedom. The experience is like the attempt to escape from the law of gravitation by defying it. The result is likely to be at least a bad fall. . . . You cannot become free physically by defying the laws of nature. And you cannot become free morally by defying the laws of ethics.

Viktor Frankl

The experiences of camp life show that one does have a choice of action. There were enough examples, often of a heroic nature, which proved that apathy could be overcome, irritability suppressed. We can preserve a vestige of spiritual freedom, of independence of mind, even in such terrible conditions of psychic stress. We who lived in concentration camps can remember the men who walked through the huts comforting others, giving away their last piece of bread. They may have been few in number, but they offer sufficient proof that everything can be taken from a man [or a woman] but one thing: the last of the human freedoms—to choose one's attitude in any given set of circumstances, to choose one's own way.

How much we can do, how much we can be, when we hold on to each other. Whatever passed between us yesterday, we can return to each other today. Thank You for this day and its great good. It can be a day of liberation from the Egypt within.

Mishnah It says (Exodus 32:16), *And the tablets [given to Moses] were God's own work, and the writing was God's own writing engraved on the tablets.*

Do not read it as *harut* (engraved) but as *herut* (freedom), for no one is free except one engaged in the study of Torah.

Unknown When the Voice of God spoke at Sinai, it did not begin by saying, *I am the Eternal One, your God, Who created heaven and earth.* It began by saying, *I am the Eternal One, your God, Who brought you out of the land of Egypt, out of the house of bondage.* Judaism is not only deliverance from external slavery, but also freedom from false fears and false glories, from fashion, from intellectual will-'o-the-wisps.

The most commanding idea that Judaism dares to think is that freedom, not necessity, is the source of all being. The universe was not caused, but created. Behind mind and matter, order and relations, the freedom of God obtains. The inevitable is not eternal. All compulsion is the result of choice. A tinge of that exemption from necessity is hiding in the folds of the human spirit.

John Dewey Freedom from restriction . . . is to be prized only as a means to a freedom which is power: power to frame purposes, to judge wisely, to evaluate desires by the consequences which will result from acting on them; power to select and order means to carry chosen ends into operation.

15 *Community and Justice*

The Week of Bo
Exodus 10:1–13:16

The Sidra *Bo* (Exodus 10) brings us to the climax of Israel's struggle for freedom. Pharaoh, seeing that Egypt has been wounded in the struggle, is willing to let some of the Israelites go for a time. Moses, however, refuses to go unless all Israel is together. Pharaoh offers a concession, but Moses has another agenda—freedom for all: *We will go with our young and our old, we will go with our sons and our daughters* (10:9).

Looking ahead to the Exodus, the Sidra turns to the communal celebration of the festival of unleavened bread, the festival of freedom for all: *There shall be one law for the native-born, and for the stranger who resides among you* (12:49).

⁘

Sunday

Gates of Prayer / cs

May this quiet moment refresh my inner life, and bring me tranquillity. May I find contentment and peace, my desire for possessions abated, my hope for advantage subdued.

But let me not be content when others lack their daily bread, let me not be serene while some have no roof over their heads. Teach me to give thanks for what I have by sharing it with those who are in need. Then shall my life be called good, and my name be remembered for blessing.

Mishnah

Hillel said:

Do not separate yourself from the community.
And let all who labor with the community labor with them
for the sake of Heaven.

For then the merit of their ancestors upholds them and their righteousness endures forever.

Paul K. Poulson No one person can change the whole world for the better; but each is needed. For each is a bit different—just as one leaf is different from the others on a tree, yet all are needed for its complete foliage.

Leo Tolstoy I sit on your back, choking you and making you carry me, and yet assure myself and others that I am very sorry for you and wish to lighten your load by all possible means—except by getting off your back.

Monday

Help me to reach out to those around me, and to welcome them when they seek me out; remind me continually that I need them as they need me, for I am part of them as they are of me.

Talmud One of the sages observed a man taking stones out of his own field and dumping them on public land.

He said: Why are you taking stones from property that isn't yours and putting them on land that does belong to you?

The man did not understand his admonition and laughed: Fool! It's just the other way around!

He had been removing the stones so that the field might fetch more money, and a few months later he sold it.

As he walked along the public road leading from that field, he stumbled over some stones he had thrown there, and bruised his leg. I am the fool, he reflected.

Elijah of Vilna If the owner of a field puts up a fence between his field and that of his neighbor, the neighbor has no obligation to share the expense, for he may say that the fence is of no use to him. This remains true even if the fence is extended to enclose three sides of his field. If, however, that neighbor then puts up a fourth fence, thus completely enclosing his property, he must share the cost of the other three fences. Similarly, we are born into a world we never made, yet by living and working in it we accept responsibility for it.

Rabbi Bunam said: The repetition of the word "justice" in the verse (Deuteronomy 16:20) *Justice, justice shall you pursue* teaches us that we may employ only justifiable methods even in the pursuit of justice. Pursue justice in your ends, and pursue justice in your means.

Chasidic

⁘

Tuesday

O chestnut tree, great rooted blossomer,
Are you the leaf, the blossom or the bole?
O body swayed to music, O brightening glance,
How can we know the dancer from the dance?

William Butler Yeats

You stand this day, all of you, before the Eternal One, your God. . . . (Deuteronomy 29:10). All of you are pledges for one another: if but one among you is righteous, all of you endure through that person's merit—you, and all the world, as it is said (Proverbs 10:25), *The righteous is the foundation of the world.*

Midrash

Strange is our situation here upon earth.
Each of us comes for a short visit,
not knowing why,
yet sometimes seeming to divine a purpose.
From the standpoint of daily life, however,
there is one thing we do know:
that we are here for the sake of others;
above all, for those on whose smile and well-being our own happiness depends;
and also for the countless unknown souls with whose fate we are connected by a bond of sympathy.
Many times a day I realize how much my own outer and inner life is built upon the labors of others,

Albert Einstein

both living and dead,
and how earnestly I must exert myself
in order to give in return
as much as I have received and am still receiving.

Wednesday

⁘

As I go about among my family, friends, and coworkers, let my eye be quick to see the good I can do. And perceiving the kindnesses I receive from the hands of others, let me be thankful and acknowledge how much I owe them.

Period of Mishnah

How hard the first human beings must have labored! They had to plough and plant, cut and bind sheaves, thresh and winnow grain, grind and sift flour, and knead and bake, before they could eat a piece of bread. They had to shear and wash wool, comb and dye and spin and weave and sew before they could wear clothes. But I rise in the morning, and find everything ready for me!

Harry Emerson Fosdick

We ask the leaf, "Are you complete in yourself?" And the leaf answers, "No, my life is in the branches." We ask the branch, and the branch answers, "No, my life is in the root." We ask the root, and it answers, "No, my life is in the trunk and the branches, and the leaves. Keep the branches stripped of leaves, and I shall die." So it is with the great tree of being. Nothing is completely and merely individual.

Talmud

The entire community will fall into ruins if its people insist on the letter of the law in every matter, however small, and show no inclination to temper justice with mercy.

Thursday

⁘

You have commanded me to love my neighbor as myself, and to love the stranger as myself. May I respond not by saying, "How odd and difficult this demand is," but let me say, "How privileged I am, and how honored, to be thought worthy of such a command."

Bar Yochai said: Some people were in a boat, and one of them took a drill, and began to bore a hole. Noticing, the others said: What are you doing? The one drilling replied: What business is it of yours? Am I not drilling under my own place? It is our business, they answered. When the water comes in, it will sink the boat with us in it.

Midrash

One of the sources of human suffering is disgust with oneself and inability to feel any self-love. There is a self-love which we ought to have in accordance with God's will. We ought to love ourselves as God's creation and love the Divine image and likeness within us. We must love our neighbors as ourselves. This implies that we must love ourselves, too, and respect the image of God within us. Such a love is opposed to egoism and egocentricity, i.e., to the madness of putting oneself at the centre of the universe.

Nicholas Berdayev

I can feel the suffering of millions
and yet, if I look up into the heavens,
I think that it will all come right,
that this cruelty too will end,
and that peace and tranquillity will return again.
In the meantime,
I must uphold my ideals,
for perhaps the time will come
when I shall be able to carry them out.

Anne Frank

Friday

Today I will make this effort: to walk with open eyes and ready heart. A moment may come when someone will need me. At that moment help me to see, and not to close eye and ear, and keep on going as though no one was there.

Small is your strength
if you faint in the day of adversity.
Reach out to help those who are being taken to death:

Proverbs / cs

if you hold back from those who stumble to the slaughter,
saying, "Why, we knew nothing of this!"
will it deceive one who weighs the heart?
Will the one who keeps watch in your soul
fail to perceive it?
Will you leave the scene
untouched,
unscathed,
unhurt?

cs How easy it is to blame the poor, the weak, the downtrodden for their sorry state. And since not infrequently they do contribute to their own misfortunes, I have no difficulty in justifying myself in my self-righteousness, preferring that to the effort it takes to be righteous. What a difference "self-" makes.

Shabbat

When I awaken to a world that seems bleak, and am uncertain of my way, I feel lonely and alone.

Then, in the psalmist's words (Psalm 43:3), I ask: *Show me Your light and Your truth; let them lead me, let them bring me to You.* Be with me in ways I can understand: in a loved one's touch, the smile of a friend, the green world's grace. Help me to see them as Your love letters, an earnest of Your care.

Show me Your light and Your truth; let them lead me, let them bring me to You.

Period of Mishnah We find that in the case of the Generation of the Dispersion, the people [building the Tower of Babel] loved one another, and for that reason were spared by the Holy One. Despite the fact that they waged war against Heaven, they did not share the fate of the Generation of the Flood, but were merely scattered over the earth. On the other hand, the people of Sodom hated one another, and therefore lost both this world and the world-to-come.

When God created iron the trees began to tremble. *Midrash*

The iron said: What are you afraid of? Just let none of you enter me and none of you will come to harm!

Anything which is at variance and enmity with itself is not likely to be in union or harmony with any other thing. *Plato*

Justice is the soil in which all the other virtues can prosper. It is the pre-condition of all social virtue, indeed of all community life. It makes civilized existence, it makes human existence possible. In every society justice must be the paramount concern, for it is the very foundation of all society. *Let justice roll down like waters, and righteousness as a mighty stream* (Amos 5:24). *Shalom Spiegel*

16 *Faith*

The Week of B'shalach
Exodus 13:17–17:16

The Sidra *B'shalach* (Exodus 13) celebrates the Exodus. Pharaoh yields to the people of Israel, then changes his mind and pursues them. The people are terrified as they enter the sea, but they pass through on dry ground, and their pursuers are overwhelmed by the waters. And *When Israel saw the great power that the Eternal One wielded against Egypt, they had faith in the Eternal One, and in Moses, God's servant . . .* (14:31).

The people had just passed safely through the waters and escaped to freedom. They saw and believed. What of the times when we don't see, when our experience betrays our expectations? Our faith is tested by such times. But can we live without it?

Sunday

Gates of Prayer / cs

There are moments when I hear the call of my higher self, the call that links me to the Divine. Then I know how blessed I am with life and love. May this be a moment of such vision, a time of deeper attachment to the godlike in me and in the world, for which I shall give thanks and praise!

Irving Greenberg

Faith is living life in the presence of the Redeemer, even when the world is unredeemed. After Auschwitz, faith means that there are times when faith is overcome. [Martin] Buber has spoken of "moment gods": God is known only at the moment when Presence and awareness are fused in vital life. This knowledge is interspersed with moments when only natural, self-contained, routine existence is present. We now have to speak of "moment faiths," moments when Redeemer and vision of redemption are present, interspersed with times when the flames and smoke of the burning children blot out faith—though it flickers again. . . .

This ends the easy dichotomy of atheist/theist, the confusion of faith with doctrine or demonstration. It is clear that faith is a life response of the whole person to the Presence in life and history. Like life, this response ebbs and flows. The difference between the skeptic and believer is frequency of faith, and not certitude of position. The rejection of the unbeliever by the believer is literally the denial or attempted suppression of what is within oneself. The ability to live in moment faith is the ability to live with pluralism and without the self-flattering, ethnocentric solutions which warp religion, or make it a source of hatred for the other.

⁘

Monday

cs / Gates of Prayer

How much I need You, O God! I need the sense of Your presence within me, giving me the strength to elevate my soul beyond the sordid to the sacred.

Your presence is the light that dispels the darkness that would envelop me, the light that shows me the path to a life of honor and truth.

Israel I. Mattuck

Belief in God is more than a simple acceptance of the idea that God exists. It involves a particular view of life, a belief that there is a spiritual quality in human life and in the universe—and a belief that this spiritual quality matters.

Blaise Pascal

Faith affirms many things respecting which the senses are silent, but nothing which they deny.—It is superior to their testimony, but never opposed to it.

August Wilhelm von Schlegel

In actual life every great enterprise begins with and takes its first forward step in faith.

Friedrich Nietzsche

One who has a why to live
can bear almost any how.

Blaise Pascal It is the heart that senses God, and not the reason. That is what faith is, God perceptible to the heart and not to the reason.

Tuesday

⁘

It has been taught that the real meaning of the word *faith* is "faithful." More than mere belief is required of me. What You call for is faithfulness as parent or child or both, as family member and friend, as worker or employer: to be honest and honorable, one who can be counted on.

Will Herberg Faith is a never-ending battle against self-absolutization and idolatry; it is a battle which has to be refought every moment of life because it is a battle in which the victory can never be final. But although never final, victory is always possible. . . .

Helen Keller A sane society whose riches are happy children, men and women, beautiful with peace and creative activity, is not going to be ordained for us. We must make it ourselves. Our destiny is our responsibility, and without faith we cannot meet it competently. Long enough have we been told that faith is impracticable, that we must trim our sails to whatever winds that blow. Now the truth is burning in us that indifference and compromise are chaos.

William James What keeps religion going is something else than abstract definitions and systems . . . and something different from faculties of theology. . . . All these things are after-effects . . . connecting themselves with feeling and conduct that renew themselves in the worldly lives of humble private men and women. If you ask what these experiences are, they are conversations with the unseen, voices and visions, responses to prayer, deliverances from fear, inflowings of help, assurances of support, whenever certain persons set their own internal attitude in certain appropriate ways.

·:·

Wednesday

How hard it is to see any meaning in my life or in anything else. And yet there are moments when it all seems so right. Between these two poles, I walk most of my days in a state of "in-between." Today, let me awaken knowing that the ground I walk on is solid, that my life has enduring meaning and value, even when I cannot see it.

cs / Chasidic

When the Baal Shem Tov was young, he lived in the mountains of southern Russia.
From time to time he would walk to the top of a mountain, and lose himself in thought.
Lost to the world, lost to himself, but found to God.
Deep in this lostness and this foundness, he once began to walk where there was no ground to walk on. As he put his foot down, he was stepping into an abyss.
But before he could hurtle downward, a nearby mountain moved, and closed the gap.
The Baal Shem, all unknowing, continued on firm ground:
lost to the world, lost to himself, but found to God.

John Greenleaf Whittier

Nothing before, nothing behind;
The steps of faith
Fall on the seeming void, and find
The rock beneath.

John Stuart Mill

There is no such thing as absolute certainty, but there is assurance sufficient for the purposes of human life.

·:·

Thursday

Is there a Heart that feels my longing, a Mind that knows me? Is there a Love that will outlast me, and bear me up "on an eagle's wings"? My questions are ceaseless, my answers few and uncertain. Might not my questions become answers, when I ask them with all my mind and heart and soul?

Leo Baeck In Judaism faith is . . . the capacity of the soul to perceive the abiding . . . in the transitory, the invisible in the visible.

David E. Roberts Once I heard a man say: "I spent twenty years trying to come to terms with my doubts. Then one day it dawned on me that I had better come to terms with my faith. Now I have passed from the agony of questions I cannot answer into the agony of answers I cannot escape. And it's a great relief."

Charles Hanson Towne

I need not shout my faith. Thrice eloquent
Are quiet trees and the green listening sod;
Hushed are the stars, whose power is never spent;
The hills are mute: yet how they speak of God!

Swami Prabharananda and Christopher Isherwood True faith is not like a picture frame, a permanently limited area of acceptance. It is like a plant which keeps on throwing forth shoots and growing.

Friday

Give me a God worthy of worship, worthy of the stars in all their radiance, and of the splendor in which we walk, and of the mystery that surrounds us at every turning. Make me aware of this grandeur, and fill me with the gratitude of faith.

Abraham J. Heschel Faith is not an insurance but a constant effort, constant listening to the eternal voice. . . . To have faith means to justify God's faith in us. . . . Religion is not a feeling for something that is, but an answer to the One who is asking us to live in a certain way. It is in its very origin a consciousness of duty, of being committed to higher ends.

Ernest M. Wadsworth

Pray for a faith that will not shrink
when it is washed in the waters of affliction.

Chasidic The Sassover Rebbe taught: Nothing is altogether without its value. Error may lead to truth, lack of faith may lead to God.

For if someone comes to you asking for help, you must not refuse, saying: Have faith; God will help. No, act as if there were no God, and none to help but you.

Chasidic

Some Chasidim of Rabbi Muttl of Tchernobyl came out to meet Rabbi David Leikes, a disciple of the Baal Shem Tov, who was on his way there. He asked them: Who are you?

They said: We are Chasidim of Rabbi Muttl of Tchernobyl.

He went on questioning them and asked: Have you perfect faith in your teacher?

They did not answer, for who can claim to have perfect faith?

He answered for himself: Then I will tell you what faith is. One Sabbath, the third meal went on into the night. Then we gave thanks and remained standing and said the Evening Prayer and made Havdalah, and at once sat down to the melaveh malkah, to escort the Sabbath Bride on her departure. Now we were all poor and had not a penny of our own. And we would not in any event have had money on the Sabbath! And yet, when the meal was over and the holy Baal Shem Tov said to me: *David, give something for a drink,* I put my hand in my pocket, although I knew I had nothing in it, and I drew out a coin.

⁘

Shabbat

I am a fish swimming in water, and I am thirsty! This day slake my thirst for You. First of all, though, I must learn how very thirsty I am, and how much I need to drink of the life-giving water in which I swim all unawares. Give me this day eyes to behold Your being in all that I see, and in all that I cannot see.

Abraham J. Heschel

To have faith is to perceive the wonder that is here, and to be stirred by the desire to integrate the self into the holy order of being.

Faith does not spring out of nothing. It comes with the discovery of the holy dimension of our existence.

Faith means to hold small things great, to take light matters seriously, to distinguish the common and the passing from the aspect of the lasting.

It is faith from which we draw the sweetness of life, the taste of the sacred, the joy of the imperishably dear. It is faith that offers us a share in eternity.

Karl Jaspers This is the vision of a great and noble life: to endure ambiguity and to make light shine through it; to stand fast in uncertainty; to prove capable of unlimited love and hope.

יתרו

17 *Revelations*

The Week of Yitro
Exodus 18:1–20:26

The Sidra *Yitro* (Exodus 18) describes the experience of the people at Mount Sinai. After a tremendous display—thunder, lightning, a dense cloud, the eerie sound of the Shofar—God reveals the Ten Commandments to Moses, beginning with the words: *God spoke all these words, saying: I AM . . .* (20:1–2).

Jewish tradition is rich in reflection on the theme of revelation. God's presence is felt as a revelation, both at Sinai and elsewhere. And what of us? Remote in time from ancient revelations, we can make them our own, and to them add the revelations of spirit and meaning that are a continuing unfolding word speaking to us, awaiting our response.

Sunday

cs / Gates of Prayer

Infinite is Your love, endless Your compassion. Day by day You teach us. Today let me reflect upon Your teaching, and then let my life be a reflection of my learning. Day and night, from waking to lying down, let me be mindful of it, seeing it as my life and the length of my days.

Midrash

Rabbi Yochanan said: When God's voice came forth at Mount Sinai, it divided itself into the seventy human languages, so that the whole world might understand it.

Rabbi Tanchuma said: All at Mount Sinai—old and young, women, children, and infants—heard the voice of God according to their ability to understand.

Moses, too, understood only according to his capacity, as it is said (Exodus 19:19), *Moses spoke, and God answered him with a voice.* With a voice that Moses could hear.

Union Prayer Book / cs

Open our eyes, O God of truth, that we may see and welcome all truth, whether shining from the annals of ancient revelations or reaching us through the seers of our own time; for Your light glows in every one of Your children who yearns for You and seeks Your truth.

Monday

⁘

Where would Torah be, without a hungry heart to taste it, a thirsty mind to drink it? Let me be one who receives Torah today, when I sit in my house, when I walk by the way, when I lie down and when I rise up, so that Torah becomes the way I live.

Chasidic

Rabbi Leib son of Sarah, the hidden saint who wandered the earth and its rivers and valleys redeeming dead and living souls, said this: I went to the Great Maggid not to hear him say Torah, but to see his way of unlacing his boots and lacing them up again.

Chasidic

It is written (Deuteronomy 4:23): *Take heed, lest forgetting the covenant that the Eternal One, your God, has made with you, you make for yourself a graven image, the likeness of anything that the Eternal your God, has bidden you.* But the text should really have said: "of anything which the Eternal your God, has *forbidden* you."

This means: The Torah warns us not to make a graven image of anything God has bidden us.

Chasidic

Rabbi Bunam was asked: It is written (Exodus 19): *And you shall be to Me a kingdom of priests, a holy nation. These are the words that you shall speak to the people of Israel.* To this our teacher Rashi comments: *These are the words*—No more, no less. What does he mean by that?

Rabbi Bunam explained: Moses wanted to reveal more Torah to the people, but he was not allowed. For it was God's will that the people make an effort on their own. Moses was to say just these words to them, no more and no less, so that they might feel: Something is hidden here, and we must strive to discover it for ourselves. That is why, further on, we read: *And he [Moses] set before them these words.* No more and no less.

⁘

Tuesday

As I receive Torah, so may I, through what I am and what I do, be a revelation of Torah to those around me. Make of me a scroll for truths You will inscribe on my heart.

Midrash

I am the Eternal One, your God. (Exodus 20:2) Because the Holy One appeared to Israel on the sea as a warrior doing battle, and at Sinai as a scribe teaching Torah, and in the days of Solomon as a youth, and in the time of Daniel as an elder filled with compassion, the Holy One was careful to say to them: Since you see Me in many different guises, do not suppose that there are many gods. It is I: I am the One at the sea, I am the One at Sinai, I am the One everywhere: *I am the Eternal, your God.*

Rabbi Levi said: . . . when the Holy One spoke to the people of Israel, each one felt personally spoken to by God, and thus it says in the singular, *I am the Eternal One, your God.*

Mishnah

Rabbi Yosé says:
Let your friend's property be as dear to you as your own.
Devote yourself to learning Torah,
for you were born without it,
yet born to learn it.
And let your every deed be for the sake of Heaven.

Chasidic

Rabbi Mendel of Kotzk said: *Set these words, which I command you this day, upon your heart* (Deuteronomy 6:6). The verse does not say "*in* your heart," for there are times when the heart is shut. But the words rest upon the heart, and when, in a holy moment, the heart is open, the words sink deep into it.

Wednesday

✣

Simone Weil Love is revelation, and revelation comes only with love.

Midrash The Torah was given in fire (Exodus 19:18):
And Mount Sinai was wrapped in smoke. . . .
The Torah was given in water (Judges 5:4):
The clouds dropped water. . . .
The Torah was given in wilderness (Numbers 1:1):
And the Eternal One spoke to Moses in the wilderness of Sinai. . . .
Why?
These three are a gift to all who live,
and the Torah is a gift,
as it is said (Isaiah 55:1),
Ho, every one who thirsts, come to the waters,
and the one who has no money, come, buy and eat!
Come, buy wine and milk
without money and without cost.

Midrash Another word:
. . . in the wilderness of Sinai . . .
Make yourself free as the wilderness:
and acquire wisdom and Torah.

Thursday

✣

Eternal God, You call to me second by second, minute by minute. Teach me to hear that call. And when I do hear You, let me find myself eager to listen, and to do.

Midrash

In public,
in the open,
in a place belonging to none
was the Torah given.
Thus no one can say:
I have no portion in it.
Do you want it?
Come and get it.

Wisdom is dear and not for sale.
This is the way of wisdom:
your food—bread with salt;
your water—measured out;
your bed—the earth;
your life—hardship;
your labor—Torah.
And if this is what you choose,
Happy are you, fortunate your lot. (Psalm 128:2)
Happy are you—here, in this world;
fortunate your lot—there, in the world-to-come.

Mishnah

⁘

Friday

Your word comes in stillness, and as I hear it, it comes to me, not to someone else. I cannot pretend that I do not have to respond with all my heart and soul because the commandment is meant for my neighbor: I am my neighbor, my nearest neighbor!

Talmud

If an oven was cut up into sections and sand placed between each one, Rabbi Eliezer said: Such an oven can never become impure. The sages said: It can.

On that day, Rabbi Eliezer employed every conceivable argument, and yet the sages were not convinced: they would not yield.

He then said: If I am right, this carob tree will prove it. And the carob tree moved a distance of one hundred cubits. (Others say: four hundred.)

The sages replied: Carob trees prove nothing.

He then said: If I am right, this stream of water will prove it. And the stream began to flow backwards.

The sages replied: A stream of water proves nothing.

He then said: If I am right, the walls of this house of study will prove it. The walls began to cave in.

Rabbi Joshua rose at this point and rebuked the walls: When sages debate the law, what business is it of yours?

The result was that, out of respect for Rabbi Joshua, the walls did not cave in, but out of respect for Rabbi Eliezer, the walls did not return to their original position. Thus do they remain inclined, to this very day!

Eliezer then said to his colleagues: If I am right, Heaven itself will prove it! And a voice from Beyond was heard to say: Why do you reject Rabbi Eliezer? The law has always been as he says.

Rabbi Joshua now rose and exclaimed (Deuteronomy 30:12): *It is not in heaven.* When we decide the law, we take no notice even of a voice from heaven, for it is already written in the Torah (Exodus 23:2): *The majority view must be followed.**

One day Rabbi Nathan encountered Elijah the Prophet and asked him: What did the Holy One do when all this happened?

Elijah answered: God laughed and said: My children have overcome Me, My children have overcome Me!

Shabbat

Shabbat is a "sign of the covenant" and Torah is the covenant in detail. May I find new Torah in my own life and deeds; may I discover it in this day's learning and teaching and doing, for You do not withhold Your truth from those who seek it.

Jiri Langer

When I was a little boy, and my teacher had just taught me to read, he once showed me two little letters, like square dots, in the prayer book, as he said: "Urele, you see these two letters side by side? That's the monogram of God's name, and whenever you see these two letters side by side, you must pronounce the name of God at that spot, even though it is not written in full."

I continued reading with my teacher until we came to a colon. It also consisted of two square dots, only instead of being side by side they were one above the other. I imagined that this also must be the monogram of God's name and so I pronounced the name of God at this spot.

* A "creative" misinterpretation of that verse.

But my teacher told me: "No, no, Urele, that does not mean the name of God. Only when there are two sitting nicely side by side, where one looks on the other as an equal—only there is the name of God; where one is under the other and the other is raised higher—there the word of God is not. . . ."

Talmud

Teach me the whole Torah,
 a heathen said, while I stand on one foot.
Shammai cursed and drove him away.
He went to Hillel.
Hillel said:
  What is hateful to you, do not do to anyone else:
  that is the whole Torah.
  The rest will follow—go now and learn it.

18 *Doing*

The Week of Mishpatim
Exodus 21:1–24:18

The Sidra *Mishpatim* (Exodus 21) sets forth significant legislation whose aim is justice and fairness in the lives of individuals and in society as a whole. When all this has been read aloud to the people, they respond with the promise: *All that the Eternal One has spoken we will do and we will hear!* (24:3).

In the sequence of the words of the people *we will do* comes first. It seems paradoxical that doing should precede hearing; we are meant to discover, perhaps, a message about the supreme importance of doing. Hearing is not hearing when there is no doing.

Sunday

Two things to think about today. First is this: What I do is not going to change the world much. Second: It's important to keep on doing what I do.

Talmud The Sages of Yavneh liked to say:

I am a creature of God and you are a creature of God. My work may be in the city; yours, in the field. You rise early to your work, I rise early to mine. You do not claim your work is superior, I do not claim my work is superior. And should one say, I do more important work and the other does lesser work, we have learned (Talmud B'rachot 5a): *More or less, it matters not, if the heart is turned toward Heaven.*

Midrash Once when Rabbi Tarfon, Rabbi Yosé the Galilean, and Rabbi Akiba were together in Lydda, the question arose: Which is more important, study or practice? Tarfon argued, "practice." Akiba argued, "study." They concluded: "Study is more important, for it leads to practice."

Rabbi Israel Salanter saw a servant girl carrying two pails of water on her shoulder. When dinner was ready, he used only a few drops in washing his hands. When asked why he did not use more water, he replied: One must not be generous with a mitzvah on another person's shoulders.

Jewish anecdote

⁘

Monday

There are things I need to do today that I intend to put off until tomorrow: Don't let me feel too guilty about it. Give me one day so free of guilt that tomorrow I'll feel liberated to do what I should have done yesterday.

Improve your own character first, then that of others.

Moses ibn Ezra

There are many fine things which you mean to do some day, under what you think will be more favorable circumstances. But the only time that is surely yours is the present; hence this is the time to speak the word of appreciation and sympathy, to do the generous deed, to forgive the fault of a thoughtless friend, to sacrifice self a little more for others. Today is the day in which to express your noblest qualities of heart and mind, to do at least one worthy thing which you have long postponed, and to use your God-given abilities for the enrichment of some less fortunate fellow traveler. Today you can make your life significant and worthwhile. The present is yours to do with as you will.

Grenville Kleiser

The Bershider Rebbe said: Don't have contempt for your ability to do good. You make the effort and God does the rest. . . .

Chasidic

When I say to myself, "I can't do everything," let it not be in order to do nothing. Let it be, instead, merely a recognition that

Chasidic / cs

I don't have to do everything, that other people, too, will do their part to right wrongs, just as they—and I—will try not to add to the wrongs we see done each day.

Tuesday

⁘

There might be something really important for me to do today, but I'm not sure I'll recognize it when I see it. Help me, then, to make sure to greet everyone I meet today with a cheerful face: What can be more important than that?

Chasidic The Baal Shem Tov said: What matters is not the number of commandments we obey, but how, and in what spirit, we obey them.

John Milton I cannot praise a fugitive and cloistered virtue, unexercised and unbreathed, that never sallies out and seeks her adversary, but slinks out of the race, where that immortal garland is to be run for, not without dust and heat.

George Eliot The growing good of the world is partly dependent on unhistoric acts; and that things are not so ill with you and me as they might have been, is half owing to the number who lived faithfully a hidden life, and rest in unvisited tombs.

Wednesday

⁘

I know I can do as I please, if I am willing to pay the price. Help me, Holy One, to be pleased with what I do. And let that doing be honest words and deeds.

Chasidic When Rabbi Moshe of Kobrin died, the Rabbi of Kotzk asked one of the Kobriner's disciples what things his master had considered to be the most important. The man answered: Always just what he was engaged in at the moment.

Talmud Rabbi Meir would say: Never press a friend to dine with you when you know he [she] won't do it; never offer gifts knowing they will not be accepted, and never open a barrel of wine that has been sold without telling your guest [that it has been sold and it has not been opened in his [her] honor]; do not, with an empty flagon, say to someone, "Anoint yourself with oil" [when you know he [she] will refuse]. But if it is done to honor someone in the sight of others, it is permitted.

The Baal Shem Tov said: No two people have the same abilities. You, like all others, must work to serve God according to your own talents. If you try to imitate another, you merely lose your opportunity to do good through your own merit; you cannot accomplish anything by imitating another person's way of service. *Chasidic*

Thursday

If today I should add to the sum of the world's pain, it will have been a day ill spent. And yet, let not the fear that I may err or do an unintended wrong keep me from acting according to what light I have. Let me aim for good, hoping that it adds up to more good than harm.

Rabbi Ber of Radishitz asked the Lubliner to teach him the best way of serving God. The Lubliner replied: The best way is the one to which your heart is drawn. Labor in it with your whole strength. *Chasidic*

In single file the days bring their gifts. We choose and pay for them with time. In the morning we have today; its hours are currency. At night they will have been exchanged. For what? For a task well done, a house lovingly cared for, for contentments or regrets, for a memory which blesses or burns, for a little more wisdom. *Ralph Waldo Emerson*

When a disciple of Rabbi Shmelke begged him to teach him how to prepare his soul for the service of God, he told him to go to Rabbi Abraham who at that time was still an innkeeper. *Chasidic*

The disciple went and lived in the inn for several weeks but saw no sign of holiness in the man, who all day long devoted himself to his business. Finally he asked him: What do you do all day? My most important job, said Rabbi Abraham, is to clean the dishes properly, so that no food is left, and to clean and dry the pots and pans, so that they do not rust. When the disciple returned and reported to Rabbi Shmelke what he had seen and heard, the rabbi said to him: Now you know the answer to your question.

Friday

It's been a long week. I've just gone along and lived. I hope I haven't done any great harm, and I hope, too, that somewhere along the days of this week I've given someone something good. I hope my hopes amount to something. Help me make it so today, whatever yesterday may have been like.

Chasidic

A man died and was brought before the Heavenly Court. When his sins and good deeds were placed on the scales, his sins far outweighed the good deeds he had done. Suddenly a fur coat was piled on the scale containing the good deeds, which then became the heavier scale, and the man was sent to Paradise. On the way, he said to the angel who escorted him: I cannot understand: what did the fur coat have to do with my judgment? The angel replied. One cold wintry night you traveled on a sled and a poor man asked for a ride. You took him in, and, noticing his thin clothes, you placed your fur coat on him to give him warmth. That was the act of kindness that offset your transgressions.

James Philip Bailey

We live in deeds, not years;
in thoughts, not breaths;
in feelings, not figures on the dial;
we should count time by heart throbs.

Do not do to others what you would not have them do to you is one of the fundamental principles of ethics. But it is equally justifiable to state: *Whatever you do to others, you also do to yourself.*

Erich Fromm

⁘

Shabbat

Today is Shabbat, and I can do something for myself, my family, my friends, my community. I can leave things alone, tell the world hello, attend to people's feelings, sing and dance. So much I can do in the peaceful palace of Shabbat!

If you do what is right in God's sight . . . (Exodus 15:26). That is, what is right in business, or in buying and selling. Thus you may learn that if you conduct your business, and buy and sell in truth and fidelity, and give people cause to be pleased with you, it is regarded as if you have fulfilled the whole Torah.

Midrash

I am only one, but I am one. I cannot do everything, but I can do something. And I will not let what I cannot do interfere with what I can do.

Edward Everett Hale

You have not done enough, you have never done enough, so long as it is still possible that you have something of value to contribute.

Dag Hammarskjöld

Rabbi Mendel of Kotzk said: The prohibition against making idols includes a prohibition against making idols out of the commandments, for the chief purpose of a commandment is its inward meaning, not its outward form.

Chasidic

Always do right.
This will gratify some people
and astonish the rest.

Mark Twain

19 *Prayer*

The Week of T'rumah
Exodus 25:1–27:19

The Sidra *T'rumah* (Exodus 25) records the instruction to Moses and the people that they build a sanctuary to take with them on their journey through the wilderness: *And let them make Me a sanctuary, that I may dwell among them* (25:8). The materials out of which the sanctuary is to be made are to be free-will offerings from the people. The sanctuary's dimensions and appearance are spelled out in minute and loving detail. Thus begins the development of organized communal worship of God in the biblical tradition. Individual prayers had already been noted in earlier portions of the biblical record.

⁘

Sunday

cs / Forms of Prayer

I thank You for this time of prayer, when I become conscious of Your presence, and lay before You my desires, my hopes, and my gratitude. This consciousness, this inner certainty of Your presence is my greatest blessing. My life would be empty without it. I would be lost if I did not return to You from time to time, to be at one with You, knowing that You are with me in all my difficulties and troubles, and that I have in You a Friend whose help is sure and whose love never changes.

cs / Chasidic

One who is about to pray should learn from a common laborer, who sometimes takes a whole day to prepare for a job. A woodcutter, who spends most of the day sharpening the saw and only the last hour cutting the wood, has earned a day's wage.

I have always found prayer difficult. So often it seems like a fruitless game of hide-and-seek where we seek and God hides. . . . Yet I cannot leave prayer alone for long. My need drives me to God. And I have a feeling that . . . finally all my seeking will prove infinitely worthwhile. And I am not sure what I mean by "finding." Some days my very seeking seems a kind of "finding." And, of course, if "finding" means the end of "seeking," it were better to go on seeking.

Gates of Prayer

Pray as if everything depended on God;
act as if everything depended on you.
Who rise from prayer better persons,
their prayer is answered.

Gates of Prayer

⁘

Monday

Look for the answer to prayer not in what you get but in what you become.

We do not even know how we are supposed to pray. All we do is call for help because of the need of the moment. But what the soul expresses is spiritual need, only we have no words to convey its meaning. That is why, when we ask God to hear our call for help, we also beg the One who knows what is hidden to hear the silent cry of the soul.

Martin Buber

Normally, we are compelled to pass from one task to another in quick succession; one duty is completed only to be followed immediately by the next; a difficulty surmounted, a problem solved is replaced with such rapidity by further worries and by other cares that we have no choice, in daily life, but to live from one minute to another, to eliminate from our minds everything but that which is immediately ahead of us and which demands immediate attention.

In worship, however, we are freed from the pressure of life. There are no immediate tasks to be performed: no insistent needs clamoring for immediate satisfaction. For once, we are

Leslie I. Edgar/ Gates of Prayer

guaranteed Time and Quietude—the rarest possessions in life today. For once, we can escape from the tyranny of the next minute with its worries, tasks and duties.

And when, as now, we do have time to take a larger view of life; when, in calm reflection, we enlarge our vision until we see life in its entirety, considerations come before us which tend to be excluded in the rush of everyday experience. We can now allow our spiritual needs to take precedence over those material satisfactions to which, usually, we pay such high regard and to which, normally, we devote so large a measure of our effort. In worship, the foremost place in our consideration is given to that which develops character, all that which lends nobility and dignity to human life, all wherein we can express the greatness of the human spirit. We consider what it means to us and for our lives that we have been endowed by God with reason, with a power to love, with a sense of the beautiful, and with a knowledge of righteousness.

Tuesday

You answer my prayer when I know You to be its answer. Let my prayer be to walk with You in the small steps I take along my life's path.

Costen J. Harrell

Prayer is opening the heart to God. It is not all petition. It has its listening side. Prayer is more than speaking to God; it is giving God an opportunity to speak to us.

Chasidic

Mendel of Vorki once said about prayer:
This is how you should pray:
Kneel—while standing up straight.
Scream—without making a sound.
Dance—without making a move.

cs

Prayer is speech. But it is not "mere" speech. The word is not to be despised. Consider, for example, the words "I love you." How great is their power! In the same way, "Hear, O Israel!" is a cry and an affirmation, a reminder of glory and martyrdom, the very essence of the history of a people. They are words, yes. But words wound and heal, they tear down, and they build up. . . . But above all, these words, laden with the tears and joys of centuries, have the power to bring us into the presence of God. Not all at once, not easily, not every time: but somehow, sometime the faithful worshippers who take heart and soul . . . and offer them up without reservation—somehow, sometime they will know that they have reached the throne of Glory, and that God has taken them by the hand.

⁘

Wednesday

Teach me how to pray as though I were planting beans, or boiling water for tea: simple, honest acts. So let my prayer be as natural as working in my garden, or in my kitchen.

When thou prayest, rather let thy heart be without words than thy words without heart.

John Bunyan

God wants the heart.

Talmud

My words fly up, my thoughts remain below:
Words without thoughts never to heaven go.

William Shakespeare

All the gates of Heaven are closed except the Gates of Tears. These are always open. (Talmud B'rachot 32a)

The "Yud" said: Why are the Gates of Tears always open? Because tears are a sign of grief, and grief cannot open gates that are closed. The other gates, however, need not be kept open, for they can be opened by joyful prayer.

Chasidic

⁘

Thursday

Through my prayer I can learn what I love, and what to work for. To be what I seem, therefore, when what I seem to be brings me honor, honorably earned—that is what I need to pray for.

Emil G. Hirsch True prayer is not a petition to God: it is a sermon to ourselves.

Chasidic The Baal Shem Tov said:

A child is conceived through pleasure and joy. In the same way, if you want your prayers to bear fruit, offer them with pleasure and joy.

William Barclay Prayer must always remain quite ineffective, unless we do everything we can to make our own prayers come true. It is a basic rule of prayer that God will never do for us what we can do for ourselves. Prayer does not do things for us; it enables us to do things for ourselves.

John Stuart Blackie The efficacy of prayer is not so much to influence the divine counsels as to consecrate human purposes.

Ernest Findlay Scott Prayer is answered when it enables us to act as God desires.

Friday

Should I pray for things that vanish? Won't I vanish along with everything else? Maybe not—maybe it only feels that way now, because I cannot imagine being, without being aware of myself. If only I could see with God's eyes! Yet if God sees me, what matter if I don't see what God sees? I pray to know that God sees me.

Leo Baeck The purpose of prayer is to leave us alone with God.

Abraham J. Heschel Sometimes prayer is more than a light before us; it is a light within us. . . . A story is told about a Rabbi who once entered heaven in a dream. He was permitted to approach the temple of Paradise, where the great sages of the Talmud, the Tannaim, were spending their eternal lives. He saw that they were just sitting around tables studying the Talmud. The disappointed Rabbi wondered, "Is this all there is to Paradise?" But suddenly he heard a voice, "You are mistaken. The Tannaim are not in Paradise. Paradise is in the Tannaim."

To pray is not the same as to pray for.

Claude G. Montefiore

We hear in these days of scientific enlightenment a great deal of discussion about the efficacy of prayer and many reasons are given us why we should not pray, whilst others are given why we should. But in all this very little is said of the reason why we do pray. . . . The reason why we do pray is simply that we cannot help praying.

William James

⁘

Shabbat

Infinite Spirit, grant me a heart of wisdom, so that on this day of rest and prayer I seek after Your light and Your truth with a whole heart.

Public worship draws out the latent life in the human spirit. Those who, when alone, do not, or cannot, pray, find an impulse to prayer when they worship with others; and some will pray together who cannot pray alone, as many will sing in chorus who would not sing solos. Many who are spiritually weak in themselves find spiritual strength in a common spiritual effort. That is the value of public worship for the individual. It also has a social value.

A congregation at worship is a society declaring its devotion to God, a community forged by faith in God. Here is an experience that can deepen the social spirit and strengthen the bond of sympathy among men and women. If in public worship I realise that my prayers are also the prayers of the person by my side, it will make us more effectively aware of our common humanity and implant a spirit which will be potent for social good. Those who worship together bring God into their mutual relations. If public worship does not produce this result, then it is but private worship in a public place. If it does bring men and women close together under the influence of God, then it is a way to the sanctification of human society.

Siddur Lev Chadash

Midrash The Holy One says to Israel: I bade you pray in the synagogue of your city, but if you cannot pray there, pray in your field, and if you cannot pray there, pray on your bed, and if you cannot pray there, then meditate in your heart and be still.

Chasidic Rabbi Uri of Strelisk said: It is written (Genesis 4:4): *And Abel, too, brought an offering. . . .* This also can be read, literally, *And Abel brought himself, too, an offering. . . .* It means: Abel brought *himself* as an offering. Only when we offer ourselves as well, is our offering acceptable.

20 *Light*

The Week of T'tzaveh
Exodus 27:20–30:10

The Sidra called *T'tzaveh* (Exodus 27) continues the account of the wilderness sanctuary by prescribing the consecration of Aaron and his sons as the first priests to minister in the sanctuary. And it begins with a task: *Command the people of Israel to bring to you pure oil of pressed olives for the light, to keep a lamp burning continually* (27:20). The lamp that burns in synagogues and churches is a descendant of that original lamp.

Light is a metaphor for the Divine, for understanding, for "enlightenment." Seeking it, we can become light-givers.

⁘

Sunday

Gates of Prayer

When justice burns within us like a flaming fire, when love evokes willing sacrifice from us, when, to the last full measure of selfless devotion, we demonstrate our belief in the ultimate triumph of truth and righteousness, then Your goodness enters our lives and we can begin to change the world; and then You live within our hearts, and we through righteousness behold Your presence.

Chasidic

A young disciple complained to his Rebbe: When I am studying Torah I feel filled with light and life, but as soon as I cease from study this feeling leaves me. What should I do?

The Rebbe replied: You are like someone who walks through a forest on a dark night, accompanied by a companion who carries a lantern. Then their paths divide, and each must go on alone.

Carry your own lantern, and you need not fear the darkness.

cs / Chasidic The Rizhiner Rebbe said: Let your light penetrate the darkness until the darkness itself becomes light and there is no longer a division between the two. As it is written (Genesis 1): *And there was evening and there was morning, one day.*

Monday

⁘

What is my task this day? Help me to find the one thing that only I can do, and give me strength to do it well. It may be that today I will find myself challenged to smile when tempted to frown, or to give when I would rather take. Help me to know the one thing to do, when the time comes to do it: To make light shine from within, to bring a light to another's eyes.

Chasidic Add oil to the lamp before the light dies, for if it does, the oil will do no good.

Theodore Ledyard Cuyler Let your religion be seen. Lamps do not talk, but they do shine. A lighthouse sounds no drum, it beats no gong; yet, far over the waters, its friendly light is seen by the mariner.

Chasidic Rabbi Baruch once said: What a good and bright world this is if we do not lose our hearts to it, but what a dark world, if we do!

Oscar Edward Maurer Waste not your life trying to push shut doors which God is opening. Neither wear yourself out in keeping open doors which ought to be forever sealed. Some episode in your life, over which you are anxious, is closed. It is in the past. Whatever its memory, you cannot change it. But you can shut the door. Go into some silent place of thought. Test your self-respect. Ask your soul, "Have I emerged from this experience with honor, or if not, can honor be retrieved?" And if your soul answers "Yes," close then the door to that Past; hang a garland over the portal if you will, but come away without tarrying. The east is aflame with the radiance of the morning, and before you stands many another door, held open by the hand of God.

✦ Tuesday

Why the dark look? Concern yourself less with yourself, stop clamoring for praise and gratitude, and take what comes with a bright eye and a warm heart. To have kindled a lamp for someone along the way—reward enough?

There are those who suffer very greatly and cannot tell you what is in their hearts, and they go their ways full of suffering. But if they meet someone whose face is bright with laughter, that person's gladness can quicken them. And it is no small thing to quicken a human being! *Chasidic*

The candle you light will give light to a hundred. *Talmud*

Rabbi Shlomo of Karlin asked: When can one see a little light? And he answered his own question: If one keeps oneself quite lowly, as it is written (Psalm 139): *If I make my bed in the lowest depths, behold, You are there!* *Chasidic*

Light that makes some things seen, makes some things invisible. Were it not for the darkness and the shadow of the earth, the noblest part of the Creation would remain unseen, and the stars in heaven invisible. *Sir Thomas Browne*

✦ Wednesday

It would be bliss to find a new virtue within me, a new form of service. My task today, it may be, is to look for it. And if I have not found it by end of day, I can at least hope that in the seeking itself there is a finding, that no one seeks altogether in vain. For by the candle I light today, many others may be kindled.

What profit have we for all our labors under the sun? (Ecclesiastes 1:3) The Koretzer Rebbe said: What reward is due us for all our labors in the service of God in addition to the reward of being alive, of beholding the sun shine on us, to bring us the joy of life and light? *Chasidic*

Who, walking in darkness and seeing a bright light ahead, would be fool enough not to hurry toward it?

Midrash A man was on his knees, searching for something.
A neighbor came along and saw him, so he asked:
What are you searching for?
My key. I've lost it.
His neighbor got on his knees, too, and both men searched for the lost key.
After a while, the neighbor asked: Where did you lose it?
At home.
Then why are you searching for it here?
Because the light is better here!

Thursday

Some days I hold a mirror to my face and what I see is the sum of my fears and griefs, my angers and disappointments. Today may I have light enough to see the world with the eyes of a child and find it the playground of my hopes and my joys. You want light enough? Radiate enough light!

Helen Keller There is no lovelier way to thank God for your sight than by giving a helping hand to someone in the dark.

Chasidic *Fire shall be kept burning upon the altar continually; it shall not go out.* (Leviticus 6:6) The Baal Shem Tov said: Your heart is the altar. Whatever your work, let a spark of the holy fire remain within you, and fan it into a flame.

Chasidic The Baal Shem once asked his disciple Rabbi Meir Margaliot: Meirl, do you still remember that Sabbath when you were just beginning to study the Torah? The big room in your father's house was full of guests. They had lifted you up on the table and you were reciting what you had learned?

Rabbi Meir replied: Certainly I remember. Suddenly my mother rushed up to me and snatched me down from the table in the middle of what I was saying. My father was annoyed, but she pointed to a man standing at the door. He was dressed like a peasant, in a short sheepskin, and he was looking straight at me. They all understood that she feared the Evil Eye. She was still pointing at the door when the man disappeared.

It was I, said the Baal Shem. In such hours a glance can flood the soul with light. But fear builds walls to keep the light away.

⁘

Friday

It is childish to suppose that the world revolves about me, that I am its center. What I do is not all that important. And yet my actions can add to the light or diminish it.

Tao / cs

Can you become like a child?
Cleansing your vision,
Can you see your inner light?
Can you keep from imposing your will?
Can you give birth and nourish?
Give birth without owning,
Act without demanding,
Lead without ruling:
This path is virtue.

Simone Weil

Love is not consolation, it is light.

Chasidic

How should you give to one in need? As a matter of duty? No, for if love is lacking the body is nourished but the soul is starved. Still, better to give only out of a sense of duty than not at all. Should you give with conscious pleasure? No, for then you are thinking of yourself, puffing yourself up and imagining you are God. How, then? Naturally, spontaneously, without thought, as the sun gives its light and a mother her milk.

Shabbat

In my daily life I live in a workaday world, occupied and all too often preoccupied with my daily needs. Today on the day of rest and re-creation, let me pause to enjoy the world and not to labor in it, to see it aright, enlarge my view and my spirit, and find the world good, even as did its Creator who said: Let there be light! and who by that light saw how very good it was.

Shifra Alon / cs

Not every day do we encounter God,
not every time is opportune for prayer,
not every hour one of grace.
We fail and fail again till journey's end.
We turn back only to lose our way
once more,
and grope in search of long
forgotten paths.
But God, holding a candle,
looks for all who wander,
all who search.

Chasidic We have not beheld the light of the divine if we think only of ourselves when serving God.

Chasidic Rabbi Moshe, the son of the Maggid of Kosnitz, said:

It is written (Exodus 27:20): *Pure olive oil beaten for the light.* We are beaten and bruised, but in order to glow with light.

21 *Quest*

The Week of Ki Tissa
Exodus 30:11–34:35

The Sidra *Ki Tissa* (Exodus 30) concludes the divine instruction to Moses and notes the impatience of the people as they await his return from Mount Sinai's summit. Unable to keep in mind the invisible God of the Exodus and of Sinai, they make for themselves a molten calf of gold. In the aftermath, as the chastened people are about to set forth toward the promised land, Moses pleads that God be present on their quest, and his own. We read: *And he said: O let me behold Your presence!* And God answers: *I will make all My goodness pass before you* (33:18–19).

⁂

Sunday

My heart is hungry, my spirit thirsts, yet much of the time I am not aware. Once in a while I have the feeling that just beyond my hearing a voice is calling to me. There is something I need to look for, without which I am in darkness even when I think I see: it is myself I must find; it is You within me, O God, that I must find. But to find I must begin to seek.

The meaning of our life is the road, not the goal. For each answer is delusive, each fulfillment melts away between our fingers, and the goal is no longer a goal once it is attained.

Arthur Schnitzler

There is deep-seated in the make-up of the ordinary person a craving for flowers that do not fade and pleasures that do not pass away. Deep down inside of every human being there is a desire for the genuine—the lasting quality of real life.

Warren Walker

Mark Van Doren

The fact that it's difficult to see the signs doesn't necessarily mean that they don't exist. The signs are there to be seen, if we could understand them. . . .

Monday

⁘

Someone said: "Do not seek for the City of God on earth, for it is not built of wood or stone; but seek it in the soul of the one who knows inner peace and is a lover of true wisdom." This, then, be my aim: to be at peace with myself, and to be a lover of wisdom.

Chasidic / cs

The Radziminer Rebbe said: In the life of the spirit you come upon door after door, each one of which you must open and pass through before you can reach the inmost entrance.

Walt Whitman

Will you seek far off? You surely come back at last, in things best known to you, finding the best, or as good as the best—Happiness, knowledge, not in another place, but in this place—not for another hour, but this hour.

Oliver Wendell Holmes

I find the great thing in this world is not so much where we stand, as in what direction we are moving.

John Ciardi

> Humanity cannot be measured by what it is;
> only by what it is trying to become.

Carl Becker

Idealism must always prevail on the frontier, for the frontier, whether geographical or intellectual, offers little hope to those who see things as they are. To venture into the wilderness, one must see it, not as it is, but as it will be. The frontier, being the possession of those only who see its future, is the promised land which cannot be entered save by those who have faith.

⁘ Tuesday

Help me to climb the mountain of my life so that at end of day I come to higher ground with a larger view of where I have come from and what I have arrived at. But teach me most of all to be glad of the joy and labor of the climb.

Let the heart rejoice of all who seek the Eternal (I Chronicles 16:10). The Apelier Rebbe said: When you're seeking an object you feel no gladness until your quest is successful. But when you seek the Eternal, the very act of seeking makes your heart rejoice. *Chasidic*

Spirituality is the sacred center out of which all life comes, including Mondays and Tuesdays and rainy Saturday afternoons in all their mundane and glorious detail. . . . The spiritual journey is the soul's life commingling with ordinary life. *Christina Baldwin*

The liberating encounter with God/ess is always an encounter with our authentic selves resurrected from underneath the alienated self. It is not experienced against, but in and through relationships, healing our broken relations with our bodies, with other people, with nature. *Rosemary Ruether*

Rabbi Mendel of Kotzk said: If you were to lose a diamond in a haystack, you would look for it and not give up until you had found it. Likewise, God's word is near to you. Don't stop looking until you find it. Does it seem beyond comprehension? Keep at it until you understand it. For it says (Deuteronomy 30:12), *This commandment I give you this day is not too far from you, nor too difficult.* . . . It is in your mouth and your heart, that you may do it. *Chasidic / cs*

⁘ Wednesday

What have I found along the way? I know I've overlooked many things, passing wonders without taking much note of them. Now, this day, let me journey with eye and mind more attentive to the marvels around me.

Talmud If someone tells you: I sought but I did not find, do not believe; I did not seek yet I found, do not believe; I sought and I found, believe.

Francis Bacon They are ill discoverers who think there is no land, when they can see nothing but sea.

cs

You fulfill the object of your existence
by asking a question you cannot answer,
and attempting a task you cannot complete.

Herman Melville God, keep me from ever completing anything. This whole book is but a draught—nay, but the draught of a draught, Oh, Time, Strength, Cash, and Patience!

Chasidic Rabbi Mendel of Kotzk told the story of the hunter whom the prophet Elijah met in the wilderness and asked why he was living there without the Torah and without the commandments. The hunter defended himself by saying: I never could find the gate that leads to the presence of God.

You were certainly not born a hunter, said Elijah. So from whom did you learn to follow this calling?

My need taught me, replied the hunter.

And was that your only need?

Thursday

I'm on my way! Where to? Who cares, as long as I'm going! No, there's something wrong with that—I do need to consider my destination. Not that I'm in control: I didn't draw the map, I didn't form the terrain, I don't make the weather, I can't decide whom I shall meet along the way. But I can choose a direction, I can steer a course and avoid some of the potholes, I can decide how to greet my fellow travelers, I can sing along the open road.

Once, Rabbi Chaim of Krosno and his disciples were watching a tightrope walker. He was so absorbed in the spectacle that they asked him what it was that riveted his gaze to this foolish performance. And he said: This man is risking his life, and I can't say why. But of this I am certain: while he is walking the rope, he is not thinking of the fact that he is earning money by his performance, for if he did, he would fall. *Chasidic*

I laugh when I hear that the fish
in the water is thirsty.
The truth is here! Go where you will—
to Benares or to Mathura;
until you have found God
in your own soul, the whole world
will seem meaningless to you.

Rabindranath Tagore

If there be anywhere on earth a lover of God who is always kept safe from falling, I know nothing of it—for it was not shown me. But this was shown—that in falling and rising again we are always kept in the same precious love. *Julian of Norwich*

⁘

Friday

Yes, God, I am on the open road, know it or not, like it or not engaged upon a quest. Make me conscious on this journey, my life. I no more know its endpoint than Abraham and Sarah did when they set forth to a land You said You would show them. And You did. Do the same for me. Give me a questing spirit, that I too may hear Your voice calling me to set forth with courage and faith.

The Koretzer Rebbe said: The Eternal accepts every invitation. You seek God? Extend an invitation. *Chasidic*

Akram was a seeker who went from sage to sage, never satisfied with what he had learnt. He came at last to a sage who knew all the secrets of life. *Sufi*

Eagerly he asked that the mysteries be revealed to him, but all the sage would say was:

First things first, and one thing at a time.

Unable to interpret this, yet thirsty for revelation, Akram remained and served the sage for a number of years. During that time he heard little and understood less.

One thing he did hear: There will be a Golden Age after several centuries.

Growing impatient, Akram determined to leave the sage and travel to the Golden Age. After a long search that spanned the oceans and continents, he found a wonder-worker who agreed to put Akram to sleep for seven hundred years.

Akram woke up and looked around. He saw the ruins of a mighty civilization.

Akram went in search of that part of earth where the Golden Age might yet be found. There was little sign of human life, however far he wandered. Finally he saw the smoke of a fire. There, beside a crude hut, was a solitary dervish, dressed in rags.

—I seek the Golden Age, said Akram.

—You have missed it by two hundred years, said the dervish.

Shabbat

⁘

On this quest of mine to make sense of my life, to discover the meaning of what I do and what is done to and for me, I come to the stillness of this day. I yearn for the insight to be grateful for the gifts that have been created in me, and for the gift of loving companions who walk at my side. On Shabbat let me put aside all doubt and sadness, and give thanks.

Ahad Ha'am

The higher and more distant the ideal, the greater its power to exalt the soul.

Helen Wodehouse

We think we must climb to a certain height of goodness before we can reach God. But God says not "At the end of the way you may find me." God says "I am the way; I am the road under your feet, the road that begins just as low down as you happen to be." If we are in a hole the way begins in the hole. The moment we set our face in the same direction as God's, we are walking with God.

The Koretzer Rebbe said: Often enough one lives out an entire lifespan for the purpose of performing a single Mitzvah or gaining a single chosen end. *Chasidic*

A ladder standing on the ground, and the top of it reached to Heaven (Genesis 28:2). Rabbi Aaron of Karlin said this: If you have yourself firmly in hand and stand solidly on the earth, your head will reach up to Heaven. *Chasidic*

ויקהל

22 *Work and Rest*

The Week of Vayakhel
Exodus 35:1–38:20

In the Sidra *Vayakhel* (Exodus 35), Moses assembles the people and tells them about the sanctuary that they are to build. Led by the master artisan Bezalel, they turn to the work of crafting the sanctuary and its furnishings. All this is preceded by the injunction concerning the Sabbath: *Six days work shall be done, but on the seventh day you shall have a holy Sabbath of complete rest, dedicated to the Eternal* (35:2).

It is well to remember that the command to rest in our Scriptural reading is preceded by a command to work. In fact, how can you rest if you haven't worked?

Sunday

Forms of Prayer / cs

God, I ask Your blessing on my daily work. Let me do it for its own sake, and let it show my service, not my selfishness. Keep me from laziness, and help me to improve myself, so that the world in which I live comes nearer to its perfection. Let humble work be honorable in my sight, and let me prefer it to works whose fruits are vanity and strife. Help me to realize that there is a goal beyond my livelihood, and that there is a purpose on earth greater than comfort. Let this knowledge save me from undue sadness and despair when I have my share of failure. I cast on You my burden of anxiety and fear, for You are with me at all times, to strengthen and uphold me.

Talmud

If need be, hire yourself out to flay carcasses in the market place, and do not say: "I am a priest, a great man, and this thing is detestable to me."

Rabbi Tarfon said: The Holy One did not let the Sh'chinah—the Divine Presence—rest on Israel until they had done work, as it is said (Exodus 25:8), *Let them make Me a sanctuary, that I may dwell among them.* First make the sanctuary; then I will dwell among you.

Period of Mishnah

⁘

Monday

My work matters to me, or should. It will not save the world; it may not even save me. But to the extent that I do mine and others do theirs, the world will be that much the better, and, to that extent, it will save us all. And since I cannot do the work of others, let me do mine.

Short is the day and
  hard the work, and
  the workers are slow.
Yet the wage is high,
And the One who employs us urges us on.
You are not called to complete the work,
  but are you free to give it up?

Mishnah

No great thing is created suddenly, any more than a bunch of grapes or a fig. If you tell me that you desire a fig, I answer you that there must be time. Let it first blossom, then bear fruit, then ripen. (Epictetus)

Epictetus

A king asked his son to hire two men to fill a deep pit. The first, upon looking into the pit, exclaimed in despair: How can I fill so deep a cavern? The other, a wise worker, said: What concern is it of mine that the pit is so deep? I am hired by the day and I shall therefore perform my day's work.

So God says to us: What concern of yours is it that the Torah is so extensive and that there is so much to learn? You are hired to do My work from day to day. All I expect of you is to perform a full day's work.

Midrash

Tuesday

Yesterday I thought: My work will not save the world. Today I wish it could, and yet what I need is not to save the world, or even myself, but to come to this day's end having done what I could. But this day is not done: I can still do a work of charity before it ends; that too is part of my day's work.

William Butler Yeats

I said: "A line will take us hours maybe;
Yet if it does not seem a moment's thought,
Our stitching and unstitching has been naught.
Better go down upon your marrow-bones
And scrub a kitchen pavement, or break stones
Like an old pauper, in all kinds of weather;
For to articulate sweet sounds together
Is to work harder than all these, and yet
Be thought an idler. . . ."

Kahlil Gibran

And what is it to work with love?

It is to weave the cloth with threads drawn from your heart, even as if your beloved were to wear that cloth. It is to build a house with affection, even as if your beloved were to dwell in that house.

It is to sow seeds with tenderness and reap the harvest with joy, even as if your beloved were to eat the fruit.

It is to charge all things you fashion with a breath of your own spirit.

And to know that all the blessed dead are standing about you and watching.

David Ben-Gurion

The true right to a country—as to anything else—springs not from political or legal authority, but from work.

Wednesday

To do a day's honest work for honest pay; to know you've done the best you can: that's good coin, not soon devalued.

Rabbi Simeon ben Elazar says: Adam, the first man, tasted nothing until he had done work, as it is said (Genesis 2:15), *God placed him in the Garden of Eden to work it and keep it.* Only after this does it say, *You may eat of any tree of the Garden.* — *Period of Mishnah*

The Holy One makes good intentions bear fruit (Talmud Kiddushin 40a). If, despite all your labors, you have not accomplished all that you set out to do, do not throw up your hands in despair: God takes note even of your labors that do not succeed, and reckons you as having accomplished your task. — *Vitry*

God gives every bird its food, but does not throw it into the nest. — *J. G. Holland*

Rabbi Baer of Radoshitz said to his teacher, the Rabbi of Lublin: Show me one comprehensive way to serve God. The Tzaddik replied: It is impossible to tell people the way they should take. For one, the way is through action, for another through prayer, for a third through fasting, for a fourth through eating. Like everyone else, you must observe carefully the way your heart directs you, and then choose that way with all your strength. — *Chasidic*

Thursday

I chose my line of work, or it chose me. It could be I fell into it without much thought. Yet here I am, working partly for myself (if only because I have to eat) and partly for others. The world needs my work. Teach me that all work faithfully done is good work, precious in Your sight.

Great is work, for it confers dignity on those who do it. — *Talmud*

What a deep faith in the rationality of the structure of the world, and what a longing to understand even a small glimpse of the reason revealed to the world there must have been in — *Albert Einstein*

Kepler and Newton to enable them to unravel the mechanism of the heavens in long years of lonely work.

Joseph ben Judah Aknin / cs

Though there is much to do, and though your days fly swifter than flight itself, do not drive yourself the way workers do who have a fixed task. If you try to do more than you can you will finally do less, because you will wear out your body, dull your mind's edge, lose enthusiasm and grow limp. And having been worn out, you will quit altogether.

Friday

⁘

Remember that as you go forth to "make a living" it is also a life you are making. It can have little or no meaning to you, or it can be holy, if you (try to) make it so. May you be wise enough to understand that the holiness lies less in doing a particular thing or in reaching a particular goal, than in making the effort with all your might.

Abraham J. Heschel

The genius of Judaism resides . . . in raising the secular to the sacred, the material to the spiritual. Just as Judaism raises the seventh day to the Sabbath, so it seeks to raise every weekday to the Sabbath.

Talmud

Ben Zoma saw a group on the Temple Mount and said:

"Blessed is the One who discerns secrets and Blessed the One who created all these to serve me." For he would say: "How hard Adam the First Man had to labor before he had a loaf to eat: he had to plow, sow, reap, bind sheaves, pound, winnow, clean, grind, sift, knead, bake—only then could he eat. And I wake up and find all this done for me! And the same is true for the clothes I find waiting for me when I wake up. Every trade and craft is here at the door of my house waiting for me to partake."

Chasidic

Once Rabbi Mendel of Kotzk said to Rabbi Yitzchak Meir of Ger: I don't know what people want of me. All week long they do as they please, but come Sabbath they put on their black gowns and gird themselves with their black belts, and set black fur hats on their heads, and there they are: best friends of the Sabbath-Bride! What I say is: *What people do in the week, so let them do on the Sabbath.*

⁘

Shabbat

Today my work is to rest from work, and to turn my mind to eternal things. Thus this day can become a gift for body and soul, helping me realize that it is not by bread alone I live—bread for the body—but by something eternal in my spirit. Even the bread I eat today will be more than bread, as I eat it bathed in the light of the Eternal. For having been created in Your image, I bear the impress of Your eternity. On Shabbat, especially, I can live in that eternity.

Talmud

> Only one who labored before the Sabbath
> can eat on the Sabbath.

Claude G. Montefiore

There are objects in life higher than success. The Sabbath, with its exhortation to the worship of God and the doing of kindly deeds, reminds us week by week of these higher objects. It prevents us reducing our life to the level of a machine. The Sabbath is one of the glories of our humanity. For if to labour is noble, of our own free will to pause in that labour may be nobler still.

Charles Williams

It will happen sometimes when one has worked hard and done all that one can for the purpose before one—it has happened then that I have stood up and been content with the world of things and with what has been done there through me. And this may be pride, or it may be the full stress of the whole being and delight in labour—there are a hundred explanations. But I have wondered whether that profound repose was not communicated from some far source and whether the life that is in it was altogether governed by time. And I am sure that state never comes when I am concerned with myself.

23 *Time and Change*

The Week of P'kudei
Exodus 38:21–40:28

In the Sidra *P'kudei* (Exodus 40), the sanctuary has been built, and the people are ready to go forth on their journey through the wilderness, toward the Promised Land. This journey was destined to be adventurous, and the people underwent many changes of fortune on their way. Through all the changes, one thing was constant, unchanging: God's presence as a guiding force. The divine presence is symbolized by a cloud: *For over the Tabernacle a cloud sent by God rested by day, and fire would appear in it by night, in the sight of all the house of Israel throughout their journeys* (40:38).

Sunday

⁘

Robert Louis Stevenson

I thank You, God, for the glory of late days and the excellent face of Your sun. I thank You for good news received. I thank You for the pleasures I have enjoyed and for those I have been able to confer. And now, when the clouds gather and the rain impends, permit me not to be cast down; let me not lose the savor of past mercies and past pleasures; but, like the voice of a bird singing in the rain, let grateful memory survive in the hour of darkness.

Israel Zangwill

Like a language, a religion was dead when it ceased to change.

Andrew Young

I saw how rows of white raindrops
From bare boughs shone,
And how the storm had stript leaves
Forgetting none

Save one left high on a top twig
Swinging alone;
Then that too bursting into song
Fled and was gone.

Autumn to winter, winter into spring,
Spring into summer, summer into fall,—
So rolls the changing year, and so we change;
Motion so swift, we know not that we move.

Dinah Mulock Craik

❖

Monday

Thank You for all the changing seasons—all that is sweet in my life, on days that swiftly pass—all that I have learned in bitter hours and days, even when they seem reluctant to end: all the changeful moments of being are a gift, the gift of life.

Force time, and time will drive you back; yield to time, and time is on your side.

Talmud

Ah, sad and strange, as in dark summer dawns
The earliest pipe of half-awakened birds
To dying ears, when unto dying eyes
The casement slowly grows a glimmering square;
So sad, so strange, the days that are no more.
Dear as remembered kisses after death,
And sweet as those by hopeless fancy feigned
On lips that are for others; deep as love,
Deep as first love and wild with all regrets;
O Death in Life, the days that are no more.

Alfred Lord Tennyson

The wintry wind blows away the snow
And knocks on the mountain window.
The bitter draught on the door
Withers the sleeping plum-blossoms,
But however much it despoils the flower,
Can it prevent the spring coming?

Yun Sun-Do

Yesterday is memory, tomorrow is hope or dread: Let me be grateful for *today.*

Abraham ben Isaac Bedersi

Time is our companion but only briefly. It flies faster than the shades of evening. We are like a child trying to capture a moonbeam. We open our hand, and it is empty, and the brightness is gone.

Sara Teasdale

It was a spring that never came,
but we have lived long enough to know
what we never had, remains.
It is the things we have that go.

Max Ehrmann

Let me do my work each day; and if the darkened hours of despair overcome me, may I not forget the strength that comforted me in the desolation of other times.

May I still remember the bright hours that found me walking over the silent hills of my childhood, or dreaming on the margin of the quiet river, when light glowed within me, and I promised my early God to have courage amid the tempests of the changing years.

Spare me from bitterness and from the sharp passions of unguarded moments.

Lift my eyes from the earth, and let me not forget the uses of the stars.

Forbid that I should judge others lest I condemn myself.

Let me not follow the clamor of the world, but walk calmly in my path. And though age and infirmity overtake me, and I come not within sight of the castle of my dreams, teach me still to be thankful for life, and for time's golden memories that are good and sweet; and may the evening's twilight find me gentle still.

⁘

Wednesday

Where are those absent friends, who gave me their hearts in days gone by? When they were no more with me, I shed tears; I felt the pain of separation, and feel it still. If I feel so deeply, I was as deeply blessed. This abides in the midst of change, and I give thanks.

Draw from the past, live in the present, work for the future.

Abraham Geiger

To be interested in the changing seasons is a happier state of mind than to be hopelessly in love with spring.

George Santayana

The supply of time is a daily miracle. You wake up in the morning and lo! Your purse is magically filled with twenty-four hours of the unmanufactured tissue of the universe of life. It is yours! The most precious of your possessions.

Arnold Bennett

Loveliest of lovely things are they,
On earth, that soonest pass away.

William Cullen Bryant

Thus time travels,
a chariot
expensive, rather decrepit.
Drive it slowly,
Drive it slowly.

Natan Alterman / cs

⁘

Thursday

How can I thank You enough for holding me in Your arms as a mother holds her young? You have held me from when I was born: You hold me always, always.

O God
give me strength to forget
evils over and done,
history's falls and failings,

Eliezer Bogatin / cs

yesterday's frozen hope.
And give me strength to keep watch
for fair weather after a stormy day,
incense of flowers
and quiet waves.
Give me strength to wait and time to hope:
until the last day
strength to keep watch and rejoice
as doves are hatched and babes are born,
as flowers bud and blossom
and visions break out and grow.
Give me strength,
O God.

P. Stebbins

After we come to mature years, there is nothing of which we are so vividly conscious as of the swiftness of time. Its brevity and littleness are the theme of poets, moralists and preachers. Yet there is nothing of which there is so much—nor day nor night, ocean nor sky, winter nor summer equal it. It is a perpetual flow from the inexhaustible fountains of eternity:—And we have no adequate conception of our earthly life until we think of it and live in it as part of forever. Now is eternity, and will be, tomorrow and the next day, through the endless years of God.

Friday

When the shadows lengthen, and evening comes, the busy world will be hushed, and my week's work done. Then, companioned by Your presence, I shall rest.

Moses ibn Ezra

Time is the teacher most sublime, and wisest of all.

Ralph Waldo Emerson

Finish every day and be done with it. You have done what you could. Some blunders and absurdities no doubt crept in; forget them as soon as you can. Tomorrow is a new day; begin it well and serenely and with too high a spirit to be cumbered with your old nonsense. This day is all that is good and fair. It is too dear, with its hopes and invitations, to waste a moment on the yesterdays.

Through loyalty to the past, our mind refuses to realize that tomorrow's joy is possible only if today's makes way for it; that each wave owes the beauty of its line only to the withdrawal of the preceding one.

André Gide

All changes, even the most longed for, have their melancholy; for what we leave behind is a part of ourselves; we must die to one life before we can enter into another!

Anatole France

Time is a very strange thing.
So long as one takes it for granted, it is nothing at all.
But then, all of a sudden, one is aware of nothing else.

Hugo von Hofmannsthal

The situation that we hoped to change because it was intolerable becomes unimportant. We have not managed to surmount the obstacle, as we were absolutely determined to do, but life has taken us round it, led us past it, and then if we turn round to gaze at the remote past, we can barely catch sight of it, so imperceptible has it become.

Marcel Proust

⁘

Shabbat

Great are Your faithfulness and Your love. I thank You for the power to begin a new day, a power You renew in me every morning. Though there are times when I lie down to troubled sleep, at sunrise I am new, for great are Your faithfulness and Your love.

Why trust in Time, when truth is not in it?
Oh, so great my task, so short my day!
We tell our neighbors not to sin:
Don't let your passions lead you astray.
But we ourselves, we sin and say:
What can I do? What I am and what I do are in the hands of the One who made me.

Judah Halevi

James Kirkup

There is a new morning, and a new day,
When the heart wakes in the green
Meadow of its choice, and the feet stray
Securely on their new-found paths, unseen,
Unhindered in the certain light of day.
There is a new time, and a new word
That is the timeless dream of uncreated speech.
When the heart beats for the first time, like a bird
Battering the bright boughs of its tree, when each
To the other turns, all prayers are heard.
There is a new world, and a new man,
Who walks amazed that he so long
Was blind, and dumb; he who now towards the sun
Lifts up a trustful face in skilful song,
And fears no more the darkness where his day began.

24 *Atonement*

The Week of Vayikra
Leviticus 1:1–5:26

The book of Leviticus takes its Hebrew name from its first word, *Vayikra,* as does its first Sidra. The Sidra speaks of sacrifices to be offered as partial atonement for one's transgressions. It is made clear (Leviticus 5) that when we trespass against others, such offerings must be accompanied by restitution: *When a person sins and commits a trespass against God by dealing deceitfully . . . or through robbery . . . or by fraud . . . and realizing his [her] guilt, would restore that which he [she] had got . . . he [she] shall repay . . . and he [she] shall be forgiven . . .* (5:21–26).

Sunday

cs / Eusebius of Caesarea

May I be . . . the friend of that which is eternal and abides. May I never quarrel with those nearest me; and if I do, may we be reconciled quickly. May I never devise evil against anyone; if any devise evil against me, may I escape uninjured and without any desire to hurt them. May I love, seek, and attain only that which is good. May I wish for the happiness of all and the misery of none. May I never rejoice in the ill-fortune of one who has wronged me. When I have done or said what is wrong, may I never wait for the rebuke of others, but always rebuke myself until I make amends.

Chasidic

Failure to repent is much worse than sin. One may have sinned for but a moment, but may fail to repent of it moments without number.

Unknown Mere sorrow, which weeps and sits still, is not repentance. Repentance is sorrow converted into action; into a movement toward a new and better life.

Chasidic Once when they asked Rabbi Mendel of Kosov with great insistence: Why doesn't the Messiah come? He gave them this answer: It is written (I Samuel 20:27): *Why did [David] the son of Jesse not come, neither yesterday nor today?* Why does the Messiah not come? Because today we are no different from the way we were yesterday.

Monday

There are days when I feel no need to repent my sins or to regret my failings. On such days I don't feel the need to improve my way of being in the world or my actions toward the people around me. Those are the days I may be most in need of repentance; on those days, especially, give me the gift of self-awareness. On other days, when my balance is more certain, keep me from too much consciousness of self.

Talmud In the place where the penitent stand, the wholly righteous cannot stand.

cs *A mended limb may be stronger than one never broken.*

William James The best repentance is to up and act for righteousness, and forget that you ever had relations with sin.

Talmud / cs

Return one day before you die.
It was asked:
—How can we know that day,
the day before we die?
—We cannot.
—What then?
—Consider each day your last,
and return.

Rabbi Yitzchak of Vorki said: On the Day of Atonement the confession of sins is arranged in alphabetical order, because otherwise we should not know when to stop beating our breasts. For there is no end to sin, and no end to the awareness of sin, but there is an end to the alphabet. *Chasidic*

∴

Tuesday

"What I do to myself affects no one but me." Even if that were true, consider that you, too, are a someone, and ask yourself whether you really have a greater right to harm yourself than to harm another.

Who says, "I will sin and return to God, sin and return," will not be given the opportunity to return; who says, "I will sin and the Day of Atonement will atone," [will find that] the Day of Atonement does not atone. For transgressions against God the Day of Atonement atones; for transgressions against other human beings, the Day of Atonement does not atone, until one has made peace with them. *Talmud*

Thus did Rabbi Elazar ben Azariah expound: *You will be made clean from all your sins before the Eternal One* (Leviticus 16:30). For transgressions against God the Day of Atonement atones; for transgressions against other human beings, the Day of Atonement does not atone, until one has made peace with them.

> This is the bitterest of all—
> to wear the yoke of our own wrong-doing.

George Eliot

I hereby forgive all who have hurt me, all who have wronged me, whether deliberately or inadvertently, whether by word or by deed. May no one be punished on my account. *Gates of Repentance*

As I forgive and pardon those who have wronged me, may those whom I have harmed forgive me, whether I acted deliberately or inadvertently, whether by word or by deed.

Wednesday

⁘

What I do and what I make of myself may have an effect far beyond me and my small circle of family and friends. Surely I sometimes have harmed others even without knowing it; may I be comforted by the knowledge that I sometimes benefit others, even without knowing it.

Chasidic

A Tzaddik would hold an audience during the Days of Repentance. People would come to hear him, and it was his way to set aside a time for them to question him.

As this was the season for atonement, a man approached him and said: We are taught to go to our family and friends to ask forgiveness for wrongs we have done in the past year. They also come to us. Please teach me how truly to forgive the people who have offended me.

The Tzaddik said to him: Here is one way: do not condemn those who offend you. Then you will not need to forgive.

Joseph Jacobs

The highest and most difficult of all moral lessons is to forgive those we have injured.

Chasidic

Turn away from any evil you have done; do not keep it in mind; do good. If you have sinned much, balance it by doing much good. Resolve today, from the depth of your heart and in a joyful frame of mind, to abstain from evil and to do good.

Thursday

⁘

There are so many ways in which I need to change; so much of me could stand improvement that I hardly know where to begin. And it is not only my failures of the past that I am thinking of, but my present shortcomings. Is there any likelihood that tomorrow will find me morally stronger, more reconciled with You? Help me to turn to You more often, more easily. Help me to put my trust in what we can accomplish together, for today I can't make it on my own.

Rabbi Bunam said to his followers: The sins we commit—that's not the great crime. After all, temptation is great and our strength is small! Our great crime is that we can turn at every moment, and we do not!

Chasidic

Nothing worth doing is completed in our lifetime; therefore, we must be saved by hope. Nothing true or beautiful or good makes complete sense in any immediate context of history; therefore, we must be saved by faith. Nothing we do, however virtuous, can be accomplished alone; therefore, we are saved by love. No virtuous act is quite as virtuous from the standpoint of our friend or foe as from our standpoint. Therefore, we must be saved by the final form of love which is forgiveness.

Reinhold Niebuhr

Whatever stress some may lay upon it, a death-bed repentance is but a weak and slender plank to trust our all upon.

Laurence Sterne

⁘

Friday

I find in myself this virtue: the sadness I feel at my weaknesses and my pity for other people in pain. Help me to keep this in mind, O Healer, when my thoughts are dark. That there is strength in me to turn, and time, is reason enough to be hopeful.

In tears a man once confessed a sin to the Rabbi of Apt and told him how he had atoned for it. The Tzaddik laughed. The man went on to tell what more he intended doing to atone for his sin, and the Rabbi went on laughing. The man wanted to continue, but the laughter robbed him of his power to speak. He stared at the Tzaddik in horror. And then his soul held its breath, and he heard a voice deep within. He realized how trivial all his fuss about atoning had been, and he turned to God.

Chasidic

Many promising reconciliations have broken down because, while both parties came prepared to forgive, neither party came prepared to be forgiven.

Charles Williams

Christina Baldwin Forgiveness is the act of admitting that we are like other people.

Chasidic As an individual you cannot be redeemed until you recognize your flaws and try to mend them. Nor can a nation be redeemed until it recognizes its flaws and tries to mend them. Whoever permits no recognition of his or her flaws—whether an individual or a nation—permits no redemption. We can be redeemed only to the extent that we recognize ourselves.

Shabbat

On Shabbat, especially, do not look into the mirror with loathing, forgetting the good in you. There can be a perverse pride in too much self-despising, for you are not a great sinner, merely average. As you need forgiveness, so do I, lest we despair of all light. But this *is* a day of light. Accept it and add to it.

Eliezer ben Judah of Worms The most beautiful thing that one can do is to forgive a wrong.

Yiddish proverb You are what you are, not what you were.

Thomas Fuller All the while thou studiest revenge, thou art tearing thy own wound open.

Charlotte Brontë Something of vengeance I had tasted for the first time; as aromatic as wine it seemed, on swallowing, warm and racy; its afterflavour, metallic and corroding, gave me a sensation as if I had been poisoned.

25 *Offerings*

The Week of Tzav
Leviticus 6:1–8:36

The Sidra *Tzav* (Leviticus 6) focuses on the ritual of sacrifice and the manner in which Aaron and his sons are to conduct themselves when they have been anointed to serve in the sanctuary on behalf of the people. They are to ensure that *a perpetual fire shall be kept burning on the altar, not to go out* (6:6).

What can we do for others? What can we offer them? Whatever that may be, it is an offering that gives light and warmth. When such service becomes an everyday thing, it is the "perpetual fire" called for by our reading.

Sunday

O God, for the good I have known, the love, kindness, and friendship that bless my days, I am very grateful. At times I feel unworthy of these gifts; therefore I hope that as the years pass I may grow more confident of my own worth.

Strengthen within me the will to give of myself to those around me. Open my eyes and my heart to their needs. As I am blessed, so may I bring blessing to others.

cs / Gates of Prayer

Who gives Tzedakah is blessed. Who lends is even better. Who gives a poor man money with which to trade and becomes his partner at half profits is better still.

Period of Mishnah

Abba and Rabbi Simeon ben Lakish [both] said: It is better to lend than to give Tzedakah, and better still to set up a business partnership with the poor.

Talmud

Marcus Aurelius

Once you have done someone a service,
what more would you have?
Is it not enough
to have obeyed the laws
of your own nature,
without expecting to be paid for it?
That is like the eye demanding a reward for seeing,
or the feet for walking.

Monday

There is something within me that demands thanks for what I give. I suppose I was taught as a child to say "Thank you," so I expect it from others. Grown from childhood now, I have—more than once—experienced ingratitude as payment for generosity. Please, God, do not let me use this as an excuse not to give, as a reason not to help.

Maimonides

There are eight degrees in the giving of charity, one higher than the other:

To give grudgingly, reluctantly, or with regret.
To give less than you should, but graciously.
To give what you should, but only after being asked.
To give before you are asked.
To give without knowing whom you are giving to, though the recipient knows your identity.
To give anonymously.
To give without knowing the recipient's identity, and vice versa.
To make someone self-supporting, through a gift or a loan, or by finding him or her employment.

Unknown

If I cannot give bountifully, yet I will give freely, and what I want in my hand, I will supply by my heart.

If I can stop one heart from breaking,
I shall not live in vain;
If I can ease one life the aching,
Or cool one pain,
Or help one fainting robin
Unto his nest again,
I shall not live in vain.

Emily Dickinson

Tuesday

There are times when you have nothing to give but yourself, for your pockets are empty of other coin. Nothing more? There is never a time, then, when you have nothing to give, so long as you have yourself.

Korah the rich asked Moses: Moses, our teacher, It is written in your Torah, Do not take from the poor, for they are poor. Who can take from the poor, since they have nothing? Moses answered him: What you should give to the poor belongs to them; what you do not give them, is what you take from them.

Midrash

This only is charity, to do all, all that we can.

John Donne

There is a gift that is almost a blow, and there is a kind word that is munificence; so much is there in the way of doing things.

Sir Arthur Helps

Benefits are only accepted so far as they can be requited; beyond that point, instead of gratitude they excite hatred.

Cornelius Tacitus

His disciples asked Rabbi Nechunia ben Hakana: What accounts for your longevity? He answered: I never accepted honor at another's expense; I never went to bed cursing a friend; I was generous with my money.

Talmud

Wednesday

Let me give without attaching strings of gratitude and obligation to my giving, but only out of a full heart. And if I cannot give with a full heart, a partially empty one will have to do—but let me give, and obligate the beneficiary not at all.

Chasidic Unlike the case of other commandments, no blessing is required before giving charity: why is this? So that we might not excuse ourselves from giving by saying we are not clean enough to recite a blessing.

Period of Mishnah If you have done your friend a small injury, let it seem like a great one to you; and if you have done your friend much good, let it seem to you a trifle.

If your friend has done you a small favor, let it seem great to you; and if your friend has done you a great injury, let it seem to you a trifle.

Nicholas Berdayev Care for the life of another, even material, bodily care, is spiritual in essence. Bread for myself is a material question: bread for my neighbor is a spiritual question.

Henri Frédéric Amiel Charity is generous; it runs a risk willingly. . . . We cannot be at the same time kind and wary, nor can we serve two masters—love and selfishness. We must be knowingly rash, that we may not be like the clever ones of the world, who never forget their own interests. We must be able to submit to being deceived; it is the sacrifice which interest and self-love owe to conscience. The claims of the soul must be satisfied first if we are to be the children of God.

Thursday

I give, but then the wheel turns. There are times when I've been on the receiving end of gifts or help or favors, and will be again. Help me, O God, to be glad for what I receive, accepting what I need with neither envy of the giver nor guilt at being the receiver, this time.

Talmud Rabbi Jonah said: It is not written, "Happy is the one who gives to the poor," but "Happy is the one who *considers* the poor." (Psalm 41:1) That is to say, one who ponders how to fulfill the command to help the poor. How did Rabbi Jonah act? If he met someone of good family who had become impoverished, he would say: I have heard a legacy has been left for you in such a place; take this money in advance, and pay me back later. When this person had accepted it, he would say: It is a gift.

We should give as we would receive, cheerfully, quickly, and without hesitation, for there is no grace in a benefit that sticks to the fingers.

Seneca

We receive everything, both life and happiness; but the manner in which we receive, this is what is still ours. Let us, then, receive trustfully without shame or anxiety. Let us humbly accept from God even our own nature, and treat it charitably, firmly, intelligently. Not that we are called upon to accept the evil and the disease in us, but let us accept ourselves in spite of the evil and the disease.

Henri Frédéric Amiel

They said to Rabbi Zusya: It is written (Exodus 25:2): *Speak to the people of Israel, and let them take for Me an offering*. Should it not rather say *and let them make for Me an offering*?

Rabbi Zusya replied: One who gives to the needy must do this in the spirit of holiness, but that is not enough. The needy must also take in the spirit of holiness. It is not enough to give in the name of God. What is given must also be taken in the name of God. That is why it is written: *let them take for Me an offering*.

Chasidic

⁘

Friday

Make me like the one of whom this was said: "*You realize that the only thing you have to do for another human being is to keep yourself really straight, and then do whatever it is you do.*"

This is hard to do, I know. Help me to keep really straight, so that others can depend on me to do what I do, knowing then that it will be done pretty well!

Sheldon Kopp

Midrash We have learned: the wicked are judged in Gehenna for twelve months.

Rabbi Eliezer asked Rabbi Joshua: What must one do to escape Gehenna?

One must occupy oneself with good deeds.

Then the nations can do good and pious deeds, and so escape the judgment of Gehenna.

My son, said Rabbi Joshua, the Torah speaks to all the living. If you like, I will tell you how I reached this conclusion.

Say on.

I once heard you teaching in the House of Study and expounding the verse (Proverbs 19:1), *Better are the poor who walk in their integrity . . .* in this manner: Everyone in this world who walks blamelessly before the Creator will escape the judgment of Gehenna in the world-to-come.

Dag Hammarskjöld To remain a recipient—and be grateful. Grateful for being *allowed* to listen, to observe, to understand.

Chasidic *When anyone brings an offering to the Eternal* (Leviticus 1:2). The Rizhiner Rebbe said: Only if you bring yourself to the "One" as an offering may you be called "one."

Shabbat

Today I know how much I take during the week, for all is a gift. Air to breathe, work to do, love to give and get—everything is a gift. The gift is life. And the gift of this day is one that enables me to reflect on all the gifts I receive from the week's first moment to the flame that ends this day of rest, as the dark settles on my patch of earth. Thank You, Eternal Source of life.

Jewish anecdote The Dubner Maggid said: Some people not only refuse to give, they take away. A charitable man who was collecting money to assist a needy person came to a certain citizen for a donation and was refused without a reason being offered. He then went to another, who began to abuse the one for whom the collection was being taken, calling him shiftless and lazy, a worthless drunkard who would not otherwise be in need. The collector said: Your neighbor gave nothing but kept quiet; you, however, not only give nothing but take away a needy man's reputation.

We make a living by what we get, but we make a life by what we give. *Norman MacEwan*

The wife of the Ropshitzer Rebbe said to him: You prayed so long today. What was it for? *Chasidic*

I was praying that the rich be more generous in their gifts to the poor.

Was your prayer successful?

Half of my prayer was successful. The poor are willing to accept them."

26 *Death*

The Week of Sh'mini
Leviticus 9:1–11:27

The Sidra *Sh'mini* (Leviticus 10) deals with the sudden and mysterious deaths of Aaron's sons, Nadab and Abihu. As priests, Aaron and his surviving sons cannot take part in the rites of mourning, but the rest of the community can mourn these deaths. *But your kin, all the house of Israel, shall bewail the death that the Eternal One has wrought* (10:6).

Sunday

From *Psalm 16 / cs*

Keep me, Eternal One, for in You I find refuge,
and in You my happiness lies.
Guardian of all my days,
You are my cup from which I drink,
my life's portion.
My life-lines have fallen in pleasant places;
a goodly heritage has been my lot.
I thank You for guiding me,
for the inner voice that instructs me.
I have set You before me always;
with You beside me I cannot fail.
So my heart is glad, my soul rejoices,
and all of me can rest secure:
for You will not abandon me in death.
You show me the path of life,
and Your presence is fullness of joy.

Midrash They said in Rabbi Meir's name:
With clenched fists we enter this world, as though to say:

The whole world is mine to acquire.
With hands wide open we leave the world, as though to say:
I acquired nothing in this world.

We come into this world crying while all around us are smiling. May we so live that we go out of this world smiling while everybody around us is weeping.

Persian proverb

⁘

Monday

Eternal God, I humbly ask Your help, for my need is great. My days fly past in quick succession, and I cannot look back without regret or ahead without misgiving. I seek to understand the mystery of my life, but in vain. And when suffering and death strike those I love, my faith all but fails me, and I forget that I am Your child. O God, help me now to feel Your presence. When my own weaknesses and the storms of life hide You from my sight, help me to know that You are with me still, and uphold me with the comfort of Your love.

cs / Gates of Prayer

I often feel that death is not the enemy of life, but its friend, for it is the knowledge that our years are limited that makes them so precious.

Joshua Loth Liebman

A NINTH-CENTURY REQUIEM FOR THE ABBESS OF GANDESHEIM WHO DIED YOUNG

Thou hast come safe to port,
I still at sea,
The light is on thy head,
Darkness in me.
Pluck thou in heaven's field
Violet and rose,
While I strew flowers that will thy vigil keep
Where thou dost sleep,
Love, in thy last repose.

Medieval period

Walt Whitman

I do not think seventy years is the time of a man or woman,
Nor that seventy millions of years is the time of a man or woman,
Nor that years will ever stop the existence of me, or any one else.

Tuesday

You are near—never more than when I feel lost and far from faith. Would that I really knew that! O give me strength when I am weary, courage when I am faint of heart! Console me when I grieve, and bless me with a quiet spirit, filled with trust that joys await me along the road.

Jacob Philip Rudin

To ask of death that it never come is futile, but it is not futility to pray that when death does come for us, it may take us from a world one corner of which is a little better because we were there.

Paul Tillich

The 90th Psalm . . . starts with a song of praise: God, You have been our dwelling place in all generations. In order to describe human transitoriness, the poet glorifies the Divine Eternity. Before looking downward he looks upward. . . . Only because we look at something infinite can we realize that we are finite. Only because we are able to see the eternal can we see the limited time that is given us. . . . Our melancholy about our transitoriness is rooted in our power to look beyond it. . . . That is what the psalmist means when he calls God our dwelling place, the only permanence in the change of all the ages and generations. That is why he starts his song of profoundest melancholy with the praise of God.

Sidney Greenberg

While on a visit to Italy with his parents, Leland Stanford, Jr., age nine, became ill and died. The grief-stricken parents returned to California and resolved to become the benefactors of other children, to give them the opportunities they could no longer lavish on their own son. Thus they erected and heavily endowed the university that bears the name of their son.

Not how long you live matters, but how well.
That is true, and not true.
Some do not get time enough to live well.
And all the "living well" does not replace the hole in my life, when you are gone.
Yet how would I have it, if I could order things?
I cannot order things.
Help me to live through them.

If some messenger were to come to us with the offer that death should be overthrown, but with the one inseparable condition that birth should also cease; if the existing generation were given the chance to live for ever, but on the clear understanding that never again would there be a child, or a youth, or first love, never again new persons with new hopes, new ideas, new achievements, ourselves for always and never any others—could the answer be in doubt?

Herbert Louis Samuel

Hers was springtime magic, bringing
music with pale harebells ringing
now an elegy.
Hers the endless summer singing
ours the winter of her going.

Anne Lewis-Smith

This dewdrop world
is a dewdrop world
and yet, and yet

Issa

What is it that troubles you? Death? Who lives for ever? Or because your foot has stumbled on the earth? There is no one who has never stumbled.

Shmuel Ha-nagid

Thursday

Earth has many pleasant things, and I take them lightly, often enough, as though I'd done something to earn them. Creation is robed in beauty and oft as I have looked at it, how often have I seen it? My home and family nurture me, yet I do not always understand how great a gift this is. I take health for granted, noticing only when it fails me. In death's dark shadow it is hard to think of gifts, hard to be thankful. May I have time enough for that, time to realize at last that what I have had and still have make life a gift beyond price. O Compassionate One, let grief teach me this, though I did not seek to learn it.

Martin Buber

We know nothing about death, nothing beyond the one fact that we shall "die"—but what is that, to die? We do not know. We must therefore assume that death constitutes the final limit of all that we are able to imagine. The desire to extend our imagination into the beyond of dying, to anticipate psychically what death alone can reveal to us existentially, seems to me a lack of faith disguised as faith. Genuine faith says: I know nothing about death, but I do know that God is eternity; and I also know that God is my God.

Buddhist parable

A young woman was so crazed by the death of her little son that she carried her dead child from house to house, demanding medicine for him. One sympathetic soul directed her to the monastery where the Compassionate Buddha taught.

It was wise of you to come, the Buddha said. Here is what you must do. Go to each house in this city, one by one, and collect tiny grains of mustard seeds. But you must only take seeds from houses where no one has ever died.

Filled with gratitude, the mother set out immediately, asking at every door, Is this a house where no one has died? Oh, no, said each owner, the dead from this house are beyond counting. On and on she went, but the answer was always the same—every family had been touched by death. Finally she understood: There is no medicine for this but the acceptance of it.

When I am oppressed by heavy burdens, be my teacher and show me how to carry them. Make them seem . . . not light but lighter, not easy to carry, perhaps, but easier than I expected. Help me to experience my grief when I need to, lest it hide within me and become too heavy to bear. When I should feel the pain of loss, give me strength to feel it, to accept it, and then to move beyond it—when the time for moving has arrived within me.

Talmud

When Rabbi Eliezer was dying, his disciples went in to visit him. They said to him: Master, teach us how to live in this world, so that we may be worthy of the life of the World to Come.

He said to them: Be careful of the honor due your colleagues; seat your children at the feet of the wise; and when you pray, know before whom you stand; then you will be worthy of the life of the World to Come.

Talmud

Elihoreph and Achijah were Ethiopians who served King Solomon as scribes (I Kings 4:3).

One day the Angel of Death came to Solomon's court. He seemed sad. Solomon said to him: What ails you?

The Angel of Death said: I have instructions to take away these two Ethiopians.

Solomon immediately gave them into the charge of the spirits that he controlled. He ordered them to take his servants to the district of Luz.

Upon their arrival at Luz, the two of them died.

On the next day Solomon again saw the Angel of Death. This time he was cheerful. Solomon asked him: Why so happy?

Because I was told to find your servants in the very place to which you sent them.

Chasidic The Psalmist says (Psalm 118:17): *I shall not die but live.* Rabbi Yitzchak of Vorki said: In order really to live, you must give yourself to death. But when you have done so, you discover that you are not to die, but to live.

Shabbat

⁂

A wise tradition forbids us to mourn on Shabbat, but it does not insist that we pretend our grief and sorrow have gone away forever. They will return, a reminder that we know the depth of our loss by the height of our pain. Though I may not weep today, I well may weep tomorrow. Help me to rest from my grief on this Sabbath day, and renew my strength for tomorrow, until I stop asking for what I had and remember what I have.

Talmud As Rabbi lay dying the sages decreed a fast and began to plead for mercy. Rabbi's servant went up to the roof, thinking: *They want Rabbi above and below: may the ones below overcome the ones above.* When she saw that he was in great pain, she thought: *May the ones above overcome,* but the sages did not cease to pray for mercy. She then took a pitcher and threw it down from the roof. The sages were startled into silence, and Rabbi's soul departed.

Abraham Lincoln Die when we may, I want it said of me, by those who knew me best, that I always plucked a thistle and planted a flower, when I thought a flower would grow.

Joseph H. Hertz According to ancient Jewish custom the ceremony of cutting our garments, when our nearest and dearest on earth is lying dead before us, is to be performed standing up. This teaches: meet all sorrow standing upright. The future may be dark, veiled from the eyes of mortals—but not the manner in which we are to meet the future. To rail at life, to rebel against a destiny that has cast our lines in unpleasant places, is of little avail. We cannot lay down terms to life. Life must be accepted on its own terms. But hard as life's terms are, life (it has been finely said) never dictates unrighteousness, unholiness, dishonor.

תזריע

27 *Health*

The Week of Tazri'a
Leviticus 12:1–13:59

The Sidra *Tazri'a* (Leviticus 13) discusses diseases of the skin and the manner in which the priest was to examine and treat a person with such afflictions: *When a person has . . . a swelling, a rash, or a discoloration* (13:2). In the time of our Sidra the art of healing was in truth an art, not a science. But the mandate to heal was clear then as now. The readings for this week are meditations and prayers for illness and healing. Of course, they might be used anytime.

Sunday

Milton Steinberg

ON TAKING GOOD HEALTH FOR GRANTED

After a long illness, I was permitted for the first time to step out-of-doors. And as I crossed the threshold sunlight greeted me. . . . So long as I live, I shall never forget that moment. . . . The sky overhead was very blue, very clear, and very, very high. . . . A faint wind blew from off the western plains, cool and yet somehow tinged with warmth—like a dry, chilled wine. And everywhere in the firmament above me, in the great vault between the earth and sky, on the pavements, the buildings—the golden glow of sunlight. It touched me, too, with friendship, with warmth, with blessing. And as I basked in its glory there ran through my mind those wonderful words of the prophet: *For you who revere My name the sun of righteousness shall rise with healing on its wings* (Malachi 3:20).

In that instant I looked about me to see whether anyone else showed on their face the joy, almost the beatitude, I felt. But no, there they walked—men and women and children, in the glory of the golden flood, and so far as I could detect, there was none to give it heed. And then I remembered how often I, too, had been indifferent to the sunlight, how often, preoccupied with petty and sometimes mean concerns, I had disregarded it. And I said to myself: How precious is the sunlight but alas, how careless of it we are.

Psalm 4:7 There are many who say: O *that we could see some good, but the light of Your presence, O God, has fled from us!*

Sir Thomas Browne Light that makes some things seen, makes some things invisible. Were it not for the darkness and the shadow of the earth, the noblest part of the Creation would remain unseen, and the stars in heaven invisible.

cs What is it that the darkness I live in can help make me see that otherwise I would not see?

בָּרוּךְ אַתָּה יי, הַמֵּאִיר לָעוֹלָם כֻּלּוֹ בִּכְבוֹדוֹ.
Baruch atah Adonai, ha-mei-ir la-olam kulo bi-ch'vodo.
Praised be the Eternal One,
the Light of the world.

Monday

ON SUFFERING

Each day must contain the service of God even if it is also a day of suffering. Like everything that is sent into our life, suffering comes to us independently of our volition; but we must mold and shape it. Our task is to make that part of our life into which suffering has entered a portion of God's dominion. We must reshape it, surmount it ethically, and therefore raise ourselves above mere causality. Thus, to suffering too the command applies: You shall love your Eternal God with all your heart, with all your mind, with all your being.

Why do You stand far off, Eternal One? Why do You hide Yourself in time of trouble? (Psalm 10:1)

You know how much I suffer, the difficulties that surround me.

Renew a steadfast spirit within me—renew it, and help me to overcome the bitterness I sometimes feel. When I am tempted to give up the struggle, let me feel Your hand holding mine, giving me courage and strength.

בָּרוּךְ אַתָּה יי, הַנּוֹתֵן לַיָּעֵף כֹּחַ.
Baruch atah Adonai, ha-no-tein la-ya-eif ko-ach.
Praised be the Eternal One,
You are strength to the weary.

⁘

Tuesday

cs

WHAT WE CAN PRAY FOR

We can't ask for lives free of problems. . . . We can't ask God to make us and those we love immune to disease. . . . We can't ask God to weave a magic spell around us so that bad things will happen only to other people, and never to us. . . . But people who pray for courage, for strength to bear the unbearable, for the grace to remember what they have left instead of what they have lost, very often find their prayers answered. They discover that they have more strength, more courage than they ever knew themselves to have.

We cannot escape suffering, but we may find God in spite of it, and even within it.

Be gracious to me, Eternal One, for I am languishing; I am so afraid, while You, O God—how long? (Psalm 6:3a, 4)

Let these words guide me:

Know how sublime a thing it is
To suffer and be strong.

O God, teach me to be strong enough to find a moment in the day when my heart is light enough to let me smile. Even in affliction I yearn for the grace of a loving spirit.

בָּרוּךְ אַתָּה יי, שׁוֹמֵעַ תְּפִלָּה.
Baruch atah Adonai, sho-mei-a t'fi-lah.
Praised be the Eternal One,
who hearkens to prayer.

Wednesday

Talmud

THE PRAYER OF THE WOUNDED

Rabbi Samuel ben Nachmani said: At times the gates of prayer are open, at times the gates of prayer are barred. But the gates of repentance are never barred.

But it is reported that Rabbi Judah the Prince taught: In truth, the gates of prayer are never barred.

Rabbi Akiba taught: The gates of prayer are open, and the prayer of those who practice steadfast love is heard.

Rav Chisda taught: Though sometimes the gates of heaven seem shut to all prayers, they are open to the prayers of the wounded and the hurt.

Many are my heart's distresses: let me know Your ways, Eternal One; teach me Your paths (Psalm 25:4, 17).

cs

May I not think merely of what I cannot do, being sick or weak, but of what I can do, in spite of weakness and sickness.

Everyone can do something.

Helen Keller said: I thank God for my handicaps, for, through them, I have found myself, my work, and my God. May something of her wisdom be mine, so that I can say: I take what is given and make my life out of it.

בָּרוּךְ אַתָּה יי, הַנּוֹתֵן לַיָּעֵף כֹּחַ.
Baruch atah Adonai, ha-no-tein la-ya-eif ko-ach.
Praised be the Eternal One,
You are strength to the weary.

Thursday

Gates of Repentance

FOR SPIRITUAL AND MORAL HEALING

I hereby forgive all who have hurt me, all who have wronged me, whether deliberately or inadvertently, whether by word or by deed. May no one be punished on my account.

As I forgive and pardon those who have wronged me, may those whom I have harmed forgive me, whether I acted deliberately or inadvertently, whether by word or by deed.

Lead me in Your truth and teach me, for You are the God of my salvation; in You do I hope all the day (Psalm 25:5).

The times of our lives that hold the deepest meaning for us, from which we learn the most, are very often those when we are face-to-face with problems that seem too great for our strength, with illness, and with death.

May I find meaning in all that I sense and feel—whether it be pain or joy.

בָּרוּךְ אַתָּה יי, הַטּוֹב וְהַמֵּטִיב.
Baruch atah Adonai, ha-tov v'ha-mei-tiv.
Praised be the Eternal One,
the Source of all good.

Friday

VISION AND FAITH

When the darkness is too dark for me, give me light, O Source of light, and renew my vision, my hope, my dream, my faith that the darkness will not last, my sense that despair is not the last word, and the courage to believe in my dreams.

Now I will lie down in peace, and sleep; for You alone, Eternal One, make me live unafraid (Psalm 4:9).

As the week turns toward Shabbat, I pray that my mind be less troubled. My thoughts are more peaceful and tranquil. My courage grows, as I reflect on these words (Psalm 71:14):

I will hope continually, and will praise You more and more.
Yes, there is hope in me, for, it may be, that
Tomorrow I shall put forth buds again,
And clothe myself in fruit.

בָּרוּךְ אַתָּה יי, שׁוֹמֵעַ תְּפִלָּה.
Baruch atah Adonai, sho-mei-a t'fi-lah.
Praised be the Eternal One,
who hearkens to prayer.

We turn to You for help,
now, and in the hour of our pain.
When we are sick and in pain, heal us.
When our bodies are broken, comfort us.
When our minds are troubled, give us rest.
O God, we pray for the children:
Comfort them and give them strength.
We pray for parents and grandparents:
Comfort them and give them hope.
We pray for healers:
Give them the wisdom and love they need.
We pray for all who suffer:
Help us to be with them, to touch them, to try to comfort them.
Be with all Your children, O God, be with us all.
Praised be the One who gives us the power to heal.

Hear me and be gracious to me, Eternal One; O God, be my helper; then I will know that You have turned my mourning into dancing, taken off my sackcloth and clothed me with joy, so that my soul may praise You and not be silent (Psalm 30:11–12).

What life has given to me matters less than what I can give to life. So I know that my illness is not what defines me; my heart and soul can rejoice, for I can find ways to be useful, I can love and be loved.

Yes, these words are true: They are ill discoverers who think there is no land, when they can see nothing but sea.

O God, help me to remember the good I can do, even when I am weak and in pain. And help me, on this and every Shabbat, to see beyond my troubles, that I may be a blessing to others—and to myself.

בָּרוּךְ אַתָּה יי, הַטּוֹב וְהַמֵּטִיב.
Baruch atah Adonai, ha-tov v'ha-mei-tiv.
Praised be the Eternal One,
the Source of all good.

מצרע

28 *Suffering and Adversity*

The Week of M'tzora
Leviticus 14:1–15:33

The Sidra *M'tzora* (Leviticus 14) continues the theme that began in the previous Sidra of cleansing a person from an affliction of the skin, and carries on with a ritual for cleansing an afflicted house. The ritual begins with an acknowledgment of affliction: *Something like a plague has appeared upon my house. . . .* (14:35). In ancient times a sage interpreted the word *affliction* more broadly, as a spiritual plague. We are all vulnerable, for suffering and adversity are part of the human condition. What can we do with our afflictions? We can accept them. Often we can overcome them. And we can try to help one another.

⁘

Sunday

Emily Dickinson

Success is counted sweetest
By those who ne'er succeed.
To comprehend a nectar
Requires sorest need.
Not one of all the purple host
Who took the flag to-day
Can tell the definition,
So clear, of victory,
As he, defeated, dying,
On whose forbidden ear
The distant strains of triumph
Break, agonized and clear.

Jacob J. Halevi

In times of darkness when my heart is grieved,
When despair besieges my mind
And my days are a weariness of living—
Then is my life like the flower that struggles to grow
Where no ray of sun ever penetrates;
Then is my spirit pent up within me
And my soul shut in like a night of darkness.
When such darkness overtakes me, O God,
Fortify my mind with trust in life.

Dag Hammarskjöld

He bore failure
without self-pity
and success
without self-admiration.

Monday

From *Psalm 25 / cs*

My soul rises toward You, Eternal One,
when I put my trust in You.
Let me know Your ways,
teach me Your paths.
Lead me in Your truth and teach me,
O God of my salvation,
for whom I wait all day long.
Remember Your compassion
and Your steadfast love,
for they are from everlasting.
Your ways are love and truth.
Turn to me and be gracious to me,
who am lonely and poor.
Many are the sorrows of my heart:
lead me out of my distress.
See my grief and my pain
and overlook my failings.

Talmud

Rabbi Joshua ben Levi said: Those who gladly accept the sufferings of this world are this world's salvation.

Rabbi Shmelke of Nikolsburg and his brother visited the Maggid of Mezeritch. They said: Some words of our sages give us no peace, because we do not understand them. They tell us to praise and thank God for suffering just as much as for well-being, and receive it with the same joy. Will you tell us how to understand this, rabbi?

Chasidic

He replied by telling them to go to the House of Study where they would find Zusya of Hanipol, who would help them understand. There they put their question to Rabbi Zusya, who laughed and said: *You have come to the wrong man! Better go to someone else, for I have never experienced suffering.* But the two knew that from the day he was born Rabbi Zusya's life had been a continual tale of need and woe. Then they saw the answer: to accept suffering with love.

Tuesday

From
Psalm 27 / cs

My Light, my God,
this only do I ask,
only this:
to live in Your house
all the days of my life.
Keep me safe in Your tent
when evil days come.
Hide me in the shelter of Your tent;
set me safe upon a rock.
When I call, hear my voice;
be gracious and answer.
My heart tells me to seek You,
to seek Your presence.
God my help,
do not hide Your face,
do not forsake me!
Teach me Your ways,
lead me in Your paths,
and help me to hope in You.
Help me to be strong

and take heart,
still to believe I shall see Your goodness
in the land of the living.

Chasidic Levi Yitzchak of Berditchev said: O God, I do not ask you to tell me why I suffer, but only whether I suffer for Your sake!

Kenneth Hildebrand On occasion I hear someone cry out in anguish of soul, "What terrible thing have I done that God should punish me so?" The answer is—nothing! Suffering, except through the universal law of cause and effect, does not come as punishment. Once and for all, we should rid ourselves of the thought that the Creator of Life sends pain as punishment. This is the basic point in the Bible's Book of Job.

Leigh Hunt Whenever evil befalls us, we ought to ask ourselves, after the first suffering, how we can turn it into good. So shall we take this occasion, from one bitter root, to raise perhaps many flowers.

Wednesday

⁘

In my darkness be a light to me,
in my loneliness help me to find
a soul akin to my own.
Give me strength
to live with courage;
and give me courage
to draw blessing from life,
even in the midst of suffering;
to hold fast against the storm,
and to smile at a loved one's glance.

Talmud Rabbi Akiba said: It was only through suffering and adversity that Israel obtained these three priceless gifts: the Torah [see Psalm 94:10], the Land of Israel [see Deuteronomy 8:5, 7], and the World to Come [see Proverbs 6:3].

We race carelessly to the precipice, after we have put something before us to prevent us from seeing it.

Blaise Pascal

The life . . . that she had complained against, had murmured at, had raged at and defied—none the less she had loved it so, joyed in it so, both in good days and evil, that not one day had there been when 'twould not have seemed hard to give it back to God, nor one grief that she could have foregone without regret.

Sigrid Undset

To be ignorant of evils to come, and forgetful of evils past, is a merciful provision in nature, and our delivered senses not relapsing into cutting remembrances, our sorrows are not kept raw by the edge of repetitions.

Sir Thomas Browne

⁘

Thursday

Psalm 23

Eternal God,
You are my shepherd,
I shall not want.
You make me lie down in green pastures,
You lead me beside still waters.
You restore my soul;
You guide me in paths of righteousness
for Your name's sake.
Yes, even when I walk through the valley of the shadow
of death,
I will fear no evil, for You are with me;
with rod and staff You comfort me.
You prepare a table before me in the presence of my enemies;
You have anointed my head with oil;
my cup overflows.
Surely, goodness and mercy shall follow me
all the days of my life,
and I shall dwell in the house of the Eternal God forever.

Not to have had pain is not to have been human.

Yiddish proverb

Janet Harrison The times of our lives which hold the deepest meaning for us, from which we learn the most, are very often those when we are face-to-face with problems which seem too great for our strength, with illness, and with death.

Archibald Rutledge Going up a mountain path one day, I met a mountaineer with an ax in his hand. I walked with him and asked him what he was going to cut. "I need a piece of timber to fix my wagon," he said. "I need the toughest kind of wood I can get. That kind always grows on top of the mountains where all the storms hit the hardest."

Juvenal We deem those happy who from the experience of life have learned to bear its ills, without being overcome by them.

Friday

⁘

Abba Kovner/cs

We are not the silent!
The only silence is Yours.
Grant perfect rest
to the scream and the hope. For
we haven't many choices,
only the one prospect of reaching the fair
at the end of it all, by filling
the Promised Cup with our spilt blood
for the soul to drink
and find strength to walk
a straight line
back
to the world.

Chasidic When you are in distress, think first upon all the good you have experienced in the past, and then you will discover yourself better able to pray for relief in the here-and-now. Thus says the Psalmist: *To You will I bring a thank-offering and then I shall call upon the name of the Eternal.*

I was, being human, born alone;
I am, being woman, hard beset;
I live by squeezing from a stone
The little nourishment I get.
In masks outrageous and austere
The years go by in single file;
But none has merited my fear,
And none has quite escaped my smile.

Elinor Wylie

I thank God for my handicaps,
for, through them,
I have found myself, my work, and my God.

Helen Keller

⁘

Shabbat

Your love, O God, is high as heaven,
Your faithfulness reaches to the skies.
Your righteousness is like the mighty mountains,
Your justice is like the great deep;
You help every human, every beast.
How precious is Your faithful love, O God!
Your children take refuge in the shadow of Your wings.
We feast on the riches of Your house;
we drink from the fountain of Your delights.
For with You is the fountain of life;
and by Your light shall we see light.
O continue to show Your love
to those who would know You,
and Your justice to the upright in heart.

From *Psalm 36*

Only the strong are strengthened by suffering; the weak are made weaker.

Lion Feuchtwanger

It is well to remember that there are all kinds of individuals and little groups who find security in abiding spiritual values, and with complete dedication seek to find ways of preserving them. During the invasion of southern Europe by "the barbarians,"

Clarence E. Pickett

copies of the original text of the Scriptures were hidden in various places so that they might not be destroyed. People in secret caves, in forests, and wherever they could find hiding places, kept alive the spirit of devotion to the needs of suffering humanity.

Booker T. Washington Character is the sum of all we struggle against.

Albert Camus In the midst of winter, I finally learned that there was in me an invincible summer.

אחרי מות

29 *And Beyond Death*

The Week of Acharei Mot
Leviticus 16:1–18:30

The deaths of two of Aaron's sons were reported in an earlier Sidra. Our present Sidra, *Acharei Mot* (Leviticus 16) takes us beyond that point, as God instructs Aaron—through Moses—about his further duties; once again he is warned about the danger of death from coming too close to the awesome power of the divine presence: *Tell your brother Aaron that he is not to come casually into the Shrine behind the curtain . . . lest he die* (16:2). Only at certain times may Aaron safely enter. A paradox: We seek the nearness of God, and it endangers us. And are we in God's presence after our death? What lies beyond the grave?

Sunday

If I dwell in Your house today, I will dwell there all days. How this may be I do not know, but that it may be is my hope.

From
Psalm 49 / cs

Shall we live forever
and avoid the sight of a grave?
Alike the wise and the foolish end their days,
leaving their wealth to others.
They imagine their houses will last forever,
their homes for countless generations;
they give their names to streets and towns.
But human splendor does not last,
we are animals, we pass away.
But God, taking me,
will redeem my soul from death's dark hand.

Henry Van Dyke There is only one way to get ready for immortality, and that is to love this life and live it as bravely and faithfully and cheerfully as we can.

Proverbs *The path of the righteous is like a shining light, ever more bright until the day is full.*

Monday

⁘

I don't know what tomorrow will bring; how, then, can I know what lies beyond this life of mine? Yet I know this: I can so live that others bless me when I am gone. Help me, O Compassionate, in my struggle to be a blessing.

Jacob Philip Rudin When we are dead, and people weep for us and grieve, let it be because we touched their lives with beauty and simplicity. Let it not be said that life was good to us, but, rather, that we were good to life.

Period of Mishnah *The wicked shall go into Sheol, and all the nations that forget God* (Psalm 9:17). Rabbi Eliezer said: That shows that all the nations [apart from Israel] shall have no share in the World to Come. Rabbi Joshua said to him: Since the verse does not end with *all the nations* but goes on to say *that forget God,* it means that only those who forget God have no share in the World to Come; the righteous among the nations do have a share in the World to Come.

Chasidic It is told: When Rabbi Moshe Leib of Sassov died he said to himself: Now I am free from fulfilling the commandments. What can I do now to fulfill the will of God? He thought for a while and concluded: It must surely be God's will that I be punished for my many sins! Immediately he began to run with all his might and jumped straight into hell. Heaven was much perturbed at this, and soon the prince of hell was told not to stoke his fires while the rabbi of Sassov was down there. Thereupon the prince begged the Tzaddik to take himself off to paradise, for hell was clearly not the place for him. It would not do to call a holiday in hell for his sake.

If that is the case, said Moshe Leib, I won't stir from here until all the souls are allowed to go with me. On earth I made it my business to ransom prisoners, and so I certainly will not let this big crowd suffer in this prison.

And they say that he had his way.

⁘

Tuesday

When I think of the times that have been before me, and the ages that will follow, I realize that I am less than a drop in time's river. And yet I feel so much more, when I consider that You have made me in Your own image. Can I hope to live when life has ceased to flow through my frame? Eternal and Infinite Spirit, I am in Your hands, now and always.

Chasidic

Once the spirit of the Baal Shem Tov was so oppressed that it seemed to him that he would have no part in the World to Come.

Then he said to himself: If I love God, what need do I have of the World to Come?

Sydney Carter

Swung by the rhythm of
a yes and no
between the living and
the dead I go.
The dance is in my bones
and though I see
that every dancing bone
will cease to be
I will believe my bones and learn to trust
my living and my dying,
for I must.
Coming and going by
this dance, I see
that what I am not is

a part of me.
Dancing is all that I
can ever trust,
the dance is all I am,
the rest is dust.
I will believe my bones
and live by what
will go on dancing when
my bones are not.

Wednesday

No one has come back to tell me anything about it, and I don't suppose anyone will. And when I go there—but where is "there"? My words shatter on stone, for I cannot see beyond them. I can only say: "You are our dwelling -place in life and in death," and hope I live a life whose significance is eternal.

Chasidic From time to time Elimelech of Lizensk would say: I will earn eternal life.

A guest asked him once how he could be so sure: Is it not written (Pirké Avot 4:4), *Be exceedingly humble, for the end of humankind is the worm.*

Elimelech replied: Never fear, I will earn it. When I arrive at the gates of Eden, they will ask me:

—Did you learn enough Torah?

I will say: No.

Then they will ask:

—Did you pray with enough fervor?

I will say: No.

And then they will ask:

—Well, did you fulfill the [other] commandments as you should have?

I will say: No.

Finally they will ask:

—What of your good deeds?

I will say: I had none.

And then they will say:
—An honest man! Come in, come in.

Like footsteps in a gallery, our lightest movements are heard along the ages. *Samuel Alexander*

*

Thursday

O God, fill me with the courage to laugh and to spend myself without worrying overmuch about a day that I may never see. Remind me today that when the next day does come, I still will have love and laughter to spend, however much I give away today.

Christina Rossetti

Does the road wind uphill all the way?
    Yes, to the very end.
Will the day's journey take the whole long day?
    From morn to night, my friend.
But is there for the night a resting-place?
    A roof for when the slow, dark hours begin.
May not the darkness hide it from my face?
    You cannot miss that inn.
Shall I meet other wayfarers at night?
    Those who have gone before.
Then must I knock, or call when just in sight?
    They will not keep you standing at that door.
Shall I find comfort, travel-sore and weak?
    Of labour you shall find the sum.
Will there be beds for me and all who seek?
    Yea, beds for all who come.

The righteous are called alive even in death; the wicked are called dead even when alive. *Talmud*

I believe in my survival after death. Like many others before me, I have experienced "intimations of immortality." I can no more explain these than the brown seed can explain the flowering tree. Deep in the soil in time's midwinter, my very stirring and unease seem a kind of growing pain toward June. *Robert Hillyer*

Friday

⁘

"I was much farther out than you thought
And not waving but drowning" (Stevie Smith).
  And nobody came to help?
  Or was she beyond their reach?

And when I come to my last days, will I feel like saying something like this? Give me the sense to ask for help when I need it, and the goodwill to give it when asked. And if at times I can offer it before being asked, let me know how to do it, and the right time for it. In other words, teach me how to live wisely. What others will say of me afterward I then can leave to them.

William Ellery Channing

What a sublime doctrine it is that goodness cherished now is Eternal Life already entered upon!

William Makepeace Thackeray

To be rich, to be famous? What do these profit a year hence, when other names sound louder than yours, when you lie hidden away under ground, along with the idle titles engraven on your coffin? But only true love lives after you—follows your memory with secret blessings—or precedes you, or intercedes for you. *Non omnis moriar*—if dying. I yet live in a tender heart or two; nor am lost and hopeless living, if a sainted departed soul loves and prays for me.

Talmud

Rabbi Yochanan said: Every prophet prophesied only for the days of the Messiah; but as for the World to Come, no eye has seen what the Holy One has prepared for us.

Albert Pine

What we have done for ourselves dies with us. What we have done for others . . . remains and is immortal.

Shabbat

⁘

Even if, on other days, I could not imagine anything about myself worthy of surviving, or capable of it, would not today bring a different way of seeing? Shabbat itself feels like eternal life, as I might imagine it: the peace, the joy, the play, the sense of life fulfilled. So these words come as a cold winter wind: Can it be that love does not abide? Can it be that the tears of everyone who ever loved do not water the Tree of Life? Ah, my very words, and the pain they issue from, are Yours.

Mishnah

Rabbi Jacob said:
Like an anteroom to the infinite is this our world,
And if you would enter the palace
make ready here.
He would say:
Better one hour of turning and good deeds here
than all the life of the World to Come,
and better one hour of bliss there
than all the life of this world.

Edward Young

Still seems it strange, that thou shouldst live forever?
Is it less strange, that thou shouldst live at all?

Robert Ingersoll

It may be that death gives all there is of worth to life. If those we press and strain within our arms could never die, perhaps that love would wither from the earth. Maybe this common fate treads from out the paths between our hearts the weeds of selfishness and hate. And I had rather live and love where death is king, than have eternal life where love is not.

30 *The Holy Life*

The Week of K'doshim
Leviticus 19:1–20:27

The Sidra *K'doshim* (Leviticus 19) begins with a chapter that has been called the Holiness Code. It is a blueprint for a holy life in imitation of the holy God. Its opening words are *You shall be holy, for I, your Eternal God, am holy,* (19:2), and its famous climax is *You shall love your neighbor as yourself.* (19:18). It speaks of holiness in terms we all can recognize. It makes us see that the "holy life" is for tzaddikim, hermits, saints, monks, gurus—and also for us, when we learn what a holy life really is.

Sunday

Anonymous

O God, grant that each one who has to do with me today is the happier for it. Each hour of this day grant me the wisdom of a loving heart that I may say the right thing rightly.

Give me a quick perception of the feelings and needs of others, and make me eager-hearted in helping them. Then shall my day be filled with blessing. Amen.

Midrash

You shall walk in God's ways (Deuteronomy 28:9). What are God's ways? As it is God's way to be merciful and forgiving to sinners, and to accept them when they repent, so should you be merciful to one another. As God is gracious, and gives freely to all, so should you give freely to one another. As God is patient with sinners, so should you be patient with one another.

William Ellery Channing

To live content with small means; to seek elegance rather than luxury, and refinement rather than fashion; to be worthy, not respectable, and wealthy, not rich; to study hard, think quietly, talk gently, act grandly; to listen to the stars and birds, to babes and sages, with open heart; to bear all cheerfully, do all bravely, await occasions, hurry never; in a word to let the spiritual, unbidden and unconscious grow up through the common.

One crowded hour of glorious life
Is worth an age without a name.

Anonymous

Monday

Holy One, Maker and Shaper, help me to live this day as if it were the first day of creation, and everything newly glistening to my eyes.

If you have been disgraced, forgive it; and do not seek honor through the disgrace of your neighbor.

Midrash

Opportunities do not come with their values stamped upon them. Every one must be challenged. A day dawns, quite like other days; in it a single hour comes, quite like other hours; but in that day and in that hour the chance of a lifetime faces us. To face every opportunity of life thoughtfully and ask its meaning bravely and earnestly, is the only way to meet the supreme opportunities when they come, whether open-faced or disguised.

Maltbie V. Babcock

Overcome anger by gentleness,
Overcome evil by good,
Overcome the miser by liberality,
Overcome the liar by truth.

The Dhammapada

Hatred is the evil spirit, the sickness of melancholy that leads you to despise the sight of your own kind and to hate all things. One then prefers the society of animals, prefers places without habitation. Without doubt this shortens a person's life.

Maimonides

Joseph Fort Newton

We cannot tell what may happen to us in the strange medley of life. But we can decide what happens in us—how we take it, what we do with it—and that is what really counts in the end. How to take the raw stuff of life and make it a thing of worth and beauty—that is the test of living.

Tuesday

⁛

I am not always wise, not always sweet enough to bear the pangs of disappointment that living with others must bring. So give me a heart more understanding, a mind clearer, a will more ready, to live with those I love without expecting a perfection lacking in myself.

Chasidic

Rabbi Bunam said: We should learn to be at least as careful in life as we are when we play checkers. Before we take any action we should think in advance whether we will have cause to regret it.

Chasidic

The Riziner Rebbe said: When we become unclean we immerse ourselves in water (Leviticus 15:13). But if the water is frozen, can we immerse ourselves in it? So, too, a frozen heart cannot serve God.

Maimonides

Do not regard yourself as wholly evil, so that you give up hope of improvement. You are not beyond redemption: exaggerate neither your virtues nor your faults.

When I have a low opinion of myself, any meanness I am guilty of does not seem surprising or outrageous to me.

Wednesday

⁛

Today enlarge my soul, O God, with the awareness that I am surrounded by love, however unclearly it may be expressed, sometimes, and fortify me with the knowledge that within me is the ability to respond to that love, in whatever form it comes to me: for come to me it does.

The Apter Rebbe said: Do not limit the form in which you wish to serve God—be what the moment calls for. Be like a vessel into which anything can be poured—wine, milk, or water.

Chasidic

The Hafetz Hayyim said: There are two kinds of heat: the heat of a fire, and the heat of an object near it. If you move that object away from the fire it will lose its heat. It follows that if you want to retain your own warmth you must be the fire, not the object that can be removed from it.

Chasidic

Perfection of means and confusion of goals seem to characterize our age.

Albert Einstein

In Pirké Avot it says: . . . *and be not wicked by facing yourself only.* This is usually understood as meaning "and do not look at yourself as completely wicked."

Rabbi Baruch said: The world has need of every single human being, for every person is born to perfect something in this world. But there are those who always sit in their room behind closed doors and study, and never leave the house to talk with others. For this they are called wicked. It is wicked to face yourself only, and not go among people, and thus in your solitude not perfect that one thing you were born to perfect.

Chasidic

Thursday

O God, give me a heart that is steadfast, a heart that no disillusion can wear out. And give me an upright spirit, which nothing unworthy can seduce for long. Then, when I fall short, I will continue to aim for the stars.

Hillel said: *What is hateful to you do not do to your neighbor* (Talmud Shabbat 31a). Rabbi Shmelke said: What in your neighbor is hateful to you, do not do yourself.

Chasidic

On every Sabbath eve Rabbi Chaim of Kosov, Rabbi Mendel's son, danced before his assembled disciples. His face was aflame

Chasidic

and they all knew that every step was informed with sublime meanings and had a cosmic effect.

Once when he was in the midst of dancing, a heavy bench fell on his foot and he had to pause because of the pain. Later they asked him about it. It seems to me, he said, that the pain made itself felt because I interrupted the dance.

Chasidic On a certain Purim when Chaim Meir Yechiel, the rabbi of Mogielnica was reading the Scroll of Esther, a young man stood by and said to him after the reading: I am afraid I did not listen closely enough and may have missed a word here and there while I was silently reciting the scroll with you.

Later the rabbi said to his friends: That's your superpious man! All he cares about is doing exactly what is prescribed. But one whose soul is directed toward God may very well fail to do something of what is prescribed, but it does not matter. For it is written (Proverbs 5:19): *In your love for her you will err constantly.*

William James

The great use of life is to spend it
for something that will outlast it.

Friday

Though I do sometimes aim for the stars, I don't need to reach them. The aiming itself is reaching enough, if I truly aim for beauty, goodness, and truth. So be with me, O Guiding Star. Show me what to aim for.

Chasidic The Bershider Rebbe said: Do you want people to love you? Love them first.

Anonymous Go placidly amid the noise and haste, and remember what peace there may be in silence. As far as possible without surrender, be on good terms with all persons. Speak your truth quietly and clearly; and listen to others, even the dull and ignorant: they, too, have their story. Avoid loud and aggressive persons, they are vexations to the spirit. If you compare yourself with others, you may become vain or bitter; for always there will be greater and lesser persons than yourself.

Enjoy your achievements as well as your plans. Keep interested in your own career, however humble; it is a real possession in the changing fortunes of time. Exercise caution in your business affairs; for the world is full of trickery. But let this not blind you to what virtue there is; many persons strive for high ideals; and everywhere life is full of heroism.

Be yourself. Especially, do not feign affection. Neither be cynical about love; for in the face of all aridity and disenchantment it is as perennial as the grass. Take kindly the counsel of the years, surrendering gracefully the things of youth.

Nurture strength of spirit to shield you in sudden misfortune. But do not distress yourself with imaginings. Many fears are born of fatigue and loneliness. Beyond a wholesome discipline, be gentle with yourself. You are a child of the universe, no less than the trees and the stars; you have a right to be here.

And whether or not it is clear to you, no doubt the universe is unfolding as it should. Therefore be at peace with God, whatever you conceive God to be; and whatever your labors and aspirations, in the noisy confusion of life keep peace with your soul. With all its sham, drudgery, and broken dreams, it is still a beautiful world. Be careful. Strive to be happy.

⁘

Shabbat

Make me know today how to be a friend to the world You made, for it is beautiful. On the day You made most precious of all—the Sabbath day—open my eyes.

Ivan N. Panin

To be forbearing to all—that is love; to be relentless toward self—that is wisdom; to be content with what one has—that is riches; to be discontented with what one is—that is piety.

David Grayson

Joy in life seems to me to arise from a sense of being where one belongs . . . of being four-square with the life we have chosen.

All the discontented people I know are trying sedulously to be something they are not, to do something they cannot do. . . .

Contentment, and indeed usefulness, comes as the infallible result of great acceptances, great humilities—of not trying to make ourselves this or that (to conform to some dramatized version of ourselves), but of surrendering ourselves to the fullness of life—of letting life flow through us.

Chasidic The Rabbi of Kobrin once looked up at the Heavens and said: Angel, little angel! It's no great trick to be an angel up there in the sky! You don't have to eat and drink, beget children and earn money. Just you come down to earth and worry about eating and drinking, about raising children and earning money, and we shall see if you keep on being an angel. If you succeed you can boast—but not now!

31 *Kindness*

The Week of Emor
Leviticus 21:1–24:23

The Sidra *Emor* contains legislation for Aaron, his sons, and future generations of priests, and also for the people as a whole (Leviticus 23). Most of the people were farmers, and the legislation spoke about the harvest; one notable purpose was to ensure that poor people were treated with kindness. *And when you reap the harvest of your land, you shall not reap all the way to the edges of your field, or gather the gleanings of your harvest; you shall leave them for the poor and the stranger.* (23:22).

Kind— the word has a familiar ring. It has another meaning, also familiar—kind as in kin—"related to." It is easier to be kind when we remember that you and I are kin, and akin.

Sunday

I can love and be loved, so long as I do not ask for a perfection beyond me, beyond you. I can care, my heart can be open to give and receive. I can give of myself, and I can be graceful when you care enough to bestow some kindness upon me.

If you give liberally, but unlovingly, and wound the heart of the poor, what good is your gift? If you give little, but give your heart with it, your deed is blessed and you are blessed. *Talmud*

One who showers you with gifts, but with a downcast face, has given you nothing; but one who greets you with a cheerful countenance, and nothing more, has given you all the gifts in the world. *Period of Mishnah / cs*

John Andrew Holmes

There is no better exercise
For the heart
Than reaching down
And lifting someone up.

Monday

✦

What gifts I could give you if only you would let me! How much I could give you if only I could find the way of it! I wanted so much to give to you, but you were elsewhere! O give up these excuses!

Mishnah

Chanina ben Dosa said:
When you ease your neighbor's heart
you make Heaven smile.

Period of Mishnah

Three things ingratiate us to others:
an open hand,
a prepared table,
a light heart.

Proverbs

Pleasant words are a honeycomb: to the soul, sweetness, and health to the body.

Tuesday

✦

I meet people who are suspicious of my motives, when all I want is to be helpful, friendly, generous. We say to ourselves: "Who is this? What does he [she] really want of me?" Help me to overcome suspicion by being patient and trustworthy. And don't let me be afraid of the kindness of others.

Mishnah

Find virtue in everyone.
Greet everyone with joy.

Joseph Addison

What sunshine is to flowers, smiles are to humanity. They are but trifles, to be sure; but, scattered along life's pathway, the good they do is inconceivable.

The Lubliner Rebbe asked that his evening meal be prepared earlier than usual, so that he would have more time to perform a good deed he had in mind. As it happened, the meal was later than usual.

About this he said: I could have lost my temper and berated my household. But I had intended to gain time to please God. Should I then displease God by becoming angry and thus double my loss?

Chasidic

I do the very best I know how; the very best I can; and I mean to keep on doing it to the end. If the end brings me out all right, what is said against me will not amount to anything. If the end brings me out all wrong, then a legion of angels swearing I was right will make no difference.

Abraham Lincoln

⁘

Wednesday

My brothers and sisters: If you are afflicted in body or mind, I would comfort and relieve you; if you are distressed, I would come to your aid; and if you are sick or in pain, I would restore you to health and ease your pain. O God, make me Your messenger, Your healing angel.

Anonymous

It is told:

One day, as Rabbi Akiba was walking through a graveyard, he came across a man bent low, carrying a load of wood like a beast of burden. Akiba said: Why such heavy labor, my son? If you are a slave and suffering from abuse on that account, let me redeem you and set you free. And if you are free, but poor, let me help you.

To this the man replied: Sir, you cannot help me. I am of the dead, not the living. It has been decreed that day after day I must gather wood, and then this wood is used to burn me.

What could you have done to earn such a fate?

The man replied: In life I was a tax-collector. I favored the rich and was a scourge to the poor. And I seduced a betrothed virgin on the Day of Atonement.

Midrash

Even so, said Akiba, is there nothing that can be done for you?

I know of nothing, said the man. But after a while he added: I did hear that my punishment would be reduced if I had a son who could stand up in the congregation and praise God. And although I had no son at the time of my death, my wife was with child. I do not know whether she bore a boy or a girl, or whether the child lived. And if I did bear a son, who would teach him?

Akiba asked his name and that of his wife, and left the suffering wretch. He then traveled from town to town asking for her. One day he came to a village where the wife was known. The villagers remembered her husband with horror. He had had a son, and the boy was still living there, in degradation. He had not been circumcised, and he had been taught nothing.

For forty days Akiba fasted, provoking a voice from Heaven to call out: For this boy you fast? Akiba answered: Yes. First he taught the boy the alphabet, then Torah. And he taught him to stand up in the congregation to recite the praise of the Holy One: Hallowed be the name of God. . . .

Then the charcoal burner appeared to Akiba in a dream and said: I have been redeemed from Gehenna. Akiba cried out in joy. He, too, sang God's praise (Psalm 135:13): *Your name is everlasting, Your remembrance for all generations.*

Thursday

What is the quality of my life? I am no judge of my own worth. This day, though, let me not reflect on questions that are without an answer, and let me instead think of problems that have a solution. For there is always something I can do to make someone glad that we met, today.

Midrash *If you pour yourself out for the hungry* . . . (Isaiah 58:10). Rabbi Levi said: If you have nothing [else] to give, give words that console; say: My heart goes out to you, that I have nothing to give you.

Some make themselves rich, yet have nothing;
others make themselves poor, yet they have much.
Those with a benevolent eye are blessed,
for they give of their bread to the poor.

Proverbs

Goodness is something so simple; always to live for others, never to seek one's own advantage.

Dag Hammarskjöld

⁘

Friday

Most of the time what I do or don't do matters to me, but not (I hope) too much; and to others, too, what I do or don't is not of cosmic import. When I remember this, I am relieved, for I see that if I don't accomplish great good, at least I don't do much harm. Help me to see myself a little more clearly today; it seems that's when I can be myself most easily, and then I find a little more generosity inside, and less fear of giving.

Once when the Baal Shem Tov was sitting with his Chasidim, a poor man entered. He had of no special distinction, yet the Baal Shem called him to the head of the table and seated him at his side. His Chasidim, astonished, asked later why he had so greatly honored this man: was he perhaps a hidden saint? The Baal Shem explained: When I want a seat of honor in the world-to-come, and I am asked what I did to deserve it, what will I have to say? The only answer I will have is that once I too gave a poor man a seat of honor.

Chasidic

In this short Life
That only lasts an hour
How much—how little—is
Within our power.

Emily Dickinson

Happiness is a perfume you cannot pour on others without getting a few drops on yourself.

Ralph Waldo Emerson

Source of good, grant that each one who has to do with me today may be the happier for it. Let me be less critical, less ill-tempered, and not too busy to say a friendly word. Let this Shabbat truly be "a delight."

Talmud

There was a drought and Rabbi opened the storehouse, saying: Let those versed in Scripture, Mishnah, Talmud, Halachah, and Agadah enter, but not the ignorant.

Rabbi Yonatan ben Amram knocked and was allowed to enter.

He said: Rabbi, give me sustenance!

Have you learned Scripture, my son?

No.

Mishnah?

No.

In that case, why should I sustain you?

Feed me as you would a dog or a bird.

He gave him food.

Afterward, Rabbi regretted it and said: Why did I give food to an ignoramus?

Rabbi Simeon his son then said to him: Perhaps that was your disciple Yonatan ben Amram, who has never allowed himself to benefit from his Torah-learning in his life.

They investigated and found it to be so.

Rabbi then said: Let everyone enter.

Johann Wolfgang von Goethe

If you treat me as if I were what I ought to be and could be, I will become what I ought to be and could be.

בהר סיני

32 *This World*

The Week of B'har Sinai
Leviticus 25:1–26:2

The Sidra *B'har Sinai* (Leviticus 25) focuses on legislation intended to ensure that people—especially people in distress—may enjoy a secure life. The land itself must be taken care of. Land sold reverts to the original owner in the fiftieth year, the year of jubilee: *When you enter the land that I am giving you, let the land observe a Sabbath in honor of the Eternal One. Six years you shall sow your field . . . but in the seventh year there shall be a Sabbath of complete rest for the land. . . . You shall proclaim liberty throughout the land to all its inhabitants* (25:2,10). We are tenants, not owners, of the ground we walk on.

Sunday

Chasidic / cs

Creator of the universe, teach me how to be alone,
and guide me.
Lead my feet toward trees/grasses/all that grows.
There let me be alone with You.

FOR FLOWERS AND HERBS

בָּרוּךְ אַתָּה יי אֱלֹהֵינוּ מֶלֶךְ הָעוֹלָם, בּוֹרֵא עִשְׂבֵי בְשָׂמִים.

Father of all being, we give praise for fragrant flowers and spices.

FOR SHRUBS, BUSHES, AND TREES

בָּרוּךְ אַתָּה יי אֱלֹהֵינוּ מֶלֶךְ הָעוֹלָם, בּוֹרֵא עֲצֵי בְשָׂמִים.

Mother of all being, we give praise for trees and their fragrance.

Midrash *When you come into the land and plant . . .* (Leviticus 19:23). Though you find the land full of goodness, don't think of sitting idle. Make sure to plant trees. As you found trees that others planted, so you must plant for your children. Never say: I am old. How many more years do I have? Why should I trouble myself for the sake of others? You found trees, so you must plant more even when you are old.

TODAY'S TASK: Plant a tree, or arrange for one to be planted.

MEDITATION: Fountain of mercy and unending love, sustain me with fruit from the Tree of Life.

Monday

Midrash Rabbi Simeon bar Yochai said: These three are equally important: earth, human beings, and rain. Rabbi Levi ben Chiyah said: He meant that the earth cannot live without rain, and that human beings cannot live without earth or rain.

UPON DOING OR BENEFITING FROM AN ACTION THAT IMPROVES THE WORLD AROUND US

בָּרוּךְ אַתָּה יי אֱלֹהֵינוּ מֶלֶךְ הָעוֹלָם, אֲשֶׁר
קִדְּשָׁנוּ בְּמִצְוֹתָיו וְצִוָּנוּ לַעֲשׂוֹת מַעֲקֶה.

Father of all being, be praised: for all who answer the call to be holy, whose labor benefits the world.

FOR EDIBLE FRUITS AND NUTS

בָּרוּךְ אַתָּה יי אֱלֹהֵינוּ מֶלֶךְ הָעוֹלָם, הַנּוֹתֵן רֵיחַ טוֹב בַּפֵּרוֹת.

Mother of all being, be praised: for the fragrance of fruits.

TODAY'S TASK: Recycle.

MEDITATION: Power beyond all earthly powers, sustain me with fruit from the Tree of Life.

⁛

Tuesday

Maimonides

Do not imagine that all other beings exist merely for the sake of the existence of human beings. On the contrary, all other beings exist for their own sakes, and not for the sake of something else.

FOR LIGHTNING OR OTHER NATURAL WONDERS

בָּרוּךְ אַתָּה יי אֱלֹהֵינוּ מֶלֶךְ הָעוֹלָם, עֹשֶׂה מַעֲשֵׂה בְרֵאשִׁית.

Father of all being, we give praise: for creation and its wonders.

FOR THUNDER

בָּרוּךְ אַתָּה יי אֱלֹהֵינוּ מֶלֶךְ הָעוֹלָם, שֶׁכֹּחוֹ וּגְבוּרָתוֹ מָלֵא עוֹלָם.

Mother of all being, we give praise: Your power and might pervade the world.

Talmud

You may eat of them, but you must not cut them down (Deuteronomy 20:19).

Whoever breaks vessels, or tears garments, or destroys a building, or does away with food in a destructive manner, violates the command "not to destroy."

TODAY'S TASK: Be less wasteful of food.

MEDITATION: You who fill my eye with beauty of earth, sky, and water, sustain me with fruit from the Tree of Life.

⁛

Wednesday

Moses Cordovero

Wisdom extends acts of love toward all things, including plants and animals.

ON SEEING TREES IN BLOSSOM

בָּרוּךְ אַתָּה יי אֱלֹהֵינוּ מֶלֶךְ הָעוֹלָם, אֲשֶׁר בָּרָא בְּעוֹלָמוֹ
בְּרִיּוֹת טוֹבוֹת וְאִילָנוֹת טוֹבִים, לֵהָנוֹת בָּהֶם בְּנֵי אָדָם.

Father of all being, we give praise: for goodly creatures and lovely trees that fill the eye and win the heart.

FOR PERFUMES OR SPICES

בָּרוּךְ אַתָּה יי אֱלֹהֵינוּ מֶלֶךְ הָעוֹלָם, בּוֹרֵא מִינֵי בְשָׂמִים.

Mother of all being, we give praise for all the world's spices.

TODAY'S TASK: When possible, walk or take a bus or train instead of driving.

MEDITATION: Eternal and unwearied Source of creation, sustain me with fruit from the Tree of Life.

Thursday

Midrash

Noah came forth from the ark, looked around and saw the whole world desolate. He cried out and said to God: How could You have done this? And God said: Ah, Noah, how different you are from Abraham. When I tell him that Sodom and Gomorrah are going to be destroyed, Abraham will plead with me on their behalf. But when I told you that I was intending to destroy the whole world, I waited for you to speak to Me on its behalf. But when you knew that you would be safe in the ark, . . . you thought of no one but your own immediate family. And now you complain?

FOR NATURAL BEAUTY

בָּרוּךְ אַתָּה יי אֱלֹהֵינוּ מֶלֶךְ הָעוֹלָם, שֶׁכָּכָה לּוֹ בְּעוֹלָמוֹ.

Mother of all being, we give praise: Your world is filled with beauty.

FOR A RAINBOW

בָּרוּךְ אַתָּה יי אֱלֹהֵינוּ מֶלֶךְ הָעוֹלָם, זוֹכֵר הַבְּרִית וְנֶאֱמָן בִּבְרִיתוֹ וְקַיָּם בְּמַאֲמָרוֹ.

Father of all being, we give praise: true to Your word, You remember Your covenant with creation.

Abraham J. Heschel

There are three ways in which we may relate ourselves to the world—we may exploit it, we may enjoy it, we may accept it in awe.

TODAY'S TASK: Waste less water, light, and paper.

MEDITATION: Glory visible in star and cell, sustain me with fruit from the Tree of Life.

✣

Friday

Midrash

Rabban Yochanan ben Zakkai would say:
If you are planting in the field and you hear them tell you the Messiah has come, continue to plant. Then you can go and greet the Messiah.

UPON EXPERIENCING A WONDER

בָּרוּךְ אַתָּה יי אֱלֹהֵינוּ מֶלֶךְ הָעוֹלָם, שֶׁעָשָׂה לִי נֵס בַּמָּקוֹם הַזֶּה.

Mother of all being, for the wonder I experience here and now, I give thanks.

Judy Chicago

And then all that has divided us will merge
And then compassion will be wedded to power
And then softness will come to a world that is harsh and unkind
And then both men and women will be gentle
And then both women and men will be strong
And then no person will be subject to another's will
And then all will be rich and free and varied
And then the greed of some will give way to the needs of many
And then all will share equally in the earth's abundance
And then all will care for the sick and the weak and the old
And then all will nourish the young
And then all will cherish life's creatures
And then all will live in harmony with
each other and Earth
And then everywhere will be
called Eden once again.

TODAY'S TASK: Ask a public servant to work harder to protect forests and rivers.

MEDITATION: Fountain of life, sustain me with fruit from the Tree of Life.

Midrash After creating the first human beings, God led them around the Garden of Eden and said: Look at my works! See how beautiful they are, how excellent! I created them for your sake. Take care not to spoil or destroy My world, for if you do, there will be none to repair it after you.

TO ACKNOWLEDGE EVENTS THAT ARE EXPERIENCED AS SUBLIME AND/OR MYSTERIOUS

בָּרוּךְ אַתָּה יי אֱלֹהֵינוּ מֶלֶךְ הָעוֹלָם, חֲכַם הָרָזִים.

Mother of all being, we give praise: You see what is hidden from our sight.

TODAY'S TASK: Let things be.

MEDITATION: Presence dwelling in flower and seed, sustain me with fruit from the Tree of Life.

Albert Einstein There is a . . . stage of religious experience that . . . I will call cosmic religious feeling. It is very difficult to explain this feeling to anyone who is entirely without it, especially as there is no anthropomorphic conception of God corresponding to it.

The individual feels the nothingness of human desires and aims and the sublimity and marvellous order that reveal themselves both in nature and in the world of thought . . . [and] looks upon individual existence as a sort of prison and wants to experience the universe as a single significant whole.

33 *Gratitude and Rejoicing*

The Week of B'chukotai
Leviticus 26:3–27:34

The Sidra *B'chukotai* (Leviticus 26), last of the book of Leviticus, promises a time of security, peace, and prosperity for those who are faithful to God. *You shall eat your fill of bread and dwell securely in your land. I will grant peace in your land, and you shall lie down untroubled* . . . (26:5). Would not a people blessed in this manner have reason to be grateful, to rejoice? But even when it goes less well for us, we are wise to count our blessings and to live with gratitude in our hearts. That, too, is faithfulness.

Sunday

Source of blessing, teach me to pursue my own happiness by contributing to the happiness of those I love, and show me that there are blessings in my life even when I lose sight of the goodness that has surrounded and sustained me all my days.

Rabbi Pinchas of Koretz said: Joy is on a higher plane than grief. Even with the newborn child, tears come first and smiles only later. Joy constitutes a higher stage, for it springs from higher worlds, from the glory of God. Thus it is that joy washes away all sin. — *Chasidic*

The door to happiness opens outwards. — *Søren Kierkegaard*

Nothing is enough for the one to whom enough is too little. — *Epicurus*

William Blake You never know what is enough, unless you know what is more than enough.

Monday

⁘

Today let me be grateful that I wakened to a new day, that the sun is shining somewhere, and, for that matter, that rains fall, too; let me be glad for the air and the soil, and for the world's simplest pleasure: the breath I draw right now.

Midrash *I have done all that You have commanded me* (Deuteronomy 26:14). That means: I have rejoiced, and caused others to rejoice.

Robert Louis Stevenson We know of some very religious people who came to doubt God when a great misfortune befell them, even though they themselves were to blame for it; but we have never yet met anyone who lost his faith because an undeserved fortune fell to his lot.

Harry Emerson Fosdick Happiness at its deepest and best is not the portion of a cushioned life which never struggled, overpassed obstacles, bore hardships, or adventured in sacrifice for costly aims. A heart of joy is never found in luxuriously coddled lives, but in men and women who achieve and dare, who have tried their powers against antagonisms, who have met even sickness and bereavement and have tempered their souls in fire. . . . If we were set upon making a happy world, then we would not leave struggle out or make adversity impossible. The unhappiest world conceivable . . . would be a world with nothing hard to do, no conflicts to wage for ends worthwhile; a world where courage was not needed and sacrifice was a superfluity.

Tuesday

⁘

For acts of kindness I do or receive, for the miracle of daily bread, for transcendent grace within ordinary things, and for the times I surprise myself with unexpected virtues, let me give thanks.

One of the finest sides to living is liking people and wanting to share activities in the human enterprise. The greatest pleasures come by giving pleasure to those who work with us, to the person who lives next door, and to those who live under the same roof. Entering into this human enterprise, feeling oneself a part of the community, is a very important element which generates happiness.

Fred J. Hafling

Happiness in this world, when it comes, comes incidentally. Make it the object of pursuit, and it leads us a wild-goose chase, and is never attained. Follow some other object, and very possibly we may find that we have caught happiness without dreaming of it.

Nathaniel Hawthorne

What is life's heaviest burden? asked a youth of a sad and lonely old man. To have nothing to carry, he answered.

E. Scott O'Connor

To love playthings well as a child, to lead an adventurous and honourable youth, and to settle when the time arrives, into a green and smiling age, is to be a good artist in life and deserve well of yourself and your neighbour.

Robert Louis Stevenson

Wednesday

What I have is so much more important than what I lack—a family, friends, enough to eat and drink, a place to live in, work to do, my thoughts, my feelings, my hopes and dreams—how can I not give thanks for all this?

The Holy Spirit rests only on one who has a joyous heart.

Talmud

There is in happiness an element of self-forgetfulness. You lose yourself in something outside yourself when you are happy; just as when you are desperately miserable you are intensely conscious of yourself, are a solid little lump of ego weighing a ton.

J. B. Priestley

Joseph Addison The grand essentials to happiness in this life are something to do, something to love, and something to hope for.

Charles Lamb I am disposed to say grace upon twenty other occasions in the course of the day besides my dinner. I want a form for setting out upon a pleasant walk, for a moonlight ramble, for a friendly meeting, or a solved problem. Why have we none for books, those spiritual repasts—a grace before Milton—a devotional exercise proper to be said before reading The Faerie Queen?

Thursday

It would be fooling myself to ask for too much of anything, including happiness; how could I be completely happy when others are not? How could I be completely happy with myself, unless I were perfect? Knowing I'm like everyone else, I know how flawed I am. Even so, let me be more grateful for what I am, and less disgruntled over what I cannot be.

Chasidic How full of wonders the world is! And yet we take our little hand, cover our eyes, and see nothing!

William Shakespeare

My crown is in my heart, not on my head;
Not deck'd with diamonds and Indian stones,
Nor to be seen; my crown is called content.

William Winter As much of heaven is visible as we have eyes to see.

Dag Hammarskjöld To rejoice at success is not the same thing as taking credit for it. To deny oneself the first is to become a hypocrite and a denier of life; to permit oneself the second is a childish indulgence which will prevent one from ever growing up.

Teach me the meaning of the word *enough*. Some things I surely have enough of, enough to be grateful for. Other things I don't have. Some I may in time acquire, others not. Do not let me enmesh myself in the web of endless desires. Let today be enough for today: Tomorrow hasn't come, and never will until—tomorrow.

The Radziminer Rebbe said: We cross an ocean and are rescued from a shipwreck, so we give thanks to God. Should we not thank God if we cross without a mishap? I am cured of a dangerous illness and recite a thanksgiving blessing. Should I not give thanks when I am well and preserved from illness?

Chasidic

In every part and corner of our life, to lose oneself is to be gainer; to forget oneself is to be happy.

Robert Louis Stevenson

It is right to be contented with what we have, not with what we are.

Sir James Mackintosh

Socrates was wont to say, They are most happy and nearest the gods that need nothing. And coming once up into the Exchange at Athens, where they that traded, asked him, What will you buy, What do you lack?, after he had gravely walked up into the middle, spreading forth his hands and turning about: Good gods, said he, who would have thought there were so many things in the world which I do not want?—and so left the place under the reproach of Nature. He was wont to say that happiness consisted not in having many, but in needing the fewest things. . . . We need heaven and earth, our senses, souls, and bodies to be enjoyed. Which, God in his mercy having freely prepared, they are most happy that so live in the enjoyment of these, as to need no accidental, trivial things, no splendors, pomps and vanities.

Thomas Traherne

⁘

I owe so much to others, O God. Some of them I know, most I will never meet, however many gifts they send me. May they receive equal gifts from me, though they never know my name. We all are known to You, and for that I give thanks.

Chasidic

It is good to sing to our God (Psalm 147:1). It is good if you can have God sing within you.

Beverly Nichols

Every moment of this strange and lovely life from dawn to dusk is a miracle. Somewhere, always, a rose is opening its petals to the dawn. Somewhere, always, a flower is fading in the dusk. The incense that rises with the sun, and the scents that die in the dark, are all gathered, sooner or later, into the solitary fragrance that is God. Faintly, elusively that fragrance lingers over all of us.

Christina Rossetti

Were there no God we would be in this glorious world with grateful hearts: and no one to thank.

George Herbert

Thou hast given so much to me.
Give me one thing more—a grateful heart.

Edward Arlington Robinson

Two kinds of gratitude: the sudden kind
We feel for what we take, the larger kind
We feel for what we give.

במדבר

34 *Finding Our Way*

The Week of B'midbar
Numbers 1:1–4:20

This week's Sidra *B'midbar Sinai* (Numbers 1) takes up the narration of the journey of Israel in the wilderness. We read: *The Eternal One spoke to Moses in the wilderness* (1:1). As they prepare to set forth, they ready themselves by taking a census of able-bodied men who can defend them on the way through the wilderness to the destination they seek: the promised land, a land that must have seemed far away, almost mythical, as our own far-off destinations may sometimes seem, when we are young.

And when we feel we're lost in a wilderness, we can remember that Moses in the wilderness heard the voice of the Eternal; perhaps we can, too.

❖

Sunday

God, I give thanks for the days to come and for Your strength within me that will bring me through its difficulties and dangers. I thank You for the joys that will lighten my days. If in the swift-passing days I fail to hear Your voice, and if in their blinding glare I do not recognize Your presence, please forgive me.

Help me, then; strengthen the goodness within me. Help me to see clearly what is worthwhile, and to keep to it more faithfully. Then when this day and this week have passed, they will mark another step on my way through life, a step taken in the awareness that You go with me.

cs / Forms of Prayer

David said: My fear comes from my joy, and my joy comes from my fear, but my love rises higher than both.

Midrash

Chasidic Rabbi Mendel often complained: As long as there were no roads, you had to interrupt a journey at nightfall. Then you had all the time in the world to recite psalms at the inn, to open a book, and to have a good talk with someone. But nowadays you can ride on these roads day and night and there is no time anymore.

Chasidic Rabbi Uri of Strelisk once said to the Chasidim who had come together in Strelisk: You journey to me, and where do I journey? I journey and journey continually toward God.

Monday

Which way should I go? When I get to a crossroads, does it matter whether I go right or left? I hear a voice saying, "Not to me it doesn't," but it does to me. Should I ask You the way? How will I know You have answered me? Help me to hearken to the still, small voice at my center, and to know that that's where I'll hear You.

Proverbs Do not be easily angered:
restraint shows insight;
a cool spirit, understanding.

Talmud Rabbi Yosé taught in Sepphoris:
Father Elijah could not control his temper.
Elijah had been accustomed to visit him frequently;
now three days passed without a visit.
When at last he did come, Rabbi Yosé asked:
—Why didn't the Master come?
—You called me a hot-head.
—You proved me right!

Chasidic A Tzaddik used to say:
I keep my anger in my pocket,
and take it out only when I need it.

It is easy to fly into a passion—anybody can do that—but to be angry with the right person to the right extent and at the right time and with the right object and in the right way—that is not easy, and it is not everyone who can do it. *Aristotle*

How much more grievous are the consequences of anger than its causes. *Marcus Aurelius*

⁘

Tuesday

"It takes two to speak truth—one to speak and one to hear," said Thoreau. I need to listen well when others speak; even when their truth is hard to swallow, it may be good medicine. Help me to listen well, for it is said, "God's seal is Truth."

One time Rabbi Israel joined a group of Chasidim who were seated together, and they asked him: Tell us, honored Rabbi, how should we serve God? The question surprised him, and he said: How should I know? But I'll tell you a story. *Chasidic*

Two friends were accused of a crime, found guilty and brought to the king for judgment. He loved them and wanted to show them mercy, but even the king must obey the law. So this was his verdict: Let a rope be stretched over a deep chasm and the two were to walk it, one after the other. If either one reached the other side, he would be granted his life. It was done, and the first one got safely across. The other then cried to him: How did you manage to walk that rope? The first called back: All I know is this—whenever I felt myself toppling over to one side, I leaned to the other.

We make our own world; when we have made it awry, we can remake it, approximately truer, although it cannot be absolutely true, to the facts. It will never finally be made; we are always stretching forth to larger and better fictions which answer more truly to our growing knowledge and experience. *Havelock Ellis*

James Harvey Robinson

We like to continue to believe what we have been accustomed to accept as true, and the resentment aroused when doubt is cast upon any of our assumptions leads us to seek every manner of excuse for clinging to them. The result is that most of our so-called reasoning consists in finding arguments for going on believing as we already do.

Wednesday

Yesterday I reflected on the truths I might hear from the lips of others; today I ask that You guard me from telling lies—and first of all to myself. And it is not so much the big lies I need to guard against, but the times I pretend to myself—or to others—just a little bit more than I need to.

Period of Mishnah / cs

Be ready to appear naked—or clothed;
to appear standing—or sitting;
to appear laughing—or crying,
as it is said (Ecclesiastes 3):
a time to weep and a time to laugh.

Robert Browning

Just when we are safest, there's a sunset-touch,
A fancy from a flower-bell, some one's death,
A chorus-ending from Euripides,—
And that's enough for fifty hopes and fears
As old and new at once as Nature's self,
To rap and knock and enter in our soul.

Tao / cs

A balanced woman who doesn't try for balance
keeps her balance;
One who wants to be admired for it
will lose it.
The "righteous" calculate profit and loss from each transaction;
The "moral" demand that all conform to their conventions.
When none respond

they roll up their sleeves and force it on the rest.
When we lose our way we seek kindness;
failing that, we seek justice;
failing that, convention.
Then honest faith fades, and chaos appears.
Don't get lost.
Go deeper into reality.
Keep close to the ground where the roots are.
Eat the fruit and not the flower.

⁘

Thursday

The biggest lie I tell myself is. . . . For a moment I thought I could complete that sentence, and that would have been the biggest lie of all! But I do understand what is the great struggle of my life: to know the inside of me better, to examine what I'm about to do, as well as what I've already done.

Keep two truths in separate pockets always, and take them out as needed: In the first, *For my sake the world was created;* in the second, *I am but dust and ashes.* — *Chasidic*

Tao / cs

It takes thirty spokes to make a wheel:
but the hole in the center
makes it useful for a cart.
It takes a lump of clay to make a pot:
but the empty space within it
gives the pot its value.
A house needs doors and windows:
but the empty space is what
we call "a room to live in."
Thus fullness has its role,
but emptiness redeems it.

We show greatness not by being at one extreme, but by touching both at once and occupying all the space in between. — *Blaise Pascal*

Chasidic Rabbi Moshe Leib of Sasov said: The way in this world is like the edge of a blade: on this side is an abyss, and on that side is an abyss, and the way of life lies in between.

Bachya ibn Pakuda First learn evil, to shun it; then learn good, to do it.

Friday

Someone said that when you're wrapped up in yourself you make a pretty small package. Help me to unwrap, O God; then help me to wrap myself in something larger than myself; help me forget the tightrope under my feet and to keep my eyes on today's destination.

Midrash

Rabbi Akiba would teach in the name of
 Rabbi Simeon ben Azzai:
Move down a step or two,
so that they tell you to ascend,
rather than go up and be told to descend.
Much better to be told: Go up, go up!
rather than: Go down, go down!
And thus said Hillel:
My descent is my ascent and my ascent is my descent. . . .

Tao / cs

What is deflated
was surely filled with air.
If it was taken away,
it must have been given.
If it was laid low,
it must have been flying high.

Samuel Butler Life is like playing a violin solo in public and learning the instrument as one goes on.

James Bissett Pratt The plover, south of Capricorn, hears the call of the Labrador Spring while yet Winter reigns, and starts out on her twelve thousand mile flight; the salmon in the sea is drawn to the breeding grounds of Maine and Scotland and Alaska; the compass-needle trembles at the influence of the distant pole; the moon draws the tides through two hundred and forty thousand miles of intervening space; light travels across the stellar universe, and through the power of gravity distant star greets distant star.

⁘

Shabbat

On Shabbat I can relax my grip on where I may be going, because I've arrived in time's favored resting place. Give me this day of rest to realize that much of my restlessness doesn't have to be; and help me bring some Shabbat rest into the week.

Yiddish proverb

We don't know what to thank God for.

Ruth F. Brin

No one ever told me the coming of the Messiah
Could be an inward thing.
No one ever told me a change of heart
Might be as quiet as new-fallen snow.

No one ever told me that redemption
Was as simple as springtime and as wonderful
As birds returning after a long winter,
Rose-breasted grosbeaks singing in the swaying branches
Of a newly budded tree.

No one ever told me that salvation
Might be like a fresh spring wind
Blowing away the dried, withered leaves of another year,
Carrying the scent of flowers, the promise of fruition.

What I found for myself I try to tell you:
Redemption and salvation are very near,
And the taste of them is in the world
That God created and laid before us.

Chasidic *Noah was a righteous man, whole-hearted in his generations* (Genesis 6:9). The Lizensker Rebbe said: The fact that Noah thought himself to be righteous and whole-hearted lessened his goodness; he had descended.

Those who labor in quest of God never stand still; they either increase the purity of their service or they decrease it.

Each such change marks a different "generation" in their life. In this way good people live in many generations, as we read in the case of Noah: *in his generations.*

35 *Gifts and Blessings*

The Week of Naso
Numbers 4:21–7:89

The Sidra *Naso* (Numbers 6) contains the most famous of all benedictions; it is called the Priestly Blessing or the Threefold Benediction. The blessings grow in richness, culminating in Shalom—a word meaning wholeness, harmony, peace. *May God bless you and keep you. May God smile upon you and be gracious to you. May God look with favor upon you and give you peace* (6:24–26). According to ancient interpreters, these blessings comprise both material and spiritual well-being.

The gift of gifts is to be born. Never take it for granted. And when we unfold that gift, how many more are waiting to be enjoyed.

Sunday

For the light and truth that come to me in my daily life, for the teachings that reach me through my experiences, Your messengers, I am grateful. Help me now to transform my gratitude into service: Let my labors add to the store of the world's goodness.

Chasidic

The Kobriner Rebbe turned to his Chasidim and said: Do you know where God is? He took a piece, showed it to them all, and continued: God is in this piece of bread. This bread would have no existence without the manifestation of God's power in all nature.

Anonymous

Now, on the gleaming jewels of dew,
the splendor of the setting sun!
And now you come to me
bearing gifts.
I cannot remember picking flowers,
yet my hands are quite full!

Friedrich Nietzsche

We take,
never asking
who it is that gives.

Monday

Some time today I'll probably hear these words: Have a good day! But what You say is: Have a day! Whether this day will be "good" or "bad" You do not say and I cannot know. I may not know this until it is long past. Either way, I am blessed to have it; thank You for today, and for all my days.

Talmud

As it is possible to abuse things that are permitted, so is it possible to sin by abstaining from the right use of these things—such as food, sex, and all else that God made and called "very good." We will be called to account for our abstinence from these permitted things.

Ralph Waldo Emerson

The days come and go like muffled and veiled figures sent from a distant friendly party, but they say nothing, and if we do not use the gifts they bring, they carry them as silently away.

David E. Roberts

Sin, at its roots, is ingratitude. It is a sort of seizure of life, as though by right, instead of the receiving of a gift.

Chasidic

Once, when Rabbi Moshe of Kobrin was young, he spent Purim with his teacher Rabbi Mordechai of Lechovitz. In the middle of the meal, Rabbi Mordechai exclaimed: This is a time for gifts. Reach out your hands and I will give you whatever gifts of spirit you crave! The other disciples present asked for a variety of spiritual gifts and received them, but Moshe was silent.

Finally, the rabbi inquired: Well, Moshe, and what do you want?

He replied: The only thing I want is to serve until I deserve what I get.

⁘

Tuesday

How I wish I could feel blessed each and every day! Remind me, O Source of blessing; remind me again and again, that I am loved however I feel, and remind me that every day is a birthday. Sometime later today may I again remember to say thanks!

Midrash

There is no blade of grass
no plant
no flower
without its own star.
That star looks down
with light,
and says:
Grow!

J. Arthur Hatfield

Nature is economic in her gifts: she will not give strength to those who will not expend it. . . . She is lavish in her gifts to those who will use them. . . . The Sea of Galilee is fresh and blue and gives life to living creatures within its sunlit waters—not because it receives waters, but because it gives them freely. The Dead Sea is dead, not because there is no supply of fresh water, but because it permits no outlet. It is a law of nature—a law of life—that only by giving shall we receive.

Chasidic

Rabbi Moshe Leib of Sasov said: How easy it is for the poor to depend on God! What else have they to depend on? And how hard it is for the rich! All their possessions call out to them: *Depend on us!*

Wednesday

❖

I know You need no thanks when you shower Your blessings upon me—life and health, healing from sickness, the beauty of heaven and earth, an infant's smile—and even more! But there are times when my thankfulness, unsought, goes out to You, O Giver of life.

Chasidic The Bratzlaver Rebbe said: You live in Paradise when you know that whatever happens to you is for your good.

cs / Lin Yutang The secret of contentment is my discovery of my own powers and limitations, finding satisfaction in a line of activity that I can do well, plus the wisdom to know that my place, no matter how important or successful I am, never counts very much in the universe. I may very well be so successful in carving a name for myself in my field that I begin to imagine myself indispensable or omnipotent, I am eaten up by some secret ambition, and then good-bye to all contentment. Sometimes it is more important to discover what one cannot do than what one can do. So much restlessness is due to the fact that I do not know what I want, or perhaps I want to be someone else, to be anybody except myself. The courage of being one's genuine self, of standing alone and of not wanting to be somebody else!

Tao / cs

Heaven begets us and sustains us,
Nourishes and develops us,
Shelters us and feeds us.
Begetting, it does not own;
Sustaining, it does not control;
Stronger, it does not compel;
Guiding, it does not intrude.
You ask for well-being, not for thanks.

Thursday

As I reflect upon the blessings I daily receive, I think above all that I am called to *be* a blessing. More than getting, let me give, give with a full heart and an open spirit. Will I not myself be blessed all the more? Giving, I will receive; blessing, I will be blessed.

Those who seek the Eternal One are in want of no good thing (Psalm 34:11). The Kobriner Rebbe said: That is because they believe that whatever they possess is enough good to meet their needs.

Chasidic

Drink, Pilgrim, here; here rest! And if thy heart
Be innocent, here too shalt thou refresh
Thy spirit, listening to some gentle sound.
Or passing gale, or hum of murmuring bees.

Samuel Taylor Coleridge

Blest, who can unconcernedly find
Hours, days and years, slide soft away
In health of body, peace of mind
  Quiet by day.
Sound sleep by night; study and ease
Together mix'd, sweet recreation,
And innocence, which most does please
  With meditation.

Alexander Pope

If I cannot give bountifully, yet I will give freely, and what I want in my hand, I will supply by my heart.

Anonymous

Friday

God, I am grateful that so many are part of me and my life, though most are strangers whose life and work make mine better than otherwise it would be. May my own life and work do an equal good to those unknown friends and neighbors.

Chasidic Rabbi Michal once said to his sons: My life was blessed in that I never needed anything until I had it.

Chasidic *We have no one to lean on except our Divine Parent* (Talmud Sotah 49a). The Gerer Rebbe said: One who knows this does not lack for anything.

Tao / cs

Life is a host who invites everyone,
without distinctions,
feeding all, refusing none.
She simply extends the invitation,
and not to display her wealth.
Nor does she send a bill to her invited guests.
Some are misled by a host so unassuming.
They don't notice her,
and imagine they are themselves
the hosts at Life's feast.
Others know her as the perfect host,
the one who, barely seen,
is always there.

Shabbat

What a blessing it is to work, and then to rest. Especially today I feel rich in blessing—the blessing of Your spirit that pervades all things living and inanimate, the joy of family love and the gift of friendship. Give me always a heart grateful as in my sunniest days, a soul thankful as in the hour of my highest joy.

Talmud *You shall meditate on it day and night* (Joshua 1:8). Rabbi Yochanan said: This is no command or obligation, but a blessing. Because Joshua loved the words of the Torah he was blessed: *they shall never depart from your mouth.* They taught in the school of Rabbi Ishmael: The words of the Torah are not to be an obligation to you; on the other hand, you are not free to release yourself from them.

Sure thou didst flourish once! and many springs,
Many bright mornings, much dew, many showers
Passed o'er thy head: many light hearts and wings,
Which now are dead, lodged in thy living bowers.
And still a new succession sings and flies;
Fresh groves grow up and their green branches shoot,
Towards the old and still enduring skies,
While the low violet thrives at their root.

Henry Vaughan

And this is the blessing with which Moses, the man of God, blessed the people of Israel (Deuteronomy 33:11).

The Lentzner Rebbe said: What was his blessing? That each of them might become the man or woman of God.

cs / Chasidic

36 *The Religious Vision*

The Week of B'ha-alot'cha Numbers 8:1–12:16

The Sidra *B'ha-alot'cha* (Numbers 11) recounts an event in the life of the community as it proceeds on its course in the wilderness. A group of elders is chosen to assist Moses in leading the people, and momentarily they speak in ecstasy: *And when the spirit rested upon them, they spoke as prophets* (11:25). When they are done, two young men, Eldad and Medad, continue. Far from restraining them, Moses applauds them, saying: *Would that all the people of God were prophets, that God put the divine spirit on them!* (11:29). The religious vision, then, is one that all may participate in: it is not the property of an elite.

Sunday

cs / Liberal Jewish Prayer Book I

Our God and God of our ancestors, we give thanks for the sense of justice You have implanted within us, and for the longings of our heart: these impel us to seek communion with You. A moment comes to each of us when we look upward and find a glory, and the heart leaps; again and again, too, we seek to embody our sense of justice in the daily relations of life. We know You are with us at all times, and especially when we strive to do Your will. For all this we give thanks.

Shmuel Sperber

Religion offers answers without obliterating the questions. They become blunted and will not attack you with the same ferocity. But without them the answer would dry up and wither away. To question is a great religious act; it helps you live great religious truth.

The men and women in the Bible are sinners like ourselves, but there is one sin they do not commit, our arch-sin: they do not dare confine God to a circumscribed space or division of life, "religion." They have not the insolence to draw boundaries around God's commandments and say: Up to this point you are sovereign, but beyond these bounds begins the sovereignty of science or society or the state.

Martin Buber

The religious need of the human mind remains alive, never more so, but it demands a teaching which can be *understood.* Slowly an apprehension of the intimate, usable power of God is growing among us, and a growing recognition of the only worthwhile application of that power—in the improvement of the world.

Charlotte Perkins Gilman

⁘

Monday

There are inspired seekers who bring us the fruits of their labors. Their minds soar to distant realms, their eyes see what is invisible, penetrating to the heart of living matter, and the gifts they bring us are tokens of Your infinite and abiding presence.

Religion is a momentous possibility, the possibility namely that what is highest in spirit is also deepest in nature—that there is something at the heart of nature, something akin to us, a conserver and increaser of values . . . that the things that matter most are not at the mercy of the things that matter least.

Henry Slonimsky

Only an existence that is not content with the mere fact of existence can have any value.

Leo Baeck

It is not my business to think about myself. My business is to think about God. It is for God to think about me.

Simone Weil

Rabbi Bunam said: Two merchants go to the Leipzig fair. One goes by a direct route, another by an indirect, but both reach the same destination. In the service of God, too, we aim at

Chasidic

holiness, and hope to arrive at the point where we make God's will our own. As long as we get there, it makes no difference how long our journey has been, how long we have served God. One may die young, yet achieve just as much as one who dies in old age. We have learned (Talmud B'rachot 5a): *More or less, it matters not, if the heart is turned to Heaven.*

Tuesday

There are great spirits who seek You by contemplating themselves, or the human condition. What they find becomes Torah for us all, as it is written (Genesis 27): *Surely God is in this place, and I did not know it!* We give thanks for these Your messengers, who teach us that You are where we are.

Abraham Geiger

Longing after the highest and noblest, attachment to the whole, soaring up to the Infinite, despite our finiteness and limitedness—this is religion.

William L. Sullivan

A religious search is a lonely labor. It is like a flight over an ocean or a desert. Its main preoccupation is not the collecting of interesting episodes as one floats along, but the keeping of one's wings aloft and the reading of one's course by constant sun and steadfast stars. And at the end one's concern is to leave a few words of guidance, if one can, for other voyagers soon to take off upon a like adventure.

Franz Werfel

Religion is the everlasting dialogue between humanity and God. Art is its soliloquy.

Wednesday

cs / Gates of Prayer

The constellations in their immensities, the mysteries of life and death, of growth and decay, alike display the miracle of Your creative power.

In the human heart, too, Your voice proclaims the law of justice and love.

May my eyes be open to Your truth, my spirit alive to Your teaching, my heart eager to serve You.

Religion is fundamentally an attitude to reality: a response of the whole of our being—mind, heart and soul—to the world in which we are placed. It is a sense of awe and wonder, an apprehension of the mystery beyond the commonplace, that produces, if only in rare moments, a feeling of joy too deep to be communicated except in music, poetry and prayer.

John D. Rayner

To be religious is to feel reverential respect for the cosmos and its Creator, for humanity and its individual members. But it doesn't stop there. It doesn't lose itself in mere contemplation. It is also an *active* response to that which elicits reverence. It is not merely a feeling of the heart but a decision of the will, a commitment to a task, a self-enrollment in a great adventure.

This has been the lesson of religion through the ages . . . that time . . . may be swallowed up in the splendor of eternity, that experience . . . may be elevated into unconquerable immortality, that little men and women, born of earth, may rise to the heavenly throne of glory by losing themselves in an overbounding love of humanity.

Joseph Baron

We define religion as the assumption that life has meaning. Religion, or the lack of it, is shown not in some intellectual or verbal formulations but in one's total orientation to life.

Rollo May

⁂

Thursday

Creator of skies, Maker of worlds:
Your glory is stamped on the heavens above;
Your love is revealed in my days as they pass.
You are my God; there is none else.
As You endow my fleeting days
with abiding worth,
so do I affirm and thank You,
Holy One, Source of my being.

Benjamin N. Cardozo

The submergence of self in the pursuit of an ideal, the readiness to spend oneself without measure, prodigally, almost ecstatically, for something intuitively apprehended as great and noble, spend oneself one knows not why—some of us like to believe that this is what religion means.

Albert Einstein

Knowledge of what *is* does not open the door directly to what *should be.* One can have the clearest and most complete knowledge of what *is* and yet not be able to deduce from that what should be the goal of our human aspirations.

. . . Mere thinking cannot give us a sense of the ultimate and fundamental ends. To make clear these fundamental ends and valuations, and to set them fast in the emotional life of the individual, seems to me precisely the most important function which religion has to perform. . . .

Ludwig Geiger

The old conceptions of religion can be overcome only through more religion, not by irreligion.

Friday

From *Psalm 139*

Whither can I go from Your spirit?
Whither can I flee from Your presence?
If I ascend to the heavens, You are there!
If I make my bed in the lower depths,
behold, You are there!
If I take up the wings of the morning,
and dwell on the ocean's farthest shore,
even there Your hand will lead me,
Your hand will hold me.
If I say: Surely darkness will conceal me,
night will hide me from view,
even the darkness is not too dark for You,
the night is clear as the day;
darkness is as light to You.

We can speak only in metaphor of the eternal and infinite. If we wish to describe the indescribable, we can do so only by poetry. All endeavors to reach God by words resolve themselves into religious poetry. When we experience the hidden, the unfathomable, we can respond with the devoutness of silence . . . or with poetry and prayer we can sing of the ineffable.

Abraham J. Heschel

Science says things are; morality says some things are better than other things; and religion says . . . that the best things are the more eternal things. . . .

William James

A religion without mystery must be a religion without God.

Jeremy Taylor

⁛

Shabbat

Draw near, Eternal God, as working day
turns to Sabbath rest.
You have been with me all the week,
and yet, I have forgotten You,
God of my hope and my salvation.
Now, in the stillness of Shabbat, I say Your name,
remembering the love You have shown to me,
and in gratitude and thanks I turn to You,
to bathe my hungry soul in Your kindness.

Siddur Lev Chadash

Religion is the vision of something which stands beyond, behind, and within, the passing flux of immediate things; something which is real, and yet waiting to be realized; something which is a remote possibility, and yet the greatest of present facts; something that gives meaning to all that passes, and yet eludes apprehension; something whose possession is the final good, and yet is beyond all reach; something which is the ultimate ideal, and the hopeless quest.

The immediate reaction of human nature to the religious vision is worship. Religion has emerged into human experience mixed with the crudest fancies of barbaric imagination. Gradu-

Alfred North Whitehead

ally, slowly, steadily, the vision recurs in history under nobler form and with clearer expression. It is the one element in human experience which persistently shows an upward trend. It fades and then recurs. But when it renews its force it recurs with an added richness and purity of content. The fact of the religious vision, and its history of persistent expansion, is our one ground for optimism. Apart from it, human life is a flash of occasional enjoyments lighting up a mass of pain and misery, a bagatelle of transient experiences.

The vision claims nothing but worship. . . . The vision never overrules. It is always there, and it has the power of love presenting the one purpose whose fulfillment is eternal harmony. . . . That religion is strong which in its ritual and its modes of thought evokes an apprehension of the commanding vision. The worship of God is not a rule of safety—it is an adventure of the spirit, a flight after the unattainable. The death of religion comes with the repression of the high hope of adventure.

37 *Courage*

The Week of Sh'lach L'cha
Numbers 13:1–15:41

In the Sidra *Sh'lach L'cha* (Numbers 13), Moses sends twelve scouts to spy out the land the people are about to enter. The twelve report that the land is good and fruitful: *it does indeed flow with milk and honey.* Joshua and Caleb, two of the scouts, urge the people to move forward, saying: *Let us by all means go up . . . for we shall surely overcome . . .* (13:30). The others, however, dissuade the people from going forward, saying: *We looked like grasshoppers to ourselves, and so we must have looked to them* (13:33). Their courage failing, the people fall into despair.

Sunday

When the light fails, help me to walk in the dark.
When it is hard to walk, help me to crawl.
Let me keep going, one more minute.

Who is brave? Who turns a foe into a friend.

Period of Mishnah

Thomas Mann

Shall we strike sail, avoid a certain experience so soon as it seems not expressly calculated to increase our enjoyment or our self-esteem? Shall we go away whenever life looks like turning in the slightest uncanny, or not quite normal, or even rather painful and mortifying? No, surely not. Rather stay and look matters in the face, brave them out; perhaps precisely in so doing lies a lesson for us to learn.

Marcus Aurelius / cs

Unhappy am I, because this has happened to me.—Not so, but happy am I, though this has happened to me, because I continue free from pain, neither crushed by the present nor fearing the future. . . . Will then what has happened prevent you from being just, magnanimous, temperate, prudent, secure, against inconsiderate opinions and falsehood; will it prevent you from being modest, free, and all else that you need in order to be yourself? Remember always to apply this thought: not that this is a misfortune, but that to bear it nobly is good fortune.

Monday

Mine is a quiet life, with few opportunities for heroism. O God, don't let me say that! I can be a hero—a hero in small ways: Teach me how those ways add up to a big life.

Chasidic

The Gerer Rebbe said: In Pirké Avot (5:23) we learn that impudence is evil and shamefacedness is good. We should bear in mind, however, that what looks like impudence may in reality be courage, and that what looks like shamefacedness may in reality be merely melancholy. The distinction is so delicate that sometimes even the keenest have failed to appreciate it.

Hugh Walpole

Don't play for safety.
It's the most dangerous thing in the world.

Martin Niemoeller

When the Nazis first came for the Communists, I didn't speak up, because I was not a Communist. Then they came for the Jews, but I didn't speak up, because I was not a Jew. Then they came for the Trade Unionists, but I didn't speak up, because I was not a Trade Unionist. Then they came for me . . . and by that time there was no one to speak up for anyone.

Michel de Montaigne

Valor has its limits like the other virtues, and these limits once transgressed, we find ourselves on the path of vice; so that we may pass through valor to temerity, obstinacy, and madness, unless we know its limits well—and they are truly hard to discern near the borderlines.

It is not from You but in You, O God, that I seek the strength to overcome whatever hurt may come this day. So I pray:

Create in me a clean heart, O God;
Renew a steadfast spirit within me. (Psalm 51)

Make me strong enough not to run away from myself and my troubles, strong enough to meet them without complaint.

A general received a message telling him that his main line of defense had been broken by the enemy. He was greatly distressed and the expression on his face showed it. His wife, hearing of the message, came to him and said: You have received bad news, I know, but I have just received worse. And what is that, he asked. I have just read discouragement on your face, she replied. Loss of courage is the worst of news.

Chasidic / cs

Pestilence once met a caravan upon the desert way to Baghdad. "Why," asked the Arab chief, "must you hasten to Baghdad?" "To take five thousand lives," Pestilence replied. Upon his way back from the City of the Caliphs, Pestilence and the caravan met again. "You deceived me," the chief said angrily. "Instead of five thousand lives you took fifty thousand." "Nay," said Pestilence. "Five thousand and not one more. It was Fear who killed the rest."

Arab folktale

You cannot run away from a weakness; you must sometime fight it out or perish. And if that be so, why not now, and where you stand?

Robert Louis Stevenson

To do wrong is base, and to do well where there is no danger, common; the characteristic of the good is to do so where there is danger.

Plutarch

It humbles me to think of the courage my ancestors needed that I might come to be. Fire and water did not persuade them to swerve from their faith. Doubtless they were not anxious to suffer and die for their God, but they seem to have been willing to. And often enough they even had the strength and fortitude to live for You, not just to die for You! God grant me some portion of such strength, and my life, like theirs, will surely be redeemed from emptiness!

Talmud

To save one's life, one may violate all the laws except three: one must accept death rather than be forced to deny God, to be unchaste, to commit murder. This rule holds only in private circumstance. In public, however, one must be willing to die rather than violate the lightest law.

Talmud

Now it was the turn of Judah ben Baba. Of him they used to say that from the age of eighteen to the age of eighty he slept as lightly as a cat.

The Romans had forbidden the ordination of rabbis, decreeing death to ordainer and those ordained, and destruction for any city in which ordination took place. Rabbi Judah ben Baba ordained five men in the hills between two cities, Shefaram and Usha. When enemy soldiers appeared on the scene, Judah told his disciples to flee. What will become of you? they cried. He answered: I will place myself before them as an immovable rock.

He did—and a hundred Roman lances pierced him. But his disciples escaped.

Ignazio Silone

Spiritual life and secure life do not go together. To save oneself one must struggle and take risks.

Søren Kierkegaard

Trusting to God I have dared but I was not successful; in that is to be found peace, calm, a confidence in God. I have not dared; that is a woeful thought, a torment in eternity.

Thursday

The courage I need is the courage to lay one foot before the other as a faithful parent, child, friend, as an honest human being. Give me, O God, courage enough to be faithful to You and Your will even when I doubt You, even when I wonder what it means to say "Your will."

Morality may consist solely in the courage of making a choice. *Léon Blum*

Courage is the human virtue that counts most—courage to act on limited knowledge and insufficient evidence. That's all any of us have, so we must have the courage to go ahead and act on a hunch. *Robert Frost*

The palm of courage will surely be judged most justly to those who best know the difference between hardship and pleasure and yet are never tempted to shrink from danger. *Thucydides*

For people sometimes believed that it was safer to live with complaints, was necessary to cooperate with grief, was all right to become an accomplice in self-ambush. . . . *Toni Cade Bambara*

Our doubts are traitors
And make us lose the good we oft might win
By fearing to attempt.

William Shakespeare

Friday

Give me the good sense to be afraid when there is something to fear, so that I make ready, as well as I can, for whatever threatens. And give me courage to stand up with grace against the troubles I cannot keep from coming my way. And make me willing to learn from what hurts me instead of feeling sorry for myself.

Midrash God asks of us to give only in the measure of which we are capable, as it says: *Moses spoke, and God answered him with the voice*—meaning, with that voice which Moses was able to hear.

Frank Crane You may be deceived if you trust too much, but you will live in torment if you do not trust enough.

Ralph Waldo Emerson

Some of your hurts you have cured,
And the sharpest you still have survived;
But what torments of grief you endured,
From evils that never arrived.

Sidney Smith A great deal of talent is lost in this world for want of a little courage.

Shabbat

⁘

Give me the courage to question my assumptions and the wisdom to wonder about statements that seem to explain everything; give me the intelligence to question my questions and the wisdom to doubt negations that explain away what we cannot touch, feel, or see.

Talmud Our Rabbis have taught: Those who are persecuted and do not persecute in turn, those who listen to contemptuous insults and do not reply, those who act out of love and are glad of sufferings, concerning them Scripture says (Judges 5:31): *They that love God are like the sun going forth in his strength.*

Midrash God gives strength in divine measure; God demands strength in human measure.

J. A. Shedd A ship in harbor is safe,
but that is not what ships are built for.

It is for facing what is painful, then, . . . that people are called brave. Hence also courage involves pain, and is justly praised; for it is harder to face what is painful than to abstain from what is pleasant.

Aristotle

Flight at the proper time, just as well as fighting, is to be reckoned, therefore, as showing strength of mind in one who is free; that is to say, one who is free chooses flight by the same strength or presence of mind as that by which he [she] chooses battle.

Baruch Spinoza / cs

38 *Character*

The Week of Korach
Numbers 16:1–18:32

The Sidra *Korach* (Numbers 16) tells of a rebellion against the leadership of Moses and Aaron. A Levite called Korach leads a group of 250 prominent Israelites, claiming to speak in the name of democracy: *All the community are holy. . . . Why then do you raise yourselves above the congregation?* (16:3). Moses, however, discerns that this claim is dishonest; God will choose between them, and, in his plea to God, Moses makes a point about character: *I have not taken the ass of any one of them, nor have I wronged any one of them* (16:15).

Job, too, points to a clean conscience as one key to character: *My heart shall not reproach me so long as I live* (Job 27:6).

Sunday

cs / Gates of Prayer

The soul that You have given me is pure!

Yet I know that within it my yearning for the sacred must struggle with my inclination for the profane. At times the profane seems the winner. Love and truth are debased. The divine gift of compassion lies dormant. The anguish of others goes unfelt and unheeded.

But there are other times, times when I can hold my head up, in the knowledge that I have done the right thing, even to my own hurt.

O God, let today be one of those times.

Maimonides

We are not born endowed with either virtue or vice, just as we are not born skilled in any particular craft.

Remember, what you possess in the world will be found at the day of your death to belong to someone else, but what you are will be yours forever. *Henry Van Dyke*

Not what you possess, but what you do with what you have, determines your true worth. *Thomas Carlyle*

If I can be firm enough to-day to do right and scorn eyes, I must have done so much right before as to defend me now. Be it how it will, do right now. *Ralph Waldo Emerson*

✦

Monday

My actions are guided by the desire to leave something for those who will come after me and remember my name. Let it be something that makes my name worth remembering.

The Ladier Rebbe said: One should so master one's nature that both the positive and negative aspects in every character trait are integrated. For example, be both conservative and progressive; be fearless and peaceable; have a strong personality and a meek one. *Chasidic / cs*

Use what talents you possess; the woods would be very silent if no bird sang there except those that sang best. *Henry Van Dyke*

We never become truly spiritual by sitting down and wishing to become so. You must undertake something so great that you cannot accomplish it unaided. *Phillips Brooks*

What utter foolishness it is to be afraid that those who have a bad name can rob you of a good one. *Seneca*

> No star is ever lost we once have seen,
> We always may be what we might have been.

Adelaide A. Proctor

Today let me reflect on who I am: Am I one who depends on others to do for me what I should be doing for myself? Am I one who will not let a loved one grow into independence? Or am I one who willingly accepts help when it is needed, helps out only when there's a need, and steps aside when someone else can do the job—and should?

Talmud Rabbi Akiba said: Rather make your Sabbath a weekday than have to depend on your neighbors to sustain you.

Chasidic The Koretzer Rebbe said: The Passover Haggadah tells us that the Torah speaks of four [types of] children. Each of us can discover our own character in the Torah.

Chasidic Reb Shmelke of Nikolsburg said: The Talmud tells us that if all the world were to repent, the Messiah would come. Knowing this, I decided to do something about it. Where to begin? The world? It was too large and I was too small. So I thought: Let me start with my own country. That, too, proved too much for me. My own town? I failed there as well. My neighborhood, my own family? Even there I did not succeed. Never mind, I thought, I shall work on myself.

With oneself, one reaches the irreducible minimum. We can each begin with ourselves.

Plutarch The enemies of Fabius thought they had sufficiently humiliated and subdued him by raising Minucius to be his equal in authority; but they mistook the temper of the man, who looked upon their folly as not his loss [but theirs], like Diogenes, who, being told that some persons derided him, made answer, "But I am not derided." He meant that only those on whom such insults made an impression were really insulted. So Fabius, with great tranquillity and unconcern, submitted to what happened, and contributed a proof to the argument of the philosophers that a just and good person is not capable of being dishonored.

Wednesday

The wise, they say, never store things up, because they know that the more they do for others, the more they do for themselves, and the more they give to others, the more they have. How I wish I had the courage to be wise!

cs / Chasidic

Rabbi Moshe Leib Sassover said: Here are some qualities that make for good character: Remove anger from your heart; be not anxious over a world that is not yours; find peace of mind, for when you have no peace, you have nothing; reprove no one until you yourself are perfect; remember that the souls of others are as much a part of the Godhead as yours is; and keep in mind that only one who has withstood temptation can be called righteous.

Ellen Glasgow

The disintegration of character is the beginning, not the end, of defeat, . . . [and] this weakening moral fiber is first revealed in the quick or slow decline of human relationships, and in the abrupt conversion to a triumphant materialism.

Aristotle

There is no middle way for every action or passion, for some are clearly bad in themselves: e.g., spite, shamelessness, envy, and with regard to actions adultery, theft, murder—for we name all these and kindred things as by themselves bad, and not the excesses or deficiencies of them. It is not possible, then, ever to be right with regard to them; one must always be wrong. Nor does goodness or badness with regard to such things depend on committing adultery with the right woman or man, at the right time, and in the right way, but simply to do any of them is to go wrong.

Thursday

Keep me from doing things—even good things—only because people will think well of me for them. Let me do them because they are right. And let me not pretend that much of the time I don't know what is right. But if in the end I do right for less than noble reasons, let me at least reflect that it is better that not doing right!

Mishnah As he was dying Akaviah ben Mehalalel said to his son: My son, concede those four things that I used to uphold.

Why didn't you concede them, then?

Because I heard them when they were the views of the majority, and they heard them from a majority. I held to my tradition and they held to theirs. But you have heard from an individual and from a group, and it is better to let go the view of an individual in favor of the larger number.

Commend me to your colleagues, his son said to him.

I will not commend you.

Have you found a fault in me?

No, but your deeds will draw you near, as your deeds will estrange you.

Thomas Paine Reputation is what men and women think of us;
Character is what God and the angels know of us.

Epictetus A good man or woman does nothing for the sake of appearances, but for the sake of doing right.

Friday

⁘

It is not out of guilt that I would act, but out of love. When loving seems hard because I don't really feel it, help me to act in a loving way. Never let me act when hate or rage are uppermost within me: Show me how to wait until they quiet down. Help me to keep in mind that nothing good can come except from a good heart and a gentle hand.

Mishnah

Rabbi Simeon says: There are three crowns:
the crown of Torah,
the crown of priesthood,
and the crown of royalty.
Rise above them
with the crown of a good name.

In the end, we are all the sum total of our actions. Character cannot be counterfeited, nor can it be put on and cast off as if it were a garment to meet the whim of the moment. Like the markings on wood which are ingrained in the very heart of the tree, character requires time and nurture for growth and development.

Thus, also, day by day, we write our own destiny, for inexorably we become what we do. This, I believe, is the supreme logic and the law of life.

Madame Chiang Kai-shek

It is the mark of a good way of life that, among other things, it satisfies and abides; bad behavior, constantly changing, not for the better, simply into different forms, has none of this stability.

Seneca

Shabbat

Let me find tasks worthy of me, but let me not imagine that the sunrise depends on what I do or who I am. Knowing it will rise, let me turn to the things that only I can do, and let me do them as well as I can. You call me to serve You by caring for the one next to me.

In a cold room you may warm yourself by heating it or by donning a fur coat. In the former case, you warm whoever else is in the room with you; in the latter, only yourself. The person who chooses to provide only for himself or herself is called in Yiddish *a tzaddik in peltz*—"a saint in furs."

Anonymous

It is a good precept that tells us not to do a thing if there is doubt whether it is right or wrong. Righteousness shines with its own brilliance. But doubt is a sign that we are possibly considering a wrong.

Cicero

Our deeds determine us, as much as we determine our deeds.

George Eliot

These three God loves; try to be all of them:
Those who do not give way to anger;
Those who do not drink more than they should;
Those who do not stand on their rights.

Talmud / cs

חקת

39 *Reward and Punishment*

The Week of Chukat
Numbers 19:1–22:1

The Sidra *Chukat* (Numbers 20) recounts an incident in the wilderness. There is no water and the people complain bitterly. God tells Moses to order a rock to flow with water for the people. But Moses strikes the rock with his rod, and this displeases God, who says to Moses: *Because you did not trust Me enough . . . therefore you shall not lead this community into the land that I have given them* (20:12).

Most of us are brought up with rewards for "being good" and punishments for the opposite. Growing older, we sooner or later come to feel a dissonance between reward and punishment. This week we reflect on a complex question, with more than one answer.

Sunday

Lizette Woodworth Reese

God is too high to measure out each thing,
This much for you, and to your neighbor that. . . .

cs

What more would I have from You,
Who have given me
A path under my feet,
And this gold-and-velvet blossom
My opened eye beholds,
As, stopping to hear
A sudden song rise and fall from yonder branch,
I stand a moment out of time?

Do the small, do the great.
One deed brings you to the next.
The reward of one deed is another.
The punishment of one misdeed is another.

Mishnah

Silently, his wife held the hungry child. It was too weak to cry. Then, for the first time, the Maggid sighed. A voice said to him: You have lost your share in the World to Come.

Well, then, he said, the reward has been done away with. Now I can begin to serve without an ulterior motive.

Chasidic

⁘

Monday

The reward I want is to feel no need for reward; the punishment I fear is to deserve punishment. Oh, how I wish I could be free to serve out of love. Alas, I know how far I am from reaching such perfection. And yet, I need to reach for it.

Why are you distraught, Hagar? Have no fear, for God has heard the boy's voice, where he is (Genesis 21:17).

Talmud

Rabbi Isaac taught: This teaches that we are judged only for what we are at the moment of judgment, as it says of Ishmael: *God has heard the boy's voice, where he is.*

Rabbi Simon added: When God took note of the boy's cry and saved Ishmael and Hagar in the wilderness, the ministering angels were astounded. They complained: Holy One, how can You provide water from a well for one whose descendants will cause Your children to die of thirst?

The Holy One replied: Here and now—tell Me—is this one righteous or wicked?

They had to say: Righteous.

The Holy One continued: Then understand: I judge My children only for what they are at the moment of judgment. The future must take care of itself. [What follows? (Genesis 21:18–19)] *God then opened her eyes. Looking up, she saw a well. She ran and filled a bottle with water, and gave it to the boy.*

Ralph Waldo Emerson

The reward for a thing well done is to have done it.

Tuesday

⁘

To be alive is a terrible punishment some days, and on other days a terrible glory. Teach me to know it as a gift even when life is a walk in the valley of the shadow and I cannot help but fear evil.

Talmud

Therefore observe faithfully the Mitzvah, the laws, and the rules of justice that I command you this day (Deuteronomy 7:11).

This day you are to do them, but not *this* day are you to receive their reward (Talmud Avodah Zarah 3a).

Do them *this* day; receive their reward the *next* day.

cs

The pharaohs of this world deserve punishment even when they carry out God's will, because their purposes are their own—not God's. God may work through them, but they know it not; they care only to carry out their own maleficent ambitions. Suppose one thief steals from another—should that thief gain our approbation? And suppose one murderer takes another murderer's life—that act would surely remain foul and deserving of retribution. No good end can justify an evil act; no bad beginning in life can justify a bad continuation.

Mencius

When we despise ourselves, others despise us.
When a family embarks on self-destruction,
others come to destroy it.
When a nation begins to smite itself,
others come to smite it.

Wednesday

⁘

Is there any work harder than being Your image? I know we are taught that You made us in Your image, yet it seems to me equally right to say that You made me able to discover Your image within me, but only if I am a good enough explorer.

Who think of reward serve themselves, not God. — *Israel Salanter*

The reward of one duty is the power to fulfill another. — *George Eliot*

Only a born artist
can endure the labour
of becoming one.

Comtesse Diane

Only our concept of time makes it possible to speak of the Day of Judgment by that name; in reality it is a summary court in perpetual session. — *Franz Kafka*

⁘

Thursday

Why should I think of pain as punishment, when it is nothing more than the fate that all flesh is born to? All flesh without exception—sinners and saints alike. Even people who are luckier than the average. . . .

The Dubner Maggid said: A father complained to a neighbor that his son was ill, and would not eat his meals. The neighbor visited the boy and offered him a toy if he would eat a meal in his home, and the boy did go and consume a goodly portion of food. When the neighbor told the father of his stratagem, the father commented: What you tell me only confirms my anxiety for my son's health. If he were really healthy, he would eat to satisfy his appetite, not because he was eager for a toy. One who is charitable and does good works in the hope of gaining a reward is spiritually ill. — *Jewish anecdote*

We are not punished for our sins, but by them. — *Leon Harrison*

Crime and punishment grow out of one stem. Punishment is a fruit that unsuspected ripens within the flower of the pleasure which concealed it. — *Ralph Waldo Emerson*

Dignity does not consist in possessing honors, but in deserving them. — *Aristotle*

Friday

⁘

What have I done to deserve this? Usually I ask this question when something painful happens. Teach me to ask it when something good happens. Then teach me not to talk of "deserving." Just to do my job, to be a mensch.

Mishnah

Who profanes here
must pay here.
Who harms now
is harmed now.

Henry Wadsworth Longfellow

To be left alone, and face to face with my own crime, had been just retribution.

Epictetus

What will be your punishment? Perhaps nothing else than, not having done your duty, you will lose the character of fidelity, modesty, propriety. Do not look for greater penalties than these.

John Milton

The mind is its own place, and in itself
can make a heaven of Hell, a hell of Heaven.

Shabbat

⁘

On Shabbat my work consists of rest and praise, to leave the world alone so it can heal from all my week's work, while I sing of the One who made it the cradle of life. This rest is work enough: Teach me to do it, teach me to let the rest be.

Talmud

Yosé ben Halafta taught: One pang of conscience is worth more than many lashes.

Ralph Waldo Emerson

Work, and thou canst not escape the reward; whether thy work be fine or coarse, planting corn or writing epics, so only it be honest work, done to thine own approbation, it shall earn a reward to the senses as well as to the thought. No matter how often defeated, you are born to victory.

Nature has observed this principle like a mother, that the actions she has enjoined on us for our need should also give us pleasure; and she invites us to them not only through reason, but also through appetite. It is unjust to infringe her laws.

Michel de Montaigne

When you have earned a good name you have earned it for yourself. When you have earned words of Torah you have earned life eternal.

Mishnah

40 *Seeing*

The Week of Balak
Numbers 22:5–25:9

In the Sidra *Balak* (Numbers 22), the Moabite king Balak, fearing the Israelites who are advancing in his kingdom's direction, engages the prophet Balaam to curse the people of Israel. Balaam agrees, and sets forth on his ass. God is incensed at Balaam and places an angel in their path. The ass, seeing the angel, goes off the road. Balaam, who sees nothing, beats the ass. After the third such beating, the ass expostulates with Baalam and Balaam finally sees: *Then the Eternal one uncovered Balaam's eyes, and he saw the divine emissary* . . . (22:31). It is one thing to look, another to see.

Sunday

⁘

God, when I look at glass, let it be a window and not a mirror. For there are times when I need to see others, when I need to look beyond me and my wants, to the needs and cares of my family and friends. And there are times when I need to remember that there are people I pass as if they weren't there: Open my eyes to them.

cs / Chasidic

The Baal Shem Tov said: It is not good to be alone, for one cannot know one's own defects. Other people are mirrors, in which you can discover your own flaws by observing the acts you dislike in them. In fact, it is only because you share them yourself in some degree, that you can see another person's flaws.

Henry Wadsworth Longfellow

If spring came but once a century instead of once a year, or burst forth with the sound of an earthquake and not in silence, what wonder and expectation there would be in all hearts, to behold the miraculous change.

To a great experience one thing is essential, an experiencing nature.

Walter Bagehot

The tree which moves some to tears of joy is in the eyes of others only a green thing which stands in the way. As a man is, so he sees.

William Blake

⁘

Monday

There are things I don't want to understand. I don't care to admit this, even to myself, but when I don't, this truth doesn't go away, it only blinds me. God, help me to see, especially those things I need to see that make me uncomfortable.

People gathered for a celebration. The fiddler's tone was so sweet that the room was filled with joy. Before long they had all begun to dance.

Chasidic

There were even some people who joined them as soon as they heard the music coming from within that room.

Just then a man was passing by. He had been deaf from birth. He looked in through a window at the people and their joyful movements and thought: These people have gone mad.

> Travelers, coming upon a place
> whose lights and music and good food
> invites them,
> will feel at home.
> How can words that point toward the Way compete?
> You look and there is nothing to be seen;
> you listen, and there is nothing to be heard.
> But go upon that Way, and it will never let you down.

Tao / cs

The Tzortkover Rebbe had a large and handsome mirror in his reception room. Once a visitor came and thought: Is then the Tzaddik so vain of his looks? The Rebbe read the man's thought

Chasidic / cs

and said: The mirror was presented to my father, the Rizhiner, when he said: It would be well if those who come here could observe the countenance with which they came to visit me.

Tuesday

⁘

Today—or it may be tomorrow or next week—the hardest thing for me to see may be what is in plain sight. It will beg to be seen and believed, and I will be too clever to trust the evidence of my senses. So when You come to the door, give me the wit to see what's in front of my face.

Chasidic Prayer / cs

May it be Your will to remove all barriers between us, and endow us with the vision to see the good in all people, and to overlook their defects.

The Dhammapada

Those who see sin where there is sin, and innocence where there is innocence, have embraced truth and entered the right path.

Yiddish proverb

Where there's smoke there's smoke.

Zen

As he lay dying, the Master rose up to impart a last word to his grieving disciples.

I will tell you, he said, one of my greatest discoveries.

Till I was twenty I cared little for what people thought of me.

Then, for many years, I worried endlessly about what people thought of me.

One day, I suddenly understood that they hardly ever thought of me at all!

This is Enlightenment: not to become divine; not to become a saint; only this: to become awake.

Wednesday

⁘

Today may I pay attention to what I can see beneath the surface. Keep my eye undeceived by beauty and undismayed by disfigurement—it too may only be skin deep. Show me a deeper beauty.

When the Rebbe of Lenchna's son was a boy, he once saw Rabbi Yitzchak of Vorki praying. Full of amazement, he came running to his father and asked how it was possible for such a Tzaddik to pray quietly and simply, without giving any sign of ecstasy. *Chasidic*

His father said: A poor swimmer thrashes around in order to stay up in the water. The perfect swimmer doesn't seem to be swimming at all.

Tao / cs

> If you want to see the world,
> don't look through the window
> before you have looked within.
> Attend to the center.
> The Sage is out there without going,
> sees without looking,
> acts without doing.

Beruriah said: Look at the end of the verse. *Talmud*

⁘

Thursday

O God, Your face is hidden, they say, yet I think I might see it if I were to look in the right place at the right time; but just now it is my own face I need to see—the face beneath the face I see reflected in the mirror, or on a pane of glass. Help me to know myself better; show this face to me.

Alas for those who see and don't know what they are seeing. *Talmud*

When you hear words that are distasteful to your mind, you must inquire whether they be not right; when you hear words that accord with your own views, you must inquire whether they be not contrary to what is right. *Shu Ching*

I cannot find redemption until I see the flaws in my own soul, and try to correct them. Nor can a people be redeemed until it sees the flaws in its own soul, and tries to correct them. But *Chasidic*

whether it be an individual or a people, if we shut out the realization of our own flaws we are shutting out redemption. We can be redeemed only to the extent that we see ourselves.

cs When I name something that I don't like "an injustice," I may be deceiving myself. It may be that it is precisely justice that I am complaining about, like being punished for cheating while others are not. Do I not remember occasions when I was the one not stopped while someone else was getting a traffic ticket? O God, keep me from self-deception, in matters small and large—except when I need it. . . .

⁘

Friday

I like to say that what I see is just the tiniest bit of the wondrous world You have created. Do I really know this? Do I really see even that little bit? If Your wonders include tomorrow, let me see then what I have said today.

Chasidic Rabbi Mendel once boasted to his teacher, Rabbi Elimelech, that every evening he saw the angel who rolls away the light before the darkness, and mornings the angel who rolls away the darkness before the light. Yes, said Rabbi Elimelech, in my youth I saw that too. Later on, you no longer [need to] see those things.

cs —*Is that because you no longer need to, or because you can't?*

Ralph Waldo Emerson The sky is the daily bread of the eyes.

Michel de Montaigne I see several animals that live so entire and perfect a life,
some without sight,
others without hearing:
who knows whether to us also
one, two, or three, or many other senses,
may not be wanting?

I often wonder how it is that I love myself more than I love others, yet I set less value on my own opinion of myself than on the opinion of others.

Marcus Aurelius

⁘

Shabbat

New every morning is Your world, created all over again, and I too am a new creation. Endless possibilities await me. No, they are not endless, and I am not new. So renew me, now, O God; renew my vision and give me a heart that cares about what it sees. Let me not be afraid to see what pains me nor too glibly think I've already earned what joys me. Renew my eyes this morning, my eyes and spirit.

Do not be like the bird that sees the grain but not the trap.

Judah ibn Tibbon

We are unknown to ourselves, we knowers: and there is a good reason for this. We have never searched for ourselves—how then should it ever come to pass that we should ever find ourselves?

Friedrich Nietzsche

Those who know do not tell,
Those who tell do not know.
Rather than wag the tongue,
Keep it in check;
Not jagged, but
Edges planed smooth;
Clear-sighted,
Clear minded:
Balanced
Beyond the dominion of love and hate,
Beyond the rule of loss and gain,
Beyond concern with praise and scorn—
You are your Master.

Tao / cs

41 *Seeing Others*

The Week of Pinchas
Numbers 25:10–30:1

In the Sidra *Pinchas* (Numbers 27), five sisters whose father has died come before Moses and plead for the right to inherit: God tells Moses that their plea is just. At a time when it was not obvious that women ought to be equal before the law, Moses, with God's guidance, sees them as real persons. Then, in contemplation of a change of leadership, Moses says: *Let the Eternal One, Source of the breath of all flesh, appoint someone over the community* (27:15).

If the Eternal is the "Source of the breath of all flesh," we are kin to "all flesh." We need to see this always.

Sunday

⁘

Siddur Lev Chadash / cs

Eternal God, let all Your children live together in peace and friendship; let oppression, discrimination and prejudice be relics of the past, and let all humanity be filled with Your spirit. Hasten the day foreseen by our prophets; the day for which we have longed during the course of a hundred generations, when all men and women will know and understand that they are brothers and sisters, and be united in humble reverence before You, and in mutual love and respect.

Talmud

Our Rabbis taught: The non-Jewish poor are to be sustained along with the Jewish poor, the non-Jewish sick are to be visited along with the Jewish sick, and the non-Jewish dead are to be buried along with the Jewish dead, for the sake of [the ways of] peace.

Jews regard Judaism as the only religion for Jews. But we neither judge nor condemn the honest, devout worshiper of any faith. The Talmud tells us: The righteous of all nations are worthy of immortality.

Morris N. Kertzer

We believe in certain basic ethical concepts: decency, kindliness, justice and integrity. These we regard as eternal verities. But we claim no monopoly on these verities, for we recognize that every great religious faith has discovered them. That is what Rabbi Meir meant some eighteen centuries ago, when he said that a Gentile who follows the Torah is as good as our High Priest.

There are many mountaintops and all of them reach for the stars.

⁘

Monday

I wish I could persuade myself that I come from better stock than most people, that I am more handsome and charming than the general run, that the people in my family are more intelligent than the average. I wish I were ignorant of the facts; then, when I am boastful, I wouldn't have such a bad conscience. Let me do this, at least: When others make foolish claims, give me permission to laugh at them—and at myself.

Do not judge another,
until you are in the other's place.

Mishnah

The first thing to learn in intercourse with others is non-interference with their own peculiar ways of being happy, provided that those ways do not assume to interfere by violence with ours. No one has insight into all the ideals. No one should presume to judge them off-hand. The pretension to dogmatize about them in each other is the root of most human injustices and cruelties, and the trait in human character most likely to make the angels weep.

William James

Alexander Pope

Teach me to feel another's woe,
To hide the fault I see;
That mercy I to others show,
That mercy show to me.

Midrash

God says: Make yourself like Me. When I created the world, I strove not to hurt a single one of My creatures, and I did not make known to any human being the name of the tree of which Adam ate [in the Garden of Eden, so that even the tree should not be put to shame].

Tuesday

O God, let me never accept the judgment of others upon me as final, nor ever decide about others before I have met them. Let me not judge others by the label on their clothes, or by their names. Keep me from forgetting that everyone, including me, speaks with an accent, and keep on reminding me that being born is a fate and privilege shared by every one of us. Maybe then someone else will give *me* the benefit of the doubt—a benefit I sorely need.

Mishnah

Joshua ben Perachiah said:
Find a teacher.
Buy a friend.
And give everyone the benefit of the doubt.

Comtesse Diane

How can we venture to judge others when we know so well how ill-equipped they are for judging us?

Robert Louis Stevenson

There is so much good in the worst of us, and so much bad in the best of us, that it behooves all of us not to talk about the rest of us.

Chasidic

On a terrible winter night Rabbi Aaron of Karlin came to a village which had only one Jewish residence. He asked for shelter there, and was not recognized. They took a long time deciding whether to admit him, and when he finally proved his identity, he was admitted, half frozen, and well entertained. He later said about this: It is plain to me now why the sages (Talmud Shabbat 127a) said that there is more merit in being hospitable to human beings than to God. When the Divine Presence finds your door barred, it returns to Heaven and you, the unwilling host, are the only one who suffers. With people it is different: if you don't let them in, they may perish.

⁘

Wednesday

Fill me, O God of all humankind, with a love of all Your creatures, a love that will keep me from wronging them, or exploiting their labor, or taking unfair advantage of them in any other way. Help me to contribute to the peace of Your world, as I learn to welcome the differences that distinguish me from others, and them from me.

Chasidic

Once, when Rabbi Levi Yitzchak of Berditchev was in the bathhouse, his coat was stolen. He returned home and his wife noticed he was without his coat and asked him where it was. The Rebbe replied that someone had taken the coat, doubtless mistaking it for his own. His wife then asked, In that case, where is his coat? Levi Yitzchak said, He must have forgotten to leave it!

A. H. R. Fairchild

The most distinctive mark of a cultivated mind is the ability to take another's point of view; to put one's self in another's place, and to see life and its problems from a point of view different from one's own.

John Stuart Mill

Such are the differences among human beings in their sources of pleasure, their susceptibilities of pain, and the operation on them of different physical and moral agencies, that unless there is a corresponding diversity in their modes of life, they neither obtain their fair share of happiness, nor grow up to the mental, moral, and aesthetic stature of which their nature is capable.

George Orwell If liberty means anything at all, it means the right to tell people what they do not want to hear.

❖

Thursday

From readiness to think ill of someone whose sole sin is to possess a different hue of skin or cast of mind, deliver me. From laughing at strangers when I am at home, forgetting that I too am a stranger almost everywhere, deliver me. And from the delusion that anyone can be a stranger on this earth, the cradle of us all, deliver me!

Deliver me, O God, from trying to rise by lowering others.

Chasidic / cs Rabbi Moshe Leib Sassover said: A conversation I overheard between two villagers taught me how we must truly love our neighbor. One said: Tell me, friend Ivan, do you love me? The other replied: I love you deeply. The first rejoined: Do you know, my friend, what gives me pain? How can I know that? demanded the other. The first then said: If you don't know what gives me pain, how can you say that you truly love me?

Yes, the Sassover concluded, to love, truly to love, means to know what gives pain to your friend.

George Eliot Nice distinctions are so troublesome. It is so much easier to say that a thing is black than to discriminate the particular shade of brown, blue, or green, to which it really belongs. It is so much easier to make up your mind that your neighbor is good for nothing than to enter into all the circumstances that would oblige you to modify that opinion.

Ignazio Silone From what source do some people derive their spontaneous intolerance of injustice, even though the injustice affects only others? And that sudden feeling of guilt at sitting down to a well-laden table, when others are having to go hungry?

⁘

How many times I have been misunderstood and thought: Why did so-and-so jump so readily to a conclusion about me, when I am so different from what he seems to think of me, or when I meant something quite other than how she took it? If that be so, then keep me from jumping to such conclusions about others; teach me to wait and learn, and to accept that they don't have to be like me, or I like them, for us to live together.

The Baal Shem Tov said: We are commanded (Leviticus 19:18) to love our neighbor as ourselves and from this the Talmud (Pirké Avot 1:6) commands us to give everyone the benefit of the doubt. You always find excuses for your own misdeeds, so make excuses also for your neighbor.

Chasidic

So companies of children march to war, hate other flags,
Worship themselves, and cling to narrow ways.
Alongside them, a thousand roads stretch out:
A thousand different visions filled with hope,
A thousand galaxies caught in the web of God,
And God would speak to us out of every wandering star.
If we could but break through the wall,
If we could hear the other—
Why, then we might hear God.

Siddur Lev Chadash

Prejudice is not held against people because they have evil qualities. Evil qualities are imputed to people because prejudices are held against them.

Marshall Wingfield

More helpful than all wisdom or counsel is one draught of simple human pity that will not forsake us.

George Eliot

⁘

cs / Siddur Lev Chadash

O keep me from seeing only black-and-white in a world of many colors. Do not let me imagine that my people are "Children of Light" while others are "Children of Darkness." Teach me to see myself in every face, to hear the human spirit in every voice. Keep me from making distinctions that are of no significance, from judgments that serve only myself, and from the urge to rise by my neighbor's fall. From prejudice preserve me, from hatred redeem me, and from self-righteousness defend me.

Chasidic

The Baal Shem Tov observed a man completely absorbed in studying a religious book. He remarked: This man is so deeply buried in his studies that he forgets there is a God in the world. All the more does he forget that there are other people in the world.

Swami Vivekananda

But how can such a variety of religions be true? If one thing is true must not its negation be false? I do not see religions as contradictory at all, but as supplementary. Each religion takes up one part of the great universal truth, and spends its whole force in embodying and typifying that part of the great truth. The religious panorama reveals the march of humanity from truth to truth . . . rather than from error to truth. All these religions are different forces in the economy of God, . . . and not one can become dead, not one can be killed.

Edwin Markham

He drew a circle that shut me out—
Heretic, rebel, a thing to flout.
But Love and I had the wit to win:
We drew a circle that took him in!

42 *Family*

The Week of Matot
Numbers 30:2–32:42

In the Sidra *Matot* (Numbers 32), two of the tribes ask permission of Moses to settle on the eastern bank of the Jordan; he agrees, provided that they will accompany their fellow tribes and help them subdue the land on the other side of the Jordan. The tribesmen of Reuben and Gad agree, but first they must provide for their families. They say: *We will build sheepfolds for our flocks and towns for our children* (32:16).

We sometimes drift away from family. When we do, it is well to remember these words of the Psalmist: *God restores the lonely to their homes . . .* (Psalm 68:6).

⁘

Sunday

I turn toward You, my God, and pray for those I love. Protect them and keep them from harm, in body, mind and spirit. Help them on their way in the world, and strengthen them as they struggle to overcome their weakness. And help me as well, so that my own life does not contradict the life I desire for them.

cs / Forms of Prayer

Three combine to make a child: the Holy One, father, mother. And of those who honor their father and mother, God says: I regard it as if I dwelt among them, and as if they honored Me.

Talmud

A happy childhood is one of the best gifts that parents have it in their power to bestow.

Mary Cholmondeley

Unknown

Days were great as lakes
And clear
When we were children
We sat a long time on their banks
And played
Or went down to swim
In the fresh water
And sometimes we wept
In our mother's apron
For life was filling us
Like jugs of wine.

Monday

Love binds me to my loved ones; thank You for its joy, its solace, and the strength it gives me. Help me to keep that love strong. May no selfishness or misunderstanding weaken it. May it bless me to the end!

Chasidic

A man asked the Kotzker Rebbe to pray for him in order that his sons might study the Torah diligently. The Rebbe replied: If you are diligent in study and your sons see it, they will imitate you. But if you neglect your own studies, and merely wish them to study, they will do likewise when they grow up. They will neglect the Torah themselves and desire that their sons do the studying.

Edmund Cahn

Where could there be a more favorable background for sympathetic instruction and effortless learning than a really harmonious family home? For security is in such a home and the awareness of being loved, guidance on the one hand and the relaxation that comes from confidence on the other. In a world full of doubts and disapprovals, here may be faith, unreserved acceptance, and fond admiration to blandish away that carking distrust of oneself.

Could I climb to the highest place in Athens, I would lift my voice and proclaim: Fellow citizens, why do you turn and scrape every stone to gather wealth and take so little care of your children, to whom one day you must relinquish all?

Attributed to Socrates

⁘

Tuesday

At first our families choose us; later we are the ones who choose. Let me always choose to be faithful to my word, and steady in showing my love. O God, give me an upright heart, that I may be worthy of the love of all who are dear to me.

All husbands and wives borrow their children. Our children are not our own; our children belong to God. . . . They are not ours to keep, but to rear. They are not given to us to mold into our image. They are not given to us so that we can force them to fulfill our lives and thus, in some way, cancel our failures. They are not tools to be used, but souls to be loved.

Thomas C. Short

Rabbi Bunam said: When it says that Jacob ordered Joseph to go and see whether it was well with his brothers (Genesis 37:14), it means as follows: Joseph was in the habit of bringing "evil reports of his brothers," so Jacob ordered him not to persist in looking for their misconduct, but rather to find the good in them.

Chasidic

This is the time to give up my home and seek for God. Ah, who has held me so long in delusion here?

God whispered I, but the ears of the man were stopped.

The man said, Who are you that have fooled me so long?

The voice said again, They are God, but he heard it not.

The baby cried out in its dream, nestling close to its mother.

God commanded, Stop, fool, do not leave your home, but still he did not hear.

God sighed and complained, Why does my servant wander to seek me, forsaking me?

Rabindranath Tagore

Wednesday

⁘

Make me worthy of the trust I see in the eyes of my loved ones. They look to me for companionship when they rejoice, for comfort when they are in pain, for consolation when they are bereaved. Help me to be equal to their needs.

Talmud

One may feed a parent the best food and be condemned, while another puts a father to work treading a mill and inherits Paradise. I give my father fatted chickens to eat, and he asks: Where did you get these, my son? and I say: Eat, old man, and be silent; dogs do not talk when they eat. In this manner I feed him the best and inherit hell. I grind at the mill when it is ordained that millers must go and grind for the government. I say: Father, come and grind here instead of me; if any trouble comes, let it befall me, and not you. In this manner I "mistreat" my father and inherit Paradise.

A. Scheinfield

Parents can't change the color of their child's eyes, but they can help give the eyes the light of understanding and warmth of sympathy.

Shirley Abbot

Within our family there was no such thing as a person who did not matter. Second cousins thrice removed mattered. We knew—and thriftily made use of—everybody's middle name. We knew who was buried where. We all mattered, and the dead most of all.

Thursday

⁘

When I am in need, help me to turn to the members of my family, and give them the will to dance with me, laugh with me, and weep with me.

Mark Zborowski and Elizabeth Herzog

"My shtetl" is the people who live in it, not the place or the buildings or the street. "My home" is the family and the family activities, not the walls or the yard or the broken-down fence.

Great ideas and fine principles do not live from generation to generation just because they are good, nor because they have been carefully legislated. Ideals and principles continue from generation to generation only when they are built into the hearts of children as they grow up.

George Benson

A father complained to the Baal Shem Tov that his son had forsaken God: What shall I do?

The Baal Shem Tov replied: Love him more than ever.

Chasidic

⁘

Friday

O God, our dwelling place in all generations, bless and keep my loved ones today and when I am no more. When it is light be their guide, and in darkness be their light. Grant them health and long life, and the gift of loving one another with a whole heart.

Alas for the children who are exiled from their parents' table. Alas for the parents who have exiled their children.

Talmud

Parents owe it to the children they bring into the world to put the tools of living in their hands—hands which we have made as strong and capable as we can. But, having given them the hands and the tools, we owe it to them not to do their digging for them.

Lenora Mattingly Weber

The family as an institution is *both* oppressive and protective and, depending on the issue, is experienced sometimes one way, sometimes the other—often in some mix of the two—by most people who live in families.

Lillian Breslow Rubin

A man made a will saying that his son should inherit nothing of his until he became a fool. Rabbi Yosé ben Judah and Rabbi Judah the Prince went to Rabbi Joshua ben Karcha to ask about this matter. They saw him outside his house, where he was crawling on his hands and knees with a reed in his mouth, and

Midrash

following after his son. Unnoticed, they watched him awhile. Later on, they asked him about the will. He laughed and said: This has happened to me! When one lives to have children, one appears to act like a fool!

Shabbat

Forms of Prayer / cs

I give thanks for this moment of prayer and quietness; in it I can feel the Divine Presence draw near, as I direct my mind toward what matters most to me. I am grateful for the goodness that every morning brings. I know it awaits me, if only I will embrace it. No day passes without its wonders, tokens of the love that surrounds me. When I open my eyes I find beauty and joy before me; when I listen closely, I hear a voice challenging me to grow, to climb upward to an ever-higher place of awareness and understanding. And I give thanks for those whom I love and who care for me: they are a treasure beyond price. For all these blessings I give praise.

Chasidic

The Koretzer Rebbe said: In the Shema we recite *Set these words . . . upon your heart. Teach them faithfully to your children. . . .* When these words go forth from your heart, they will truly influence your children for good.

John Stuart Mill

Moral and religious education consists in training the feelings and daily habits. . . . It is the home, the family, which gives us the moral or religious education we really receive.

Leo Tolstoy

The pleasure married people get from one another . . . is only the beginning of marriage and not its whole significance, which lies in the family.

43 *Marriage*

The Week of Mas'ei
Numbers 33:1–36:13

In the Sidra *Mas'ei* (Numbers 36), we are reminded that whatever else it might be, marriage has always been an economic and social arrangement. The sisters who earlier (Numbers 27) established that they, and all Israelite women like them, could inherit from their fathers are told they can marry anyone they like, with this proviso: *This is what the Eternal has commanded concerning the daughters of Zelophehad: they may marry anyone they wish, provided they marry into a clan of their father's tribe. . . . Thus no inheritance shall pass over from one tribe to another* (36:6–7).

Marriage has changed some since the above words were recorded, but not as much as we might suppose.

Sunday

Eternal God, in this moment of quiet reflection I discover anew how blessed I am, to have a partner who is my companion in all the vicissitudes of life, someone I can turn to in times of joy as in times of sorrow, someone who sees me when I am strong and leans on me, who sees me when I am weak and upholds me, who sees my victories and rejoices with me, who sees my defeats and comforts me. For all this I give thanks.

True love is . . . a divine gift, without which it is a sin . . . to enter into marriage.

Karl Emil Franzos

Life has taught us that love does not consist in gazing at each other, but in looking outward together in the same direction.

Antoine de Saint-Exupéry

Anne Morrow Lindbergh The best marriages, like the best lives, were both happy and unhappy. There is even a kind of necessary tension, a certain tautness between the partners that gave the marriage strength, like the tautness of a full sail. You went forward on it.

Monday

However hard it sometimes may be, keep open my heart and soul. When I incline to close myself off, make me understand my fearfulness and help me overcome it. And when she or he turns away from me, let me be the one to reach out.

Talmud It was the custom in ancient Judea to plant a cedar when a boy was born, and a pine when a girl was born. When they married, the canopy was made of branches woven from both trees.

Joseph Addison Two persons who have chosen each other out of all the species, with the design to be each other's mutual comfort and entertainment, have, in that action, bound themselves to be good-humoured, affable, discreet, forgiving, patient, and joyful, with respect to each other's frailties and perfections, to the end of their lives.

John Keats

But who, of men, can tell
That flowers would bloom, or that green fruit
would swell
To melting pulp, that fish would have bright mail,
The earth its dower of river, wood, and vale,
The meadows runnels, runnels pebble-stones,
The seed its harvest, or the lute its tones,
Tones ravishment, or ravishment its sweet,
If human souls did never kiss and greet?

George Sand Whoever has loved knows all that life contains of sorrow and of joy.

Tuesday

You give to me, I give to you: let that be the spirit of our marriage, a marriage of true minds, a marriage in which each of us feeds and is fed. This is what I would say today to my mate: Teach me how to say it. And if it be said to me, teach me how to hear it.

Midrash

A Roman matron said to Rabbi Yosé ben Chalafta: In how many days did the Holy One create the world? In six days, was his answer. And what has your god been doing since that time? she asked. Since that time the Holy One has been sitting and arranging marriages, deciding who should marry whom.

She laughed: Anyone can do that! I own many slaves; I could put them together in no time.

It may be easy for you, remarked Rabbi Yosé, yet for God this is as difficult as splitting the Red Sea.

Later on the woman brought a thousand male slaves and a thousand female slaves together, arranging them in two facing rows. Each one is to marry the one opposite him, she commanded. That very night was to be their marriage-night.

The next morning the couples appeared before her—this one had a concussion, that one a missing eye, another a broken leg, and so on. One said: *I cannot stand this woman!* The other: *This man displeases me!*

The matron sent for Rabbi Yosé ben Chalafta and said to him: You were absolutely right!

Louis K. Anspacher

Marriage is that relation between man and woman in which the independence is equal, the dependence mutual, and the obligation reciprocal.

Wednesday

Yet sometimes I feel abandoned and alone: more often than I like to admit. And I don't always know why. Nor do I easily find the way back from this isolation. Teach me to be patient. The time always comes.

Talmud If you marry for money your children will not turn out well.

André Maurois Some truths between husband and wife must be spoken, but let them be spoken with sweetness. Wounded vanity is fatal to love. It makes one hate the person who inflicted the wound. In married conversation, as in surgery, the knife must be used with care.

Vita Sackville-West There is nothing more lovely in life than the union of two people whose love for one another has grown through the years from the small acorn of passion to a great rooted tree. Surviving all vicissitudes, and rich with its manifold branches, every leaf holding its own significance.

Ursula K. Le Guin Love doesn't just sit there, like a stone, it has to be made, like bread; re-made all the time, made new.

Thursday

However much my mate and I may depend on each other, we remain separate beings. We don't always have to be underfoot, writing the script for a play the other doesn't want to be part of.

Barnett Brickner Success in marriage does not come merely through finding the right mate, but through being the right mate.

Talmud It is forbidden to compel a minor daughter to marry. Wait until she is grown up and says: *I want so-and-so.*

Jeremy Taylor Marriage has in it less of beauty, but more of safety, than the single life; it has not more ease, but less danger; it is more merry and more sad; it is fuller of sorrows and fuller of joys; it lies under more burdens, but is supported by all the strengths of love and charity; and those burdens are delightful.

What greater thing is there for two human souls than to feel that they are joined for life, to strengthen each other in all labour, to rest on each other in sorrow, to minister to each other in pain, to be with one another at the moment of last parting? *George Eliot*

⁘

Friday

I am not the person I was when we married. My tastes have changed. I toss and turn in bed, more than I used to. My temper is not always even, though my income has gone up. If you thought I was wonderful the day before we wed, you probably, for good reason, have moderated your admiration for me. From where you stand today, love, you could probably say something like this to me. But I love you still, and know you love me, too.

Love tastes sweet, but only with bread. *Yiddish proverb*

The particular charm of marriage is the duologue, the permanent conversation between two people who talk over everything and everyone until death breaks the record. It is this back-chat which, in the long run, makes a reciprocal equality more intoxicating than any form of servitude or domination. *Cyril Connolly*

The happiness of married life depends upon making small sacrifices with readiness and cheerfulness. *John Seldon*

One advantage of marriage, it seems to me, is that when you fall out of love with him, or he falls out of love with you, it keeps you together until you maybe fall in again. *Judith Viorst*

⁘

Shabbat

O God, today let me be thankful for the blessing of marriage. I pray for a love that will deepen with the passing years, and be a refuge against the storms of life, and in the sunshine a garden of delight.

Jewish anecdote Although the Hafetz Hayyim strove at all times to make peace between litigants, there were exceptions. Once a man and his wife came to the rabbi and told him they were completely incompatible. The rabbi advised the husband to grant his wife a divorce. He said: If it were always possible to bring about peace between a husband and a wife, the Torah would not have countenanced divorce. There are times when divorce is the only pathway to peace for both parties.

Thomas Merton Love is our true destiny. We do not find the meaning of life by ourselves alone—we find it with another. We do not discover the secret of our lives merely by study and calculation in our own isolated meditations. The meaning of our life is a secret that has to be revealed to us in love, by the one we love.

Douglas Jerrold The last word is the most dangerous of infernal machines, and the husband and wife should no more fight to get it than they would struggle for the possession of a lighted bombshell.

Dinah Shore Trouble is a part of your life, and if you don't share it you don't give the person who loves you enough chance to love you enough.

44 *Wisdom*

The Week of D'varim
Deuteronomy 1:1–3:22

In the first Sidra of Deuteronomy, *D'varim* (Deuteronomy 1), Moses begins a grand oration to the people of Israel, who are about to enter the promised land. He opens his words with a look back upon the years that began with the revelation at Mount Sinai. He reminds them that he could not lead them without help, so that he said to them: *Pick from each of your tribes people who are wise, insightful, and seasoned . . .* (1:13).

How did they choose? Did they rely on age and experience? What do we mean when we say: So-and-so is wise? What *is* wisdom? Is it another term for good judgment? Common sense? How do we acquire it?

⁘

Sunday

"It is not wisdom only to be wise," but I do ask for wisdom to shape my life through all its changing circumstances. Give me enough lightness of spirit so that I am free of compulsiveness and ready to meet whatever comes with a ready and willing heart, with "courage, gaiety and . . . quiet mind."

Who is wise? One who learns from everyone. — *Mishnah*

You are wise if you are willing to seem foolish in order to learn Torah, for those afraid to ask questions show themselves to be fools. — *Vitry*

Rabbi Nachum of Tchernobyl was a friend of the poor. One day a rich Chasid asked him: Does not the Talmud (Shabbat 92a) — *Chasidic* teach that the Divine Presence rests on the one who is wise, strong and rich?

He smiled and said: Do you really believe that God values what is external? The one on whom the Divine Presence rests is the one described elsewhere in the Talmud, in Pirké Avot (4:1): *Who are wise? Those who learn from everyone. Who are strong? Those who control their passions. Who are rich? Those who are content with what they have.*

Heinrich Heine If you have never in your life made a fool of yourself, you have also never been wise.

Monday

Today let my wisdom be to lose myself completely in the world. Whatever my worries, let them fall from my mind, like leaves on an autumn day. Whatever my troubles and fears, let them be quiet today.

Talmud Their wisdom leaves the wise who give way to anger; and if they are prophets, they lose the spirit of prophecy. And even if Heaven has destined them for greatness, those who let anger control them will be abased.

David Starr Jordan Wisdom is knowing what to do next;
virtue is doing it.

Confucius They must often change who would be constant in happiness or wisdom.

Chasidic The Kobriner Rebbe said: Some people say: "It is hard to serve God nowadays. In the old days there were many good people whose example we could follow."

This notion is absurd, and I say to them: Have you really tried to seek God and failed? Then seek God in the way the people you so admire did, and you will succeed as well as they. As Ecclesiastes (7:10) has taught us: *"Do not say, 'How is it that the former days were better than these?' for you are not wise to ask this question."*

✦

Tuesday

So often my words precede my thoughts, and I feel humiliated: I am a fool more frequently than I am a sage! O God, show me how to keep quiet more often, at least until I have something real to say and someone who wants to hear it.

The talkative listen to no one, for they are ever speaking. And the first evil that attends those who know not how to be silent is that they hear nothing.

Plutarch

Knowing and not acting is to wisdom as plowing without planting is to farming.

Unknown

You may say: I have not learned wisdom, I have not studied Torah, what am I to do? God said: All wisdom, and all Torah, is a single easy thing: If you revere Me, and fulfill the words of the Torah, you have all wisdom and all the Torah in your heart.

Midrash

> A fool and a sage both have seven traits:
> The wise never speak before the wiser.
> They do not interrupt their companions;
> they are not afraid to reply;
> they ask to the point and reply as they should;
> they speak of first things first and of last things last.
> If they have not heard they say, I have not heard.
> They acknowledge the truth.
> The reverse is true of fools.

Mishnah

✦

Wednesday

So much of the time I am unaware—unconscious, almost—when the world is begging for my notice and encouraging me to rejoice. For this, all I need is a wise heart, a mind open to challenge, a soul alive to wonder.

Solomon ibn Gabirol

We are wise only while in search of wisdom;
when we imagine we have attained it, we are fools.

Plato

Socrates, when the young Theatetus was introduced to him as a lad of brilliant promise, said to him that he felt sure he had thought a great deal. The boy answered: Oh, no—not that, but at least I have wondered a great deal. Ah, said Socrates, but that shows the lover of wisdom, for wisdom begins in wonder.

Confucius

Of neighborhoods
benevolence is the most beautiful.
How can one be considered wise who,
when given the choice,
does not settle there?

Thursday

⁛

My passion for self-improvement is far exceeded by my determination not to change.

My passion for self-improvement is far exceeded by my unwillingness to be caught out.

My passion for self-improvement is far exceeded by my penchant for self-exculpation.

If any of this is true, O God, how can I hope to attain wisdom? Give me at least credit for being honest!

Jewish anecdote

It has been said: This is the way of the wise: to be silent, to listen carefuliy, to remember what you hear, and then proceed to teach. This is the way of the unwise: to be hasty in giving advice.

Talmud

Who is wise? One who has foresight.

Elbert Hubbard

Learn from your mistakes, but don't cry over them. We best redeem the past by forgetting it.

William James

The art of being wise is the art of knowing what to overlook.

John Churton Collings

To profit from good advice requires more wisdom than to give it.

Friday

Without foresight I will be in trouble the moment I start out. Often enough, we stumble and fall despite our best efforts to plan ahead. But keep me from walking without looking merely because I cannot foresee everything to come! I need the wisdom to look ahead before I begin the journey, and I need the courage to begin it without knowing how it will end.

Rabbi Samuel bar Nachman said in the name of Rabbi Jonathan: It says (Proverbs 17:16), *What good is money in the hands of a fool to buy wisdom?*—This refers to those sages who engage in the [study of] Torah but who have in them no fear of Heaven! — *Talmud*

To finish the moment, to find the journey's end in every step of the road, to live the greatest number of good hours, is wisdom. — *Ralph Waldo Emerson*

The invariable mark of wisdom is to see the miraculous in the common. — *Ralph Waldo Emerson*

The Belzer Rebbe said: We often observe how thoroughly the wicked plan a deed, and the untiring effort with which they execute it. Should we not imitate them when we endeavor to perform a good deed? As it says in the Psalms (119:98): *From my foes You teach me wisdom in doing Your commandments.* — *Chasidic*

Shabbat

How can I be at rest when I am busy jumping to conclusions? Keep me from knowing before I know, from arriving before I get there; teach me that I must earn my wisdom by attending to my experience; and although the only experience I can have is my own, show me how to learn from the experience of others, and thus make it my own.

Marcel Proust

We do not receive wisdom,
we must discover it for ourselves,
after a journey through the wilderness
which no-one else can make for us,
which no-one can spare us.
For our wisdom is the point of view
from which we come at last
to regard the world.

Solomon Schechter

The Gaon of Vilna is . . . reported to have said on one occasion, that he would not like to have an angel for his teacher who would reveal to him all the mysteries of the Torah. Such a condition is only befitting the world to come, but in *this* world only things that are acquired by hard labor and great struggle are of any value.

Jonah ben Abraham

However much you know,
if you think you know enough
you are a fool.
However little you know,
if you seek to know more
you are wise.

45 *A Tree of Life*

The Week of Va'et-chanan
Deuteronomy 3:23–7:11

The Sidra *Va'et-chanan* (Deuteronomy 6) turns from a review of history to a restatement of Scripture's laws. Moses pleads to the people that they diligently observe the laws and commandments that he is expounding—for the love of God. And Moses calls upon Israel to pass the Teaching on.

What is your tree of life? A tree of life—the soul's place of discernment, the mind's place of enlightenment, the heart's place of connection. Would we know the way to live without the fruit of this tree? For Jews, the Tree of Life is a metaphor for Torah, God's breath felt in and between the letters of the word. It is what Moses meant when he said: *Teach them diligently to your children . . .* (6:7).

Sunday

I give thanks for the heritage that has come to me from the past. It calls upon me to show mercy, to practice justice, to walk with humility. When I follow this path I enlarge my life and the life of those near to me. Grant me, O God, wisdom and strength always to walk the way of Torah.

Chasidic

Rabbi Elazar said:

The light that the Holy One created on the first day—

With it Adam could see to the end of the world.

Upon seeing the corrupt ways of the generations of the future, the Holy One hid that first light.

And for whom did the Holy One store away this light?

—For the righteous in the time to come.

Where did the Holy One hide it?

— In the Torah.

If so, cannot the righteous, when they learn Torah, find at least some of the hidden Light?

— They can find it, it can find them.

And what should the righteous do when they find some of that hidden Light?

— Let them reveal it by their way of life!

Midrash First do good deeds and then ask Heaven for knowledge of Torah; first emulate the righteous and upright, and then ask Heaven for wisdom; first take hold of the way of humility, and then ask Heaven for understanding.

Monday

⁘

When I pray, let it be for a wise mind and a strong will to live by Your word—the word I hear within me, that never ceases to teach.

Midrash Once when Rabbi Tarfon, Rabbi Yosé the Galilean, and Rabbi Akiba were together in Lydda, the question arose: Which is more important, study or practice? Tarfon argued, "practice." Akiba argued, "study." They concluded: Study is more important, for it leads to practice.

Mishnah Rabbi Ishmael . . . says:

Learn in order to teach, and it is given you to learn and to teach.

Learn in order to do, and it is given you to learn and teach, to keep and do.

Talmud Better not to be born, than to learn without intending to put into practice what one has learned.

cs How can we do more—or better—than we know? Scripture tells of Israel's acceptance of the Torah before knowing its details, as it is said (Exodus 24:7), *And they said: All that the Eternal One has spoken we will do and we will hear.*

Rabbi Judah Zvi of Stretyn said: It is written (Deuteronomy 4:35): *It has been shown you, that you might know, that the Eternal is God, and there is no other.* *Chasidic*

There are two names of God in this verse, *Adonai* and *Elohim, Eternal* and *God.* Tradition teaches that the former denotes the divine attribute of mercy, the latter the attribute of [strict] justice. But in reality they are one. That is the real meaning of the people's cry, when the prophet Elijah had overcome the prophets of Baal: *Adonai hu ha-Elohim, The Eternal is God!* The Eternal and God are One, there is no other: justice and mercy are one thing.

⁘

Tuesday

Let me be ready this day to hear the need beneath the surface of the words that people address to me; let me listen with special attention to the words of old people, for they have seen much, and to the words of the young, for they see with new eyes what I may have come to take for granted. Their words, too, may be Torah.

> Shammai said:
> Set aside regular times for study.
> Say little, do much.
> Greet everyone with a cheerful countenance.

Mishnah

Rabbi Elazar said: When Moses received the Torah, he said this blessing: *Praised be the One who has chosen the Torah and sanctified it, and who delights in those who fulfill it.* He did not say, "those who *labor to learn* it," or "those who *meditate* on it," but "those who *fulfill* it." You may say: I have not learned the Torah, what am I to do? But God says: All wisdom and all Torah is one easy thing: if you revere Me and fulfill the words of the Torah you have all wisdom and all Torah in your heart. *Midrash*

Wednesday

⁘

What is the sum of my life? If on this very day I were called to account, what could I say, in what could I take pride? Some days I understand that when I make the effort to learn and to act on what I learn, I have done enough for that day. May this be for me one such day!

Talmud Raba said: At the final judgment we are asked: Did you conduct your business honestly? Did you set aside times for Torah? Did you cultivate your mind? Did you try to understand the inner meaning of things? Did you wait hopefully for redemption? And if, in addition, reverence for God was your treasure, then it is well with you.

Period of Mishnah *And make a fence for the Torah* (Pirké Avot 1:1). A vineyard with a fence is better than one without it. But one must not make a fence higher than the object it is to guard, lest the fence fall and crush the plants.

Midrash You may learn the entire Law and Teachings, but if you have no fear of sin you have nothing. I say to my neighbor: I have a thousand measures of wheat, wine, and oil. My neighbor responds: Have you storehouses in which to put them? If yes, you have all; if no, you have nothing. So with you: you may have learned everything; only if you have the fear of sin is it yours.

Thursday

⁘

Remind me to do the good that lies to hand, and not to worry about what is beyond me; remind me that it is my own work that I am obliged to do, and that the rest belongs to others. Together, we water the Tree of Life!

Rabbi Elazar says:
Be eager to learn Torah.
And know before whom you labor,
who your employer is,
who will pay you for your labor.

Mishnah

Rabbi Elazar ben Azariah says:
Without wisdom, how can there be reverence?
Without reverence, how can there be wisdom?
Without understanding, of what use is knowledge?
Without knowledge, where is understanding?
Without bread, what good is Torah?
Without Torah, what good is bread?

Mishnah

⁘

Friday

Behold, You desire wisdom in my inner life;
and there it is that You make me to know it.
Create in me a clean heart, O God,
and renew a steadfast spirit within me.

From *Psalm 51*

Rabbi Judah said in the name of Rav:

When Moses climbed the mountain to receive the Torah, he found the Holy One sitting and fashioning little crowns for the Torah's letters.

Moses said: *Ribbono shel olam,* for whose sake are you doing this?

The Holy One replied: Some day a man named Akiba ben Joseph will enter the world; he will discover heaps and heaps of teachings from every one of these little hooks.

Moses said: Ruler of the world, let me see him.

—Turn around.

Moses turned around and found himself sitting in the eighth row of the House of Study where Akiba was teaching. He listened eagerly to the discussion; to his amazement and dismay, he did not understand it! Then a student asked Akiba how he knew a particular thing, and he answered: This is a teaching given to Moses on Sinai.

Talmud

And Moses was comforted.

Turning back, he said to the Holy One: Ruler of the world, You have such a man as this, yet You give the Torah through me!

God replied: Be still; that is how I have ordained it.

Moses then said: Ruler of the world, You have shown me his Torah; show me his reward.

—Turn around.

Moses turned around and saw Akiba's flayed flesh hanging in a butcher's shop. He turned back and said before God: Ruler of the world, this is Torah and this its reward!?

The Holy One said: Be still; that is how I have ordained it.

Midrash

Even if Israel be exiled among the nations, if it immerses itself in Torah, it is as though it were not in exile.

Shabbat

God, teach me how to be Your agent, Your messenger of help to the needy and comfort to the afflicted, a companion to the lonely, and an encouragement to the faint of heart. Teach me that this is the wisdom You would have me know, the eternal wisdom that brings life and light to the soul.

Talmud

As he lay dying,
Rabban Yochanan ben Zakkai blessed his disciples:
—Fear Heaven as much as you fear your neighbors.
—No more than that?
—As much as that! When you are about to transgress, whom do you fear? Your great fear is that a passer-by may see you!

Talmud / cs

Raba bar bar Hunah said:
In that room is a safe, and
here are its keys.
But if the door is locked,
and the doorkey is lost:
What good are the keys to the safe?

If Torah is in your mind
but the fear of Heaven is not in your heart,
of what avail is it?
Rabbi Yannai added:
You have no courtyard,
yet you build a gate for it!

46 *Self*

The Week of Ekev
Deuteronomy 7:12–11:25

In the Sidra *Ekev* (Deuteronomy 8), Moses concentrates on reminding the people of their connection to and dependence upon the divine. He says: *Remember the long way that the Eternal your God caused you to travel in the wilderness . . . to test you by hardships . . . in order to teach you that a human being lives not on bread alone, but on all that goes forth from the mouth of the Eternal* (8:2–3).

You and I are spiritual beings, and our spirits need nourishment; we are also formed of matter, so we literally need bread. What then am I, who am compounded of dust and spirit? What is it that makes me conscious that I am who I am?

Sunday

What do I want? And if I want it, do I need it? And if I need it, will I get it? And if I get it, can I keep it? Do the answers depend on who I am? Help me to be what I am becoming. Is that "becoming" more than I am right now? Help me to trust the dawning hour. Help me to know myself better. Help me to become myself.

Midrash

Each of us has three names: what our parents call us, what others call us, and what we call ourselves.

William Wordsworth

Dust as we are, the immortal spirit grows
Like harmony in music; there is a dark
Inscrutable workmanship that reconciles
Discordant elements, makes them cling together

In one society. How strange that all
The terrors, pains, and early miseries,
Regrets, vexations, lassitudes interfused
Within my mind, should e'er have borne a part,
And that a needful part, in making up
The calm existence that is mine when I
Am worthy of myself! Praise to the end! . . .

⁘

Monday

I seem to be at least two people: the one within and the one that others see. Which of me is the real me? Both, surely. I cannot be the only one who feels this: everyone must. Maybe what I must do with myself is to stop contemplating it and get on with my work.

I am afraid of things that cannot harm me, and I know it.
I yearn for things that cannot help me, and I know it.
What I fear is within me, and within me, too, is what I seek.

cs / Chasidic

Tell me what you pay attention to and I will tell you what you are.

José Ortega y Gasset

Shibli was asked: Who guided you in the Path?

He said: A dog. One day I saw him, almost dead with thirst, standing by the water's edge.

Every time he looked at his reflection in the water he was frightened and withdrew, because he thought it was another dog. Finally, such was his necessity, he cast away fear and leaped into the water—and the "other" dog vanished.

He himself, it turned out, had been the barrier keeping him from what he sought.

At that moment I understood that I myself was the obstacle, and it vanished!

Sufi

Chasidic / cs The Baal Shem Tov said:
You must be a complete person,
in possession of every human trait. Therefore:
Learn pride, but be not proud;
learn anger, but do not feel angry.
Does not God possess both justice and mercy?

Tuesday

"*The soul that You have given me, O God, is pure! You created and formed it, breathed it into me, and within me You sustain it*" (Gates of Prayer).

Keep this realization before me, O God, when I am down on myself. And remind me of this especially, when I am down on other people, for these words were not meant for me alone!

Mishnah / cs What do you really want—your self or your fame?
What gives you more—your self or your possessions?
What would be more expensive to replace?
A name sought is a name lost.
Add to life, or you will subtract.

Chasidic Reb Zisha lay dying, and he said: Zisha will come to judgment soon. Zisha is afraid, very much afraid.

His disciples responded with astonishment: If you are afraid, Master, what hope is there for us? Your life has been blameless. You have upheld the world. Did Abraham fear, or Isaac, or Jacob? What did Moses have to fear?

Reb Zisha whispered in reply: How can you say this of Zisha? *What does Zisha have to fear?* Do you think that when Zisha comes before the Court of Heaven they will ask him: Why weren't you like Abraham? Why weren't you as great as Moses? No, they will ask: *Why weren't you like Zisha?* And what will I be able to say to that?

Dag Hammarskjöld The only kind of dignity which is genuine is that which is not diminished by the indifference of others.

✣ **Wednesday**

The less I let others determine my worth for me, the more I own myself. The less I obsess about my self, the more I am myself. Look more often for virtue and less for praise.

When we leave our own ground and take that of a friend, we end up unsuccessful everywhere. Many followed the example of Rabbi Simeon bar Yochai, and their work did not succeed because they were not of his quality, but only did as he did, in imitation of his quality. *Chasidic*

It is as hard to see one's self as to look backwards without turning around. *Henry David Thoreau*

The vices we scoff at in others laugh at us within ourselves. *Sir Thomas Browne*

How easy to see another's fault, how hard to perceive one's own! We winnow our neighbor's faults like chaff and conceal our own, like a cheat with loaded dice. *The Dhammapada*

Rabbi Noah, son of Rabbi Mordecai, was his father's successor. He conducted himself differently from his father in a number of ways, and his disciples questioned him. *Chasidic*

I do as my father did, said he. He did not imitate, and I do not imitate.

✣ **Thursday**

God, I was meant to flower in the company of my family, meant to form friendships, meant to love. I cannot be myself without others, without loving, without laughing at jokes and hugging children, without sitting at the feet of the wise and good of the generation that begot me. When I forget this, may I be helped to remember; when I lose my sense of direction, let me be shown how to find a compass. Help me to become what I am meant to be. Help me to be myself through life with other selves.

Leo Baeck Our life is fulfilled by what we become, not by what we were at birth. Endowment and heritage mean much . . . and then again nothing; the essential thing is what we make of them.

François de la Rochefoucauld Were we to take as much pains to be what we ought to be, as we do to disguise what we really are, we might appear like ourselves without being at the trouble of any disguise whatever.

Talmud The Holy One does not do as people do. Human beings do not fill a full vessel, they fill one that is empty; the Holy One fills the full. If you have heard, you will hear; if you have not heard, you will not hear. If you have heard the old, you will hear the new; if you have turned your heart away, you will not hear.

Emily Dickinson

I'm nobody! Who are you?
Are you nobody, too?

Friday

⁘

There is a darkness that is not dark, when I am aware that in Your presence I can find my way. There is a suffering that does not embitter, when I can feel the love of Your messengers, the angels who surround me with care. There is an ignorance that seems like knowledge, when all the answers I have learned turn into the one question You keep asking me: Who are you? And when I hear this as Your question, I know that You are its answer; when You are with me, I know before whom I stand: I know who I am.

Robert Mallet

It is not impossibilities
which fill us with the deepest despair,
but possibilities
which we have failed to realize.

Chasidic

There is no room for God
in those who are full of themselves.

None are so empty,
as those who are full of themselves.

Benjamin Whichcote

·:·

Shabbat

At certain times this burden, my consciousness of self, seems to fall from me. I hear myself called up, I am not alone, I know that I matter and that I don't matter. There is peace within me. And I know it will not last. Tomorrow, or the day after, I will again feel bound in a prison of my own making. Let the peace of Shabbat and the love that enters me now come back to me then, when I need it. On such days let the memory of this day reassure me, and give me strength.

Chasidic

The Maggid of Mezeritz said:

—Our good deeds go up to God. Do you know what God does with them?

God is a gardener, using our good deeds as seeds. God plants them in the Garden of Eden, and out of them, trees grow.

Thus we each create our own Paradise. . . .

Period of Mishnah

Rabbi Akiba would say:
Here is a good sign for you—
your spirit is one with your deeds.

Mishnah

A boor does not fear sin.
The ignorant cannot be pious.
The bashful cannot learn.
The hot-tempered cannot teach.
One too steeped in business cannot grow wise.
Where none are real persons, try hard to be one.

cs / Chasidic

I prefer the wicked who know they are wicked to the righteous who know they are righteous. Each has a flaw, but there is hope for both. But I cannot abide the wicked who think they are righteous. For, thinking as they do, mired in self-deception and illusion as they are, how can they ever hope to repent and change their ways?

ראה

47 *This Day's Path*

The Week of R'ei
Deuteronomy 11:26–16:17

In the very first words of the Sidra *R'ei* (Deuteronomy 11), Moses challenges the people, as he sounds one of the great recurrent themes of Deuteronomy—we are free to choose, and our choices have lasting consequences: *See, this day I have set a blessing and a curse before you* (11:26). That is to say, on this day's path we will come to many a crossroad, and we need to choose our direction with care.

When we stand staring at the horizon we see many things. At times, however, that's not the wise thing to do, because there's something closer that claims our attention: the ground we stand on, the walk we're walking.

Sunday

From *Psalm 26 / cs*

Innocent I walk,
trusting in You.
I walk
with eyes on Your love
and Your truth.
I come to Your altar
to give thanks,
and I sing of Your wonders.
My hands are washed clean.

Marcus Aurelius

Make no noise over a good deed, but pass on to another as a vine bears grapes season after season.

Bachya ibn Pakuda

If you do no more than your duty,
you are not doing your duty.

When the morning's freshness has been replaced by the weariness of midday, when the leg muscles quiver under the strain, the climb seems endless, and suddenly nothing will go quite as you wish—it is then that you must *not* hesitate.

Dag Hammarskjöld

The lesson which life repeats and constantly enforces is "look under foot." You are always nearer the divine and the true sources of your power than you think. The lure of the distant and the difficult is deceptive. The great opportunity is where you are. Do not despise your own place and hour. Every place is under the stars, every place is the centre of the world.

John Burroughs

⁘

Monday

As I walk the path of my life today, let me remember from time to time to look up to the stars, but let me not miss the flowers growing along the road—on both sides.

There are those who serve by walking the high road.
There are those who serve by walking the side road.
There are those who serve by walking a road of their own making: They get there first.

cs / Chasidic

The best things are nearest: breath in your nostrils, light in your eyes, flowers at your feet, duties at your hand, the path of Right just before you. Then do not grasp at the stars, but do life's plain, common work as it comes, certain that daily duties and daily bread are the sweetest things in life.

Robert Louis Stevenson

The time came to leave the cave [to which they had fled to escape the Roman persecution], and they looked about at the world they had not seen so long a time. Bar Yochai was surrounded by disciples. The sun dazzled his eyes. In the distance farmers could be seen tilling the soil, as though nothing had changed in all this time.

Turning to the men around him, Bar Yochai said: Look! See how those people neglect eternal life for the needs of an hour!

Talmud

All the scene before them was consumed by flames.

A voice from Heaven came to them:

Have you come out in order to destroy my world? Go back to your cave!

Tuesday

⁘

Maimonides

I know how many paths there are, and sometimes I worry that mine cannot be right. I look to others for reassurance, or I imitate them, feeling all the while a faint unease. Awaken me to faith in myself, and in the path that I can choose for myself, as others choose theirs.

Period of Mishnah

The way of life is like a path between fire and ice. The slightest bend in either direction is fatal. What to do? Walk in the middle.

Maimonides

Follow the middle path again and again, until it involves little effort, and by repetition becomes a fixed habit.

George Eliot

The years seem to rush by now, and I think of death as a fast approaching end of a journey—double and treble reasons for loving as well as working while it is day.

Antoine de Saint-Exupéry

Life has a meaning only if one barters it day by day for something other than itself.

Henry David Thoreau

Only that day dawns to which we are awake.

Chasidic

Rabbi Yitzchak of Vorki said: Adam's real sin was that he worried about the future. The serpent reasoned with him: How can you serve God, when you cannot tell the difference between good and evil? How can you make a choice? Just eat of this fruit, though, and you *will* be able to tell; then you will choose the good and receive its reward. Adam's fault lay in accepting this argument. He worried that he would not be able to serve, yet at that very hour he had his duty: to obey God and resist the serpent.

Wednesday

If I take a wrong turning today, may I find others who can direct me. Even if paths diverge, we might walk together a little while, a pleasant walk along a way I might not have seen had I not gone astray.

Plan for this world as if you were going to live forever; plan for the World to Come as if you were going to die tomorrow.

Solomon ibn Gabirol

Live your life each day as you would climb a mountain. An occasional glance toward the summit keeps the goal in mind, but many beautiful scenes are to be observed from each new vantage point. Climb slowly, steadily, enjoying each passing moment; and the view from the summit will serve as a fitting climax for the journey.

Harold V. Melchert

Alas! I have done nothing this day! What? Have you not lived? It is not only the fundamental but the noblest of your occupations. *Had I been placed or thought fit for the managing of great affairs, I would have shown what I could have performed.* Have you known how to manage your life? You have accomplished the greatest work of all. . . . Have you known how to compose your conduct? You have done more than the one who has composed books. Have you known how to take rest? You have done more than the one who has taken empires and cities. The glorious masterpiece of humanity is to live properly. . . .

Michel de Montaigne

The gayety of life, like the beauty and moral worth of life, is a saving grace, which to ignore is folly, and to destroy is crime. There is no more than we need,—there is barely enough to go round.

Agnes Repplier

Thursday

Today, with imagination, I won't need to climb a mountain to see the landscape. Today, let me proceed along my path with a mind awake to beauty, and with adventures awaiting only my arrival.

Chasidic / cs Rabbi Yechiel Michal said: *Who shall ascend the mountain of the Eternal One? Who shall stand in God's holy place?* (Psalm 24).

You ride up a mountain in your carriage and when you are half-way up, the horses are tired and you must stop and give them a rest. Now, while the carriage is standing you will take a stone and put it under the wheel to keep it from rolling back. Later, resuming your journey, you will be able to reach the top.

If you can keep from falling when forced to interrupt your service, and know how to pause, you will ascend the mountain.

Thomas Dekker To awaken each morning with a smile brightening my face; to greet the day with reverence for the opportunities it contains; to approach my work with a clean mind; to hold ever before me, even in the doing of little things, the Ultimate Purpose toward which I am working; to meet men and women with laughter on my lips and love in my heart; to be gentle, kind, and courteous through all the hours; to approach the night with weariness that ever woos sleep and the joy that comes from work well done—this is how I desire to waste wisely my days.

Elisabeth Kübler-Ross It's only when we truly know and understand that we have a limited time on earth—and that we have no way of knowing when our time is up—that we will begin to live each day to the fullest, as if it was the only one we had.

Friday

Today—and probably tomorrow again—I shall have to reprove myself for not advancing further along the path to which I am called. Teach me, O Infinite Source of Being, that at the moment of regret I shall already have advanced along my path!

James Baldwin Not everything that is faced can be changed; but nothing can be changed until it is faced.

John Ruskin Let every dawn of morning be to you as the beginning of life and every setting sun be to you as its close; then let every one of these short lives leave its sure record of some kindly thing done for others, some goodly strength or knowledge gained for yourself.

The only life we can live is lived today. Yesterday . . . cannot be lived again but only remembered. Tomorrow is before us; and however sweet its expectations, the clock must tick its patient course before we can test our hope against reality. We can live no more than a day at a time. If we do not live today, we do not live at all; and each day that we live is a lifetime complete in itself. . . . "If only I could live again!" we sometimes sigh. And we can, indeed we do! We live over and over again as day follows day with its heights to be scaled and its depths to be plumbed.

Roy Pearson

Rabbi Leib, Sarah's son, said: A Tzaddik is one who lives Torah, not one who preaches it. Your actions, not your words! You have to *be* Torah: your habits, your motions, [even] your motionless way of being, are what count. So when I visit Tzaddikim, I go not to listen to their interpretations of Torah, but to see how they behave from waking to sleeping.

Chasidic / cs

Shabbat

Today I stop walking and sail a river that effortlessly bears me on its way. Grateful to know that I can be who I am, I rest from my endless striving to become someone else.

The Hafetz Hayyim said: If you have decided to do God's will, you should begin your good deeds today, not tomorrow.

Jewish anecdote

I began to have an idea of my life, not as the slow shaping of achievement to fit my preconceived purposes, but as the gradual discovery and growth of a purpose which I did not know.

Joanna Field

Rabbi Mendel of Kotzk said: Few things are worse than these: to learn the Torah and not be troubled by it, to sin and forgive yourself, to pray today merely because you prayed yesterday.

Chasidic

Thomas Aquinas

The road that stretches before our feet
is a challenge to the heart
long before it tests the strength of our legs.
Our destiny is to run to the edge of the world
and beyond,
off into the darkness;
sure, for all our blindness;
secure, for all our helplessness;
strong, for all our weakness;
gaily in love, for all the pressure on our hearts.
In that darkness beyond the world,
we can begin to know the world and ourselves.
We begin to understand
that we are not made
to pace out our lives behind prison walls,
but to walk into the arms of God.

48 *Righteousness and Truth*

The Week of Shof'tim
Deuteronomy 16:18–21:9

The Sidra *Shof'tim* (Deuteronomy 16) begins with a grand declaration: *You shall appoint judges and officials for your tribes . . . and let them govern the people with justice. Do not judge unfairly: show no partiality; take no bribes, for bribes blind the eye of the discerning and subvert the cause of the just. Justice, justice shall you pursue, that it may go well with you* (16:18–19). This may well be the *sine qua non* for a society that is civilized, where people can live with a sense of security, knowing they will be treated fairly and honestly.

Sunday

From *Psalm 15*

Eternal God:
Who may abide in Your house?
Who may dwell in Your holy mountain?
Those who are upright; who do justly;
all whose hearts are true.
Who do not slander others,
nor wrong them,
nor bring shame upon their kin.
Who give their word and, come what may, do not retract.
Who do not exploit others,
who never take bribes.
Those who live in this way
shall never be shaken.

Maimonides You are forbidden to accustom yourself to use smooth and deceptive language. Do not say one thing when you mean another, but let your inner thoughts be in accord with the impression you give; say what you really think. Even one word of smooth talk or misrepresentation is forbidden; you should, rather, have truth on your lips, a sincere spirit, and a heart free of trickery and deceit.

Socrates The surest way to live with honor in the world,
is to be in reality what we appear to be. . . .

Midrash *You shall not take a bribe* (Deuteronomy 16:9). Not even to acquit the innocent or condemn the guilty.

Monday

In all the temptations of the day, O God, help me to be true to my better self; keep me from deception of others and from self-deception; from condemning others while justifying myself; from calling evil good and good evil; and cleanse me from all within me that is false. I know this is the labor of a life and not of one day, but today help me to do what I can in one day.

Kitzur Shulchan Aruch Do not invite your neighbor to eat at your table when you know quite well the invitation will be refused. Do not pretend to offer a gift that you know will not be accepted. All in all, do not say one thing while you mean something else. Your mouth and your heart should be one and you should train your lips to speak honestly, your spirit to be one of integrity, and your heart pure.

Chasidic Rabbi Mendel of Kotzk said:

One can imitate everything in the world except truth, for truth that is imitated is no longer truth.

Anne Morrow Lindbergh The most exhausting thing in life, I have discovered, is being insincere.

Noah was a righteous man, whole-hearted in his generation (Genesis 6:9). According to Rabbi Yochanan, this means: *in his generation*—but not in other generations. In the view of Resh Lakish, this means: *in his generation*—all the more in other generations.

Talmud

Rabbi Chanina said: How expound Rabbi Yochanan's view? If you put a flask of wine into storage with vinegar, its scent, in that place, will be outstanding, but elsewhere not so.

Rabbi Hoshaya said: How expound the view of Resh Lakish? If you put a flask of perfume among foul odors, and if it is pleasant even there, how much the more would it be pleasant in a place that smells sweet!

⁘

Tuesday

O God, there are times when I rejoice to be true and upright, when my soul delights in following a course that is honorable without counting the cost. Strengthen the impulse to be honest that You have implanted within me, for I know that as it grows stronger, the more I choose it as my way.

Let the truth and right by which you are apparently the loser be preferable to you to the falsehood and wrong by which you are apparently the gainer.

Maimonides

There are people in whose presence you would be ashamed to do something dishonorable or say something improper; keep in mind, then, that you are always in the presence of the Holy One, and conduct yourself accordingly.

Jonah ben Abraham

Never think you gain from something that compels you to break a promise, lose your self-respect, hate, suspect, curse, act the hypocrite, or desire anything that needs to be hidden from the sight of others.

Marcus Aurelius

Rabbi Bunam said: We are taught by the Talmud (Shabbat 55a) that *God's seal is truth*. Why did God select that virtue above all

Chasidic

others? Because if we are clever we may be able to counterfeit any other virtue, but any imitation of the truth is falsehood.

Chasidic

A man came to Rabbi Levi Yitzchak of Berditchev and complained: Rabbi, what shall I do with the lie that keeps sneaking into my heart? He stopped and then cried aloud: Oh, even what I just said was not said honestly! I shall never find the truth! In despair he threw himself on the ground.

How fervently you seek the truth! said the rabbi. With a gentle hand he raised him from the ground and said: It is written (Psalm 85:12): *Truth shall grow out of the ground.*

Wednesday

Grant me the wisdom to understand that to be honest in word and deed is more than one option among others. Help me to live by the light of truth that is eternal, acknowledging that some things do not change with the seasons.

Judah he-Chasid

No blessing rests on one who oppresses a worker or who buys stolen goods.

Michel de Montaigne

I find that people fool around chastising harmless faults in children very inappropriately, and tormenting them for thoughtless actions that leave neither imprint nor consequences. Only lying, and a little below it obstinacy, seem to me the actions whose birth and progress one should combat insistently. They grow with the child. And once the tongue has been put on this wrong track, it cannot be called back without the most amazing difficulty.

Talmud

Rabbi Ze'era said: Never promise to give something to a child and then fail to do it, because thereby you teach a child to lie.

Shem Tob ibn Falaquera

If something is true, it is on account of its intrinsic worth, not on account of its source.

Rabbi Mordecai of Tchernobyl said: If you want to acquire the habit of truthfulness, then, whenever you catch yourself shading the truth or uttering a falsehood, make a point of saying unashamedly, I have just been guilty of an untruth, and you will soon discipline your tongue.

Chasidic

⁘

Thursday

You call me to righteousness, and I pray that this will be one of those days when everything will comes together and I will respond to that call as a bird glides on a current of air. Sometimes it seems that easy; sometimes I see my faults clearly enough, and for a while they lose control of me. I seem not to need to hide from myself. May this be such a day.

Accept truth from any quarter. Who calls logic a "foreign" science, or speaks contemptuously of Plato or Aristotle because they were not Jews, is like the sluggard who cries, "There is a lion in the streets."

Immanuel of Rome

What is accomplished through lies can assume the mask of truth; what is accomplished through violence can go in the guise of justice, and for a while the hoax may be successful. But soon people will realize that lies are lies at bottom; that in the final analysis violence is violence, and both lies and violence will suffer the destiny history has in store for all that is false. I sometimes hear it said that a generation must sacrifice itself, "take the sin upon itself," so that the coming generation may be free to live righteously. But it is self-delusion and folly to think that one can lead a dissolute life and raise one's children to be good and happy; they will usually turn out to be hypocrites or tormented.

Martin Buber

Almost all our faults are more pardonable than the methods to which we resort to hide them.

François de La Rochefoucauld

And ofttimes excusing of a fault
Doth make the fault the worse by the excuse.

William Shakespeare

⁘

"O my God, guard my tongue from evil and my lips from deceitful words" (Gates of Prayer).

Keep me from following the crowd, when I know it is bent on dishonest gain, and keep me from falling victim to my own appetites, when others must pay for what I take without their knowing. So often I hear untruth: let me not pass it on to others; so often I hear gossip whose truth I cannot judge: keep me from going about as a talebearer among my people. Let no harmful word or deed come from me, but let my words and my other actions be only such that add to the peace and well-being of my community.

Jewish folktale

A man who had told many malicious untruths about a Rebbe was finally overcome by remorse. He went to the Rabbi and begged his forgiveness. The Rebbe cheerfully forgave him, but this did not altogether ease the man's conscience.

Rebbe, he pleaded, tell me how I can make amends for the wrongs I have done.

The Rebbe sighed. Take two pillows, go into the public square, and there cut the pillows open. Then wave them in the air. Then come back.

Quickly the penitent went home, got two pillows and a knife, hastened to the square, cut the pillows open, waved them in the air, and hurried back to the Rebbe's chambers. I did just what you said, Rebbe!

Good! Now go back to the square . . .

Yes?

. . . and collect all your feathers.

Ralph Waldo Emerson

In this kingdom of illusions we grope eagerly for stays and foundations. There is none but a strict and faithful dealing at home and a severe barring out of all duplicity or illusion there. Whatever games are played with us, we must play no games with ourselves, but deal in our privacy with the last honesty and truth. I look upon the simple and childish virtues of veracity and honesty as the root of all that is sublime in character. Speak as you think, be what you are, pay your debts of all kinds. . . . At the top or bottom of all illusions, I set the cheat which still leads us to work and live for appearances; in spite of our conviction, in all sane hours, that it is what we really are that avails, with friends, with strangers, and with fate or fortune.

⁘

Shabbat

I am thankful that I have had teachers who reveled in seeking out the truth, without or despite fear and discomfort. I have learned something from them, and hope I may continue to hold them before my mind's eye as I go my way. I am grateful for all who by their honest thought blazed a trail for me to follow.

What? Pass a law against counterfeit money? You must be a scoundrel indeed if you need such a law to keep you honest!

Solomon ha-Cohen

Spend your time in nothing which you know must be repented of; in nothing on which you might not pray for the blessing of God; in nothing which you could not review with a quiet conscience on your dying bed; in nothing which you might not safely and properly be doing if death should surprise you in the act.

Richard Baxter

There are many ways to offend against truth. One way is simply to deny it: the way of the liar. . . . Another way is to keep silence when the truth should be spoken: the way of the coward. . . . At the other end is the cruel use of truth, which involves harshly and unfeelingly proclaiming the truth when silence is clearly the better part: the way of the oaf or of the insensitive True Believer. . . . Another assault on truth, common enough, is made by twisting, distorting, and holding back the little truths in order to serve the large, capital 'T' Truth. Here is the way of the propagandist . . . who lies for truth. . . .

John Cogley

49 *Love*

The Week of Ki Teitzei
Deuteronomy 21:10–25:19

The Sidra *Ki Teitzei* restates many of the Torah's laws, and it gives us some new ones. In chapter 24 the Sidra speaks of marriage and married love. A man who marries is exempt from military duty the first year of his marriage. Moses says: *He shall be free at home one year, to be happy with the wife whom he has married* (24:5). Our Torah reading focuses on the love of husband and wife, but the Torah knows that love has many faces, and this week we will consider how love is more than one thing.

Sunday

⁘

You touch me with Your love, and in Your compassion walk with me on the path of my life. I cannot be where You are not, and in Your presence my life is true and filled with hope. Even in deep darkness, when I know I am loved, I see Your light. Then I find comfort and am restored.

Talmud

Rabbi Simeon ben Elazar said:
Why do out of fear
When you can do out of love?
They taught in his name:
Love makes you disregard your self-regard.

C. S. Lewis

Do you not know how it is with love? First comes delight; then pain; then fruit. And then there is joy of the fruit, but that is different again from the first delight. And mortal lovers must not try to remain at the first step: for lasting passion is the dream of a harlot and from it we awake in despair. You must not try to keep the raptures: they have done their work. Manna kept, is worms.

Love is . . . not . . . necessarily . . . a rational choice, but rather a willingness to be present to others without pretense or guile.

Carter Hayward

•⁘•

Monday

Loving God, how much I need the balm of friendship and the warmth of understanding! How greatly I need to be needed and cherished! Let me know, therefore, the joy of love given and received.

When I feel lonely and forsaken, let the faith that You are with me give me strength, and the solace of friendship bring me courage. Keep me from imagined hurts, from seeing only foes where friends are to be found. And give me insight into my own heart, that I may uproot my weaknesses. Help me to be patient when I am misunderstood, and quick to forgive hurts. As a friend to others, may I neither judge them too harshly, nor slavishly follow them in paths that are not mine. And as we walk through life together, let me and my dear ones go with that integrity which leads to peace, that love which brings harmony and joy, that regard whose fruit is enduring friendship.

cs / On the Doorposts of Your House

It is written (Proverbs 27:19): *As in water face answers to face, so the heart of one to another.* Why does the verse speak of water rather than of a mirror?

We see our reflection in water only when we bend close to it; so, too, your heart must lean down to another's; then it will see itself in the other's heart.

Chasidic

If a woman told us that she loved flowers and we saw that she forgot to water them we would not believe in her "love" for flowers. Love is the active concern for the life and growth of that which we love.

Erich Fromm

Tuesday

⁘

James R. Scher

Whenever two people begin
to write
Their lives' poem
On a single leaf,
Of hammered paper,
The angels sing,
And the ends of the universe,
Bright with stars,
Move somehow closer.
So
Their joy together
Eternally
Becomes
God's smile.

cs / Chasidic

Love your neighbor as yourself; I am the Eternal One (Leviticus 19:18). Rabbi Israel Isaac of Alexander said: God is saying: Love your neighbor as yourself, and include Me. I, too, am your neighbor.

Christopher Morley

If one were given five minutes' warning before sudden death, five minutes to say what it had all meant to us, every telephone booth would be occupied by people trying to call up other people to stammer that they loved them.

Erich Fromm

Why is spontaneous activity the answer to the problem of freedom? . . . Love is the foremost component of such spontaneity; not love as dissolution of the self in another person, not love as the possession of another person, but love as spontaneous affirmation of others, as the union of individuals with others on the basis of the preservation of the individual self. The dynamic quality of love lies in this very polarity; that it springs from the need of overcoming separateness, that it leads to oneness—and yet that individuality is not eliminated.

One thing today I ask of myself, O God: that I not neglect to show my love. Strangely, I can think of many reasons to live so far inside (or outside) myself that the deep love I feel will stay that way—deep inside. There is my work, and my busy-ness even when I am not working. And then I may be tired. Or something may have annoyed me. Or I may feel hurt and determined to wait to be told I'm loved, before I offer my own words. From all these, O God, deliver me today.

Chasidic / cs

Rabbi Pinchas of Koretz said: When someone despises you and injures you, strengthen yourself and love that person more than before. Through such love you [may] cause that person to turn. Therefore one should also love those who are evil, hating only their evil deeds.

Max Ehrmann

Love someone—in God's name
love someone—for this is
the bread of the inner life, without
which a part of you will
starve and die; and though you
feel you must be stern,
even hard, in your life of affairs,
make for yourself at least
a little corner, somewhere in the
great world, where you may
unbosom and be kind.

Chasidic

Rabbi Shmelke of Nikolsburg said: You sometimes will inadvertently hit yourself with your own hand. Are you going to punish yourself for being careless, and so add to your pain? Your neighbor, whose soul is one with yours, may hurt you out of a lack of understanding. If you strike back, you are adding to your pain.

⁘

There may come a time when I will lose the one I most love and care for: What will I say then, and what will I do? What do I do now, with the sense that time will run out on our life? Just to think of this turns my knees to water. "You'll get over it"—but will I? Will I really? No, I won't. So many questions. Perhaps it's not answers I need, O God. Help me.

Moses ibn Ezra

When we love, we are blind to the faults of those we love; when we hate, we are blind to their virtues.

Thornton Wilder

This assumption that she need look for no more devotion now that her beauty had passed proceeded from the fact that she had never realized any love save love as passion. Such love, though it expends itself in generosity and thoughtfulness, though it give birth to visions and to great poetry, remains among the sharpest expressions of self-interest. Not until it has passed through a long servitude, through its own self-hatred, through mockery, through great doubts, can it take its place among the loyalties. Many who have spent a lifetime in it can tell us less of love than the child that lost a dog yesterday.

François de La Rochefoucauld

There are two kinds of faithfulness in love: one is based on forever finding new things to love in the loved one; the other is based on our pride in being faithful.

Chasidic

When Rabbi Eleazar of Kosnitz, the son of Rabbi Moshe, the son of the Maggid of Kosnitz, was young, he was a guest in the house of Rabbi Naftali of Ropshitz. They were standing in a room where the curtains had been drawn, and he looked at them with surprise. When his host asked him the cause of his surprise, he said: If you want people to look in, why the curtain? If you don't, why the window?

Rabbi Naftali then said: And what is the answer, do you think?

When you want someone you love to look in, said the young rabbi, you draw aside the curtain.

⁘

Friday

O God, let me love without asking for greater reward than I get from loving with all my heart and soul; for at my best, at least, I know that there is no greater reward than to love without reservation. So let me not attach conditions.

A love that depends on one thing lasts only as long as that thing. *Mishnah*

Love that does not depend on a particular thing never dies away.

What sort of love depends on a particular thing? The love of Amnon and Tamar (II Samuel 13:15).

What sort of love does not depend on a particular thing? The love of David and Jonathan (I Samuel 18:1).

The Magelnitzer Rebbe, who had a low opinion of the Kotzker Rebbe, heard that the Vorker Rebbe was a frequent companion of the Kotzker. He asked him once: What reason have you for liking the Kotzker? I love him without a reason, said the Vorker, and as you know, such a love lasts forever. *Chasidic*

Let grace and goodness be the principal lodestone of thy affections. For love which hath ends, will have an end; whereas that which is founded on true virtue, will always continue. *John Dryden*

⁘

Shabbat

The peace of Shabbat is something I carry within me, a layer of my consciousness that can rise to the top when I call it up. And loving, too, is part of me. I can call it up today. But what I ask, O God, is an even greater gift: Let the love within me need no calling; let it well up in me as easily as my breath.

Love that does not include reproof is not love. *Midrash*

Aldous Huxley

"When we dote upon the perfections and beauties of some one creature, we do not love that too much, but other things too little. Never was anything in this world loved too much, but many things have been loved in a false way, and all in too short a measure." Traherne might have added (what many poets and novelists have remarked) that, when "we dote upon the perfections and beauties of some one creature," we frequently find ourselves moved to love other creatures. Moreover, to be in love is, in many cases, to have achieved a state of being, in which it becomes possible to have direct intuition of the essentially lovely nature of ultimate reality. "What a world would this be, were everything beloved as it ought to be!" For many people, everything is beloved as it ought to be only when they are in love with "some one creature." The cynical wisdom of the folk affirms that love is blind. But in reality, perhaps, the blind are those who are not in love and who therefore fail to perceive how beautiful the world is and how adorable.

Marcel Proust

What we suppose to be our love or our jealousy is never a single, continuous and indivisible passion. It is composed of an infinity of successive loves, of different jealousies, each of which is ephemeral although by their uninterrupted multiplicity they give us the impression of continuity, the illusion of unity.

50 *Teaching*

The Week of Ki Tavo
Deuteronomy 26:1–29:8

The Sidra *Ki Tavo* (Deuteronomy 27) describes a ceremony that Moses enjoined upon the people, to be enacted when they entered the promised land. They were to set up large stones and carve the Teaching on them, so that future generations might be able to see them and learn the Teaching for themselves. Moses says: *You shall inscribe upon the stones all the words of this Teaching very clearly* (27:8).

Thus the reading anticipates that the time to understand, to see, and to hear what will be taught is always today. The Teaching is not for one generation only, but for all time.

Sunday

Gates of Prayer

Eternal our God, make the words of Your Torah sweet to me, that I may be a lover of Your name and a student of Your Torah. Praised be the Teacher of Torah.

Talmud

Rav Huna's son refused to study with Rav Chisda, who was known to be a great teacher.

Rav Huna asked his son: How is it that you do not go to learn from Rav Chisda?

His son replied: I have gone to him. I saw that he does not teach Torah. He talks only of worldly things like eating and excreting, and how one should act in connection with such matters.

That is true, said his father. Rav Chisda does teach of worldly things. He speaks of the life of God's creatures, and you disdain him! This is our world and Rav Chisda is just the one you should be learning from.

George H. Palmer

You put yourself into people; they touch other people; these others still, and so you go on working forever.

Chasidic

Rabbi Aaron of Karlin once came to the city where little Mordecai was growing up. His father brought the boy to the visiting rabbi and complained that he did not persevere in his studies. Leave the boy with me for a while, said Rabbi Aaron. When they were alone he took the child to his heart. Silently he held him until the father returned.

I have given him a good talking-to, he said. From now on he will be diligent.

Mordecai later became the rabbi of Lechovitz.

Monday

To paraphrase a Yiddish saying, I could teach many tunes but just now I have a sore throat. May I refrain from teaching those who know better than I how to live their own lives.

James Truslow Adams

There are obviously two educations. One should teach us how to make a living, and the other how to live.

Period of Mishnah / cs

Ben Azzai said:
They take you for a fool:
You humble yourself,
eat carobs,
sit and keep watch at the doors of the wise—
but in the end they find all wisdom within you.

Harry Emerson Fosdick

Some parents say that religion is an intimate, personal matter, which every child has a right to choose for himself [herself], and they propose to leave the child neutral while he [she] is growing up, and then let him [her] freely select his [her] own religion. Even if we try we cannot keep the child neutral religiously. Religion is not an addition to life, but the very climate that pervades the whole of living. As soon as the child is born in any home, it begins creating in him [her] a spiritual climate teaching him [her] basic relations to life, feelings about life, which inevitably enter into the very substance of any religion that he [she] will ever possess.

✧ Tuesday

What have I learned, what do I know? What have I got to teach? Keep me from false humility and self-doubt. Let me teach what I can, and if anyone, young or old, gleans something from my life and thought, I will have been a true teacher.

They asked Dov Baer of Mezeritch: There are many teachers, and each has a particular way of teaching Torah. Which is best?

After a while he replied: The great teacher teaches as a flower gives off its fragrance—you must be a voice for your teaching, not the other way around.

As soon as you hear yourself talking, stop.

Chasidic / cs

The first question written on the blackboard was: Which of the required readings in this course did you find least interesting? Then, after members of the class had had ten minutes in which to expatiate on what was certainly to many a congenial topic, he wrote the second question: To what defect in yourself do you attribute this lack of interest?

Joseph Wood Krutch

The true aim of everyone who aspires to be a teacher should be, not to impart his [or her] own opinions, but to kindle minds.

Frederick W. Robertson

✧ Wednesday

Someone said, "The most certain way to hide from others the limits of our knowledge is not to go beyond them." He must have been thinking about me. Help me to think about this when I undertake to enlighten someone else.

Since you are under an obligation to do good yourself and help others do the same, it is not enough to see to it that you yourself walk in right paths; you must also show others a right path.

Midrash

That is why Hillel says, *If I am only for myself, what am I?* What have I accomplished? Have I fulfilled my obligation? Not yet—for I must also try to teach others a right way.

Albert Einstein Education is that which remains when one has forgotten everything learned in school.

George Santayana A child educated only at school is an uneducated child.

Thursday

⁘

What I have learned is not mine but belongs to all, and I would teach it if only I knew how and to whom. What I have learned is a secret I would share if only I could. Let me learn to teach with sincerity, to share without arrogance or condescension.

Israel Knox There is a beautiful saying that comes to us from Hasidic lore: *There is only one thing that is whole in the entire world, and that is a broken heart.* Reflect for a moment: here is a world that has not yet been redeemed, a world in which there is tragedy at the root of things. How could a moral and sensitive man or woman walk about with a heart that is not broken? The broken-hearted—paradoxically and profoundly—are the whole-hearted. And the task of education, especially of Jewish education, should be to break your heart. Unless it breaks your heart it is a false education, a pseudo-education. The gift of education will be a heart that is whole.

Henri Frédéric Amiel The highest function of a teacher consists not so much in imparting knowledge as in stimulating the pupil in its love and pursuit.

Henry David Thoreau One young man of my acquaintance, who has inherited some acres, told me that he thought he should live as I did, *if he had the means.* I would not have anyone adopt *my* mode of living on any account; for, beside that before he has fairly learned it, I may have found out another for myself, I desire that there may be as many different persons in the world as possible. . . .

Friday

Teach me to be diligent but not impatient,
Teach me to be persistent but not obstinate,
Teach me to be enthusiastic but not fanatic.
Then, O God, I may be worthy to teach.

The disciples of the Baal Shem Tov heard that a certain man was a sage. Some of them were anxious to see and hear his "Torah." The master gave them permission to go, but first they asked him: How will we know that he is a true teacher? The Baal Shem replied: Ask him for advice on how to pray and learn without distraction. If he answers, you will know there is nothing to him.

Chasidic

Whenever I have been afraid that my work was so personal that no one could understand it, everybody did understand it. When I tried to speak for others, they didn't know what I was talking about.

Mark Van Doren

Advice is like snow; the softer it falls, the longer it dwells upon, and the deeper it sinks into, the mind.

Samuel Taylor Coleridge

Shabbat

This day is a great teacher; may I be eager to learn. It teaches me the value of labor—and of rest; of Torah and its application in my weekday life; of companionship with loved ones, and, in prayer, of being alone with the Alone. May I always be open to the influence of this day, and find in it Your infinite presence endlessly teaching me to be human.

The Gerer Rebbe once studied with a man of great learning and intellectual agility. One time, as they were studying from the Talmud, the Gerer Rebbe noticed that a folio was missing from the volume. The other failed to notice this, and connected the previous page with what followed by a clever interpretation. The Gerer would no longer study with that man.

Chasidic

Unknown We owe our lives to our parents; but to our teachers we owe the knowledge of how to live.

John Ruskin Education does not mean teaching people what they do not know. It means teaching them to behave as they do not behave. It is not teaching the youth the shapes of letters and the tricks of numbers, and then leaving them to turn their arithmetic to roguery, and their literature to lust. It means, on the contrary, training them into the perfect exercise and royal countenance of their bodies and souls. It is a painful, continual and difficult work, to be done by kindness, by watching, by warning, by precept and by praise, but above all—by example.

51 *Choosing*

The Week of Nitzavim
Deuteronomy 29:9–30:20

In the Sidra *Nitzavim*, Moses nears the end of his oration, and he reminds the people once more of the great choice that is before them: *I call heaven and earth to witness before you this day, that I have set before you life and death, blessing and curse; choose life, then, for yourselves and your children* (30:19). And immediately before, he had encouraged them: *For this commandment that I enjoin upon you this day is not too difficult for you, nor is it beyond your reach* (30:11).

Some days we see ourselves as free choosers; other days we feel the constraints of nature and circumstance so tight, it seems we cannot choose to do other than what we do.

Sunday

Seek the Eternal, your God, whom you shall find, if you seek with all your heart and soul (Deuteronomy 4:29).

We can choose the way of our life. Not in all things of life have we a choice: fortune, fate or circumstance have a hand in the succession of events that make up my life; and even in what I am, environment or heredity, or both, have had a share, limiting my capacities and powers, and so putting bounds to the possibilities of achievement. But life presents to every person the power to choose how one shall live.

Liberal Jewish Prayer Book I / cs

The sages would say:

Everything is in the hands of Heaven, except the fear of Heaven.

Talmud

Talmud If you come to defile yourself, you are permitted; if you come to purify yourself, you are helped.

Monday

⁘

My life is the sum of my choices, small and large, but mostly small. O God, keep me from thinking that this or that small decision will not matter, that no one will notice or care. Make *me* notice, make *me* care, so that I take my choices seriously.

Menachem ben Solomon Meiri O the seas that have run dry! O the stones that have brought forth water! Your ancestors may have been sages, they may have been illiterate: which one you will be depends on you.

Edith Hamilton When the freedom they wished for most was freedom from responsibility, then Athens ceased to be free and was never free again.

Midrash We are led along our chosen path.

Dag Hammarskjöld The most dangerous of all moral dilemmas: when we are obliged to conceal truth in order to help the truth to be victorious. If this should at any time become our duty in the role assigned us by fate, how strait must be our path at all times, if we are not to perish.

Period of Mishnah They drink the dregs and throw out the wine.

Tuesday

⁘

I have to remember today that I can not be responsible for decisions made by others for me; and I have to remember that I am responsible for the decisions I will make—but not for the decisions of others. Neither they nor I will receive reward or blame for decisions we do not make.

The real moral peril consists not so much in choosing what in our best judgment seems to be the lesser evil; such choice is entailed by the very process of living. The real moral peril consists in trying to make a virtue out of necessity, in converting the lesser evil we choose, merely because we choose it, into a positive good.

Will Herberg

You cannot have power for good
without having power for evil too.
Even mother's milk nourishes murderers
as well as heroes.

George Bernard Shaw

We are not born all at once, but by bits. The body first, and the spirit later; and the birth and growth of the spirit, in those who are attentive to their own inner life, are slow and exceedingly painful. Our mothers are racked with the pains of our physical birth; we ourselves suffer the longer pains of our spiritual growth.

Mary Antin

⁘

Wednesday

Save me from too much thought of reward or blame when I decide what to do. Keep my thought on doing the right thing as well as I can, insofar as I can see it. Then let me go forward with a clear head.

If we cannot do what we will, we must will what we can.

Yiddish proverb

It is perfectly possible for you and me to purchase intellectual peace at the price of intellectual death. The world is not without refuges of this description; nor is it wanting in persons who seek their shelter, and try to persuade others to do the same. The unstable and the weak have yielded and will yield to this persuasion, and they to whom repose is sweeter than the truth. But I would exhort you to refuse the offered shelter, and to scorn the base repose; to accept, if the choice be forced upon you, commotion before stagnation, the leap of the torrent before the stillness of the swamp.

John Tyndall

Ralph Waldo Emerson God offers to every mind its choice between truth and repose. Take which you please—you can never have both.

Samuel Johnson All theory is against freedom of will; all experience for it.

Thursday

Even when it seems that I have to choose what I choose, and that I haven't freely chosen, I must accept the fact that I was the one who made the choice. Were I to win the lottery with such a "forced" choice I likely would keep the proceeds. So if the choice I make turns out to hurt me, let me accept it as though my choice had been truly free.

Mishnah

Rabbi Akiba said:
All is foreseen, yet free choice is given.
The world is given the benefit of the doubt.
And everything depends on this:
Is more good done, or more evil?

William James If your heart does not *want* a world of moral reality, your head will assuredly never make you believe in one.

cs / Chasidic This world is like a concert-hall, filled with many instruments and musical scores. Each of us can select our own instrument and sing our own song. This gives pleasure to God, our Maker.

Russell Herman Conwell

I ask not for a larger garden,
But for finer seeds.

Friday

Do I always know who has made the choices that have put me where I am today? Some were made before I was born, others may have been made across the continent. All the choices in the world come together, somehow, and bring me to the present moment, to my particular time and place as a particular person. And I am always choosing. Help me, O God, to find my own good in choices that will be also good for others.

Rabbi Samuel Kariver said: Do not hate those who offend you, simply because you have not done the same. If they had your nature, they too might not have sinned; if you were like them, you might have done as they have done. Our transgressions are not entirely freely chosen; often they depend on many other circumstances.

cs / Chasidic

One summer a college friend who had some sort of muscle paralysis decided to sell books, and he began by visiting the home of the college president. The wife of the president informed him that they did not need any books. As he turned to leave, she saw the limp in his walk and said: Oh, I am so sorry! I did not know you were lame. The young man, who was not seeking pity, bristled all over; and the woman, realizing that she had perhaps said the wrong thing, hastened to add, I did not mean to imply anything except admiration, but doesn't being lame rather color your life? *Yes,* he replied, *but thank God I can choose the color.*

Frank A. Court

If we must accept Fate, we are not less compelled to affirm liberty, the significance of the individual, the grandeur of duty, the power of character.

Ralph Waldo Emerson

⁘

Shabbat

I have heard it said that "never in this world can hatred be stilled by hatred." As I think of this I realize how, when I am self-possessed, my response to thoughtlessness can be thoughtful, my response to folly, wisdom. Teach me to rule myself and my responses.

Whenever the Chasidim would enter into competition, each claiming to have the most trouble and to have endured the greatest suffering [and had therefore earned the right to be the first to complain], the Rebbe would tell them the story of the Tree of Sorrows.

Chasidic

On Judgment Day, said he, I, like everyone else, will be

allowed to hang all my unhappiness on a branch of the great Tree of Sorrows. Then, when I have found a limb from which my sorrows can dangle, I will walk slowly around that tree.

Do you know what I will do on that walk? I will search for a set of sufferings I might prefer to those I have hung on the tree.

But search as I may, I will not find any. In the end, like everyone else, I will freely choose to reclaim my own personal set of sorrows rather than that of another.

I will leave that tree wiser than when I got there.

I will be ready to turn my back on the Tree of Sorrows and walk toward the Tree of Life.

Learned Hand

It is enough that we set out to form the motley of our life into some form of our own choosing; when we do the performance is itself the wage.

John Greenleaf Whittier

The tissue of Life to be
We weave with colors of our own,
And in the field of Destiny
We reap as we have sown.

52 *Learning*

The Week of Vayeilech
Deuteronomy 31

In the Sidra *Vayeilech* (Deuteronomy 31), Moses tells the people that because of his advanced age he can no longer lead them; Joshua will be his successor. To ensure that the Teaching will survive, Moses writes it down and entrusts it to the priests and elders, ordering them to read it to the people every seventh year, so that all the people, young and old, may learn it: *that they may hear and learn . . .* (31:12).

This week's theme is fundamental. The child begins to learn from the moment of birth; some say, before birth.

⁘

Sunday

cs / Gates of Prayer

Trusting in You, I seek Your guidance, as did my fathers and mothers, whom You taught the laws of life. As You taught them, so teach me. Enlighten my mind and strengthen my heart, so that I may joyfully cling to Your commandments. Enable me to learn, to understand, and to fulfill the teaching that You send to me through the pages of tradition and through the experiences of my life.

Chasidic

They asked Rabbi Levi Yitzchak of Berditchev: Why does every tractate of the Talmud begin on the second page?

He replied: However much we learn, we should always remember that we have not even reached to the first page.

Mishnah

There are four styles of learning:

Quick to learn and quick to forget: the gain is canceled by the loss.

Slow to learn and slow to forget: the loss is canceled by the gain.

Quick to learn and slow to forget: a sage.

Slow to learn and quick to forget: a misfortune.

Mishnah

Here are four who learn:
a sponge, a funnel, a strainer, and a sieve.
A sponge absorbs good and bad alike.
A funnel takes in and pours out.
A strainer passes the wine and keeps the dregs.
A sieve passes the chaff and keeps the wheat.

Monday

It seems to me that lessons come at me day after day, but I am not always quick to understand what they are trying to teach me. So I ask for understanding, and I pray not only to learn, but to learn how much I have to learn.

Mishnah / cs

Your learning is not a crown to wear,
nor a spade to dig with.
And in the end, is it your learning that matters,
or is it not rather your doing?

Henry David Thoreau

A truly good book teaches me better than to read it. I must soon lay it down and commence living on its hint. . . . What I began by reading I must finish by acting.

Zen

Nan-in, a Japanese master during the Meiji era, received a university professor who came to inquire about Zen.

Nan-in served tea. He poured his visitor's cup full, and then kept on pouring.

The professor watched the overflow until he no longer could restrain himself. It is overfull. No more will go in!

Like this cup, Nan-in said, you are full of your own opinions and speculations. How can I show you Zen unless you first empty your cup?

We should rather examine, who is better learned, than who is more learned.

Michel de Montaigne

∴

Tuesday

Within the word *learn* is the word *earn*. Help me to penetrate the meaning of this lesson, to realize that nothing important is learned without an effort. Then I may earn what I want to learn.

Curiosity is,
in great and generous minds,
the first passion and the last.

Samuel Johnson

No one who wants to learn should think, *How can a fool like me ask questions of a brilliant sage? I neither know nor understand enough to ask*. Feeling like this, how will you ever acquire wisdom? This is the meaning of the maxim, "Ask like a fool and save like the generous."

Jonah ben Abraham

Rabbi Ber of Radeshitz once met an old man. Recognizing him as a boyhood friend, he asked: How are you doing?

The old man answered: Berel, Berel, I will tell you. What one does not work out for oneself, one does not have.

The Rabbi was struck by the response, and thereafter repeated it frequently to his Chasidim.

Chasidic

∴

Wednesday

I can readily agree that learning does not and should not end with the end of my schooling. But I have only said it. Now I must prove it, and acknowledge one question that is always before me: When are you going to act on what you say you have learned?

Elisha ben Abuyah said:

Learning as a child: what is that like? Ink inscribed on new paper. Learning in old age: what is that like? Ink inscribed on blotted paper.

Mishnah

Mishnah Rabbi Yosé bar Judah of Kefar Habavli said:

Who learns from the young is like one who eats unripe grapes and drinks wine straight from the vat. Who learns from elders is like one who eats ripe grapes and drinks vintage wine.

Mishnah Rabbi Judah the Prince said:

Do not look at the flask but at what it contains. There are new flasks full of old wine, and old ones that don't even contain new wine.

Midrash Learning when young has two advantages: it is easier to impress knowledge on the mind, and one has time left in which to teach others. Learning when old has the correlative disadvantages: it is harder to absorb learning, and there is little time left for teaching others.

Thursday

⁘

Today I need to be attentive to my experiences, to listen with special care to the words others say to me, so that I really learn what they mean, what they are giving me, and what they want from me. And let them learn from this how much I care for them.

Midrash *On this day Israel came to Mount Sinai* (Exodus 19:1). Why on this day? When you learn Torah, do not let its commands seem old to you. Regard them as though the Torah were given this day. Hence it says, "on this day," and not, "on that day."

Chasidic "All these words" (Exodus 19:7)—and only these words! Moses wanted to reveal more [Torah] to the people, but he was not permitted. For it was God's will that the people make an effort on their own. Moses was to say just these words to them, no more and no less, so that they might feel: Something is hidden here, and we must strive to discover it for ourselves. That is why we read (Exodus 19:7): *And he set before them all these words.*

My doctrine shall drop as the rain (Deuteronomy 32:2). Rabbi Pinchas of Koretz said: Rain falls on many kinds of plants, and each grows according to its own nature. So let all learn the Teaching; all will profit according to their own ability.

Chasidic

⁘

Friday

There are ways of learning that surprise. I learn from animals, I learn from small children, I learn from hurt, I learn from joy. All the world is a school, if only I will let myself be taught.

Who is wise? One who learns from everyone.

Mishnah

As elders would feel no shame to ask the young for water, so should they feel no shame to ask the young to teach them a chapter, verse, or even a letter of Torah.

Midrash

We think so because other people all think so;
Or because—or because—after all, we do think so;
Or because we were told so, and think we must think so;
Or because we once thought so, and think we still think so;
Or because having thought so, we think we *will* think so.

Henry Sidgwick

A holy man once had an apprentice who worked very hard for him. In fact, the holy man only kept him because of his great effort, since otherwise he thought the apprentice was rather stupid.

One day, a rumor spread that the apprentice had walked on water, crossing a river as easily as if he were crossing a street. The master questioned him: Is this true? Can you really cross the river by walking on the water?

Ah, yes, the apprentice replied, thanks to you. Every step of the way I repeat your saintly name and that is what holds me up.

The holy man thought to himself: If it is in my name that this miracle occurs, I must possess power I did not suspect. But, after all, I have never tried it.

Sheldon Kopp

So, the master hurried to the river, stepped off the bank unto the water, chanting with complete faith: *Me, me, me.* And he sank.

Shabbat

❖

I do not have to go far afield to find teachers who have something rich and valuable for me. This Shabbat speaks to me of silence, the silence of places, and the silence within me, to which I am invited to listen: a still, small voice will speak, when I grow quiet enough, and when my "I" is willing to stop shouting long enough to begin to listen. Teach me the blessed silence that Shabbat can bring to me, O God who speaks within the quiet soul.

Nachmanides When you rise from your book, probe into what you have learned, to discover whether there is in it anything you can translate into reality.

Mishnah

Make your home a meeting-place for the wise.
Sit at their feet in the dust.
With thirst drink in their words.

Talmud Rabbi Nachman son of Isaac said: Why are the words of the Torah compared to a tree, as it is said (Proverbs 3:18): *It is a tree of life to those who hold fast to it?* To tell you that as a small log may set fire to a large log, so do the lesser scholars sharpen the wits of the greater. And Rabbi Chanina said the same: Much have I learned from my teachers, and more from my colleagues than from my teachers, and from my students most of all.

Chasidic They asked Levi Yitzchak of Berditchev: Why does every tractate of the Babylonian Talmud always begin with page 2?

He said: However much we learn, we must remember that we have not even reached the first page.

53 *Perseverance*

The Week of Ha'azinu
Deuteronomy 32

The Sidra *Ha'azinu* (Deuteronomy 32) is taken up for the most part by a long poem in which Moses describes God's care for Israel, pointing out that God has been patient with this people through all its troubles and failings. The divine perseverance is to be emulated. Moses then says: *Take to heart all the words with which I have warned you this day. Enjoin them upon your children, that they may observe faithfully all the words of this Teaching. For this is not a trifling thing for you: it is your very life . . .* (32:46–47).

In Proverbs 16 we read that *the just fall seven times, and rise up again. . . .* And we who dare not call ourselves "just" may wish to add: *not only the just.*

⁂ Sunday

There are the days I want to quit, and
there are the days whose coming I dread.
There are days—
I can imagine disasters that never will be, and
gains I might never enjoy.
Make me
strong enough to lift this load,
faithful enough to carry it till the day's end,
wise enough not to carry tomorrow's load
today.

Rabbi Yerachmiel said: At first every way of reaching your goal seems endless, and the goal distant—high as the heavens above; *Chasidic / cs* but after laboring to achieve, the way is easier and the goal is near. Then you will be shown new goals, higher still—higher than the heavens you have already reached—and then, will you give up? No, for you have already achieved. So begin in a modest way; work hard to go higher and higher; and before the end you will have attained undreamt-of heights.

Solomon Schechter The realization of great ideas . . . is not accomplished without travail and woe, deep sorrow and repeated disappointment.

Epictetus Sickness is a hindrance to the body, but not to the will, unless the will consent. Lameness is a hindrance to the leg, but not to the will. Say this to yourself at each event that happens, for you shall find that though it hinders something else it will not hinder you. . . .

Monday

"I tried it, but it didn't work." How many times this has happened, O God! I am fed up with the struggle to get it right. It's as though there were a demon abroad who keeps thwarting me! And yet: Let's try it one more time.

cs "If I persist in my desire to get Heaven to accept my request, I will succeed," said the Tzanzer Rebbe. "But I must use wisdom in my persistence" (Chasidic). *And, one might add, wisdom in what I request.*

Saint Francis of Sales Have patience with all things, but chiefly have patience with yourself. Do not lose courage in considering your own imperfections, but instantly set about remedying them—every day begin the task anew.

Albert Einstein . . . Knowledge of truth alone does not suffice; on the contrary, this knowledge must continually be renewed by ceaseless effort, if it is not to be lost. It resembles a statue of marble which stands in the desert and is continuously threatened with burial by the shifting sands. The hands of service must ever be at work, in order that the marble continue lastingly to shine in the sun.

⁘

Tuesday

"Who said you have to finish the job? But you're not allowed to stop working at it!" Isn't this what You teach me? After all, You did Your part in the work of creation . . . and left a little to me and my kind. . . .

cs / Chasidic

The Baal Shem Tov said: The Talmud says that of the fifty gates of understanding, forty-nine were opened to Moses. But since we always aspire to know more, how did Moses continue, after he had reached the fiftieth gate? When Moses found that the fiftieth gate could not be opened by the human mind, he stood fast in faith, and returned in meditation to deepen the knowledge he *could* acquire.

Katherine Logan

To have faith where you cannot see; to be willing to work on in the dark; to be conscious of the fact that, so long as you strive for the best, there are better things on the way, this in itself is success.

Elbert Hubbard

Genius is only the power of making continuous efforts. The line between failure and success is so fine that we scarcely know when we pass it: so fine that we are often on the line and do not know it. How many a man has thrown up his hands at a time when a little more effort, a little more patience, would have achieved success. As the tide goes clear out, so it comes clear in. In business, sometimes, prospects may seem darkest when really they are on the turn. A little more persistence, a little more effort, and what seemed hopeless may turn to glorious success. There is no failure except in no longer trying. There is no defeat except from within, no really unsurmountable barrier save our own inherent weakness of purpose.

Wednesday

⁘

There is the frustration of knowing that I will never accomplish all that I set out to do. And so sometimes I am tempted to give it all up. The ideals I cherish for the world—peace and contentment, justice for all, and food for the hungry—likewise seem so distant of realization. God, at such a moment as this, remind me to do what I can, for that is something I can keep on doing.

Moses ibn Ezra You will not attain what you love if you do not endure much that you hate, and you will not be freed from what you hate if you will not endure much from what you love.

Charles R. Brown Is anything vital ever accomplished without persistent effort? Farmers plow and sow, and keep on plowing and sowing. Miners dig, and keep on digging, deeper and deeper. Musicians practice and keep on practicing. Scholars study, and keep on studying. And so must we—if we would know how prayer purifies, fortifies, enriches the inner life, we will have to persist.

Henry Ward Beecher The difference between perseverance and obstinacy is, that one often comes from a strong will, and the other from a strong won't.

Talmud How can you compare a hundred efforts to understand with a hundred and one?

Thursday

⁘

No, I won't always have the satisfaction of seeing a completed piece of work, even when I set out upon it with high hopes. On the other hand, I am alive to the degree that I still have work to do. And what a gift it is to be alive, and still to be making plans and working away at their accomplishment.

Max Arzt Worry has been defined as the act of borrowing trouble from the future for present-day consumption; and courage has been defined as the act of borrowing hope from the future for present-day consumption. . . . One of the by-products of religious faith is the hopeful outlook described by Isaiah (26:3): *Those of steadfast mind, You keep in perfect peace because they trust in You.*

People spend their lives in anticipations, in determining to be vastly happy at some period or another, when they have time. But the present time has one advantage over every other: it is our own.

Charles C. Colton

We learn wisdom from failure much more than from success. We often discover what will do, by finding out what will not do; and probably he who never made a mistake never made a discovery.

Samuel Smiles

All the performances of human art, at which we look with praise and wonder, are instances of the resistless force of perseverance.

Ben Jonson

Friday

I have to get myself right, and it's taking an almighty long time! God of time and space, why is it so hard to change for the better? Why are the changes so slow to come, and so small? Couldn't You have made it a bit easier? I wish I could be sure that the struggle to improve is building my character, when often enough it feels as though it were tearing it down. What's that You said? You know I can do it, if only I'll keep on going just a few minutes longer?

A sage who was asked, Why are you wiser than your friends? replied, Because I spent more on oil than they on wine.

Solomon ibn Gabirol

There are two types of strength. There is the strength of the wind that sways the mighty oak, and there is the strength of the oak that withstands the power of the wind. There is the

Harold Phillips

strength of the locomotive that pulls the heavy train across the bridge, and there is the strength of the bridge that holds up the weight of the train. One is active strength, the other is passive strength. One is the power to keep going, the other is the power to keep still. One is the strength by which we overcome, the other is the strength by which we endure.

Robert Bolt

We speak of being anchored to our principles, but if the weather turns nasty you up with an anchor and let it down where there's less wind, and the fishing's better.

Polybius

Some . . . give up their designs when they have almost reached their goal; while others, on the contrary, obtain a victory by exerting, at the last moment, more vigorous efforts than before.

Shabbat

Eternal God, with Your encouragement I made it to Shabbat, and now I'm thinking: If I made it this far, I can keep going a little longer. And here is a day when I needn't struggle, when I can take a breather and be quiet. God, help me to see that what I do has a point and a use, even when it's hard to tell. Then, on Shabbat, I can let go and gain strength for the week to come.

Period of Mishnah

Until the age of forty, Rabbi Akiba could not read or write. One day, he saw how a stone had been worn away at a point where water from a spring had been dripping upon it, and as he recalled the saying: "Waters wear stones," he thought: If soft water can bore through a rock, surely Torah, which is like iron, should penetrate a tender mind. And he turned to study.

Jacob Riis

When nothing seems to help, I go and look at a stonecutter hammering away at his rock perhaps a hundred times without as much as a crack showing in it. Yet at the hundred and first blow it will split in two, and I know it was not that blow that did it—but all that had gone before.

C. S. Lewis

I heard in Addison's Walk a bird sing clear,
"This year the summer will come true. This year. This year.
"Winds will not strip the blossom from the apple trees
This year, nor want of rain destroy the peas.
"This year time's nature will no more defeat you,
Nor all the promised moments in their passing cheat you.
"This time they will not lead you round and back
To Autumn, one year older, by the well-worn track.
"This year, this year, as all these flowers foretell,
We shall escape the circle and undo the spell.
"Often deceived, yet open once again your heart,
Quick, quick, quick, quick!—the gates are drawn apart."

וזאת הברכה

54 *Humility*

The Week of V'zot ha-B'rachah
Deuteronomy 33:1–34:12

With the Sidra *V'zot ha-B'rachah* (Deuteronomy 33), we come to the end of the Torah cycle. Just before he dies, Moses characteristically speaks not of himself but of the people and their God, saying to them: *O Jeshurun, there is none like God . . .* (33:26). Thus Moses demonstrates at the end of his life that humility of which the Torah earlier spoke: *Now Moses was a very humble man, more so than any other man on earth* (Numbers 12:3).

There is of course no way one can claim to be humble; one can only *be* humble. This quality, humility, is not one we value much these days. Might it not be better if we did?

Sunday

Psalm 131

My heart is not proud, O God,
and my eyes are not haughty;
on things beyond my scope
no more I brood.
But I have calmed and quieted my soul,
like a child at its mother's breast;
my soul is like a comforted child.
O Israel, trust in God,
now and forever.

cs When I was very young I thought I could do anything; times came when it seemed I could do nothing. Keep from both of these errors.

This is what a pious man once said to the Baal Shem Tov: I have labored long and hard in the service of God, yet all my labors have not improved me. I am still an ordinary, ignorant person.

He answered: You have come to understand that you are ordinary and ignorant, and this is no small accomplishment.

Chasidic

Should we, then, always walk in meekness? No—there are moments when haughtiness becomes a duty. For when the Yetzer approaches and whispers in your ear that you are unworthy to fulfill the Law, you must say: *I am worthy.*

Chasidic

Monday

When I suddenly get a glimpse of myself as others must view me, I laugh! Give me this gift more often, O God, a perspective that keeps me from taking myself too seriously.

As water flows from the high ground and settles in the low, so are the words of Torah alive only in the humble.

Talmud

Do not put a crown on your own head; let others do it, as it is said (Proverbs 27:22), *Let another praise you and not your own mouth, a stranger and not your own lips.*

Period of Mishnah

When we see our own grotesqueries, how droll our ambitions are, how comical we are in almost all respects, we automatically become more sane, less self-centered, more humble, more wholesome. To laugh at ourselves we have to stand outside ourselves—and that is an immense benefit. Our puffed-up pride and our touchy self-importance vanish; a clean and sweet humility begins to take possession of us. We are on the way to growing a soul.

A. Powell Davies

They asked the Maggid of Zlotchov: All the commandments are written in the Torah. But humility, which is worth all the other virtues put together, is not given as a commandment. All we read about it is the words in praise of Moses, saying that he was

Chasidic

more humble than all other people. What is the meaning of this silence concerning humility?

He replied: If you were humble in order to keep a commandment, you would never attain to true humility. To think that humility is a commandment is the prompting of Satan, who bloats our hearts by telling us that we are learned and righteous and devout, masters in all good works, and worthy to think ourselves better than ordinary people. Satan then tells us that to think this way would be prideful and impious, since it is a commandment that we must be humble and see ourselves as on a par with others. So when we see humility as being a commandment, fulfilling it only feeds our pride all the more.

Tuesday

⁘

Again and again this vast universe reminds me how feeble my thought is, how fleeting my days. I know almost nothing, and am not likely to know much more when my time here is done. And yet, strangely enough, O God, my littleness is a comfort to me, more than it is a burden. Why that should be is another thing I don't know, but it is. . . .

cs / Talmud

When you humble yourself, God exalts you.
When you pursue greatness, greatness flies away.
When you fly from greatness, greatness seeks you out.
When you force the moment, the moment drives you back.
When you give way, the moment is yours.

Isaac Newton

I do not know what I may appear to the world; but to myself I seem to have been only like a boy playing on the seashore of knowledge; and diverting myself in now and then finding a smoother pebble or a prettier shell than ordinary, whilst the great ocean of truth lay all undiscovered before me.

Charles Haddon Spurgeon

The doorstep to the temple of wisdom is the knowledge of our own ignorance.

Pride is so anchored in the human heart that everyone, high or low, brags and looks for admirers. Even philosophers look for them. Those who write against it want to have the glory of having written well; and those who read it want the glory of having read it. I who write this have perhaps this desire, and perhaps so do those who will read it.

Blaise Pascal / cs

Wednesday

By no means do I always feel small. Most of the time I don't think about it at all, and then I fail at something, and it makes me feel not small but low, and angry at myself. Keep me from that kind of anger, O God; teach me to accept the fact that I'm imperfect, and always will be.

Once it happened that the arranger of the worship service called on Rabbi Akiba, a giant of his times, to stand up and read the Torah, but he did not stand up. When they had left the synagogue he calmed his disciples, saying: I assure you that it was not out of arrogance that I declined to stand up and read the Torah! Why, then? Because I had not prepared myself. His words astounded them.

Midrash

Rabbi Meir said:
Be humble in spirit before every person.
If you neglect Torah, many occasions of neglect will arise
  for you.
And if you labor in Torah, it has good wages for you.

Mishnah

We do not expect a vine to bear figs or an olive grapes, but when it comes to ourselves, if we do not possess the combined advantages of millionaire and scholar and general and philosopher, of the flatterer and the plain speaker, of the frugal and the extravagant, we calumniate ourselves and are irked with ourselves and despise ourselves as leading a drab and curtailed life.

Plutarch

Chasidic Rabbi Azriel Hurwitz, an opponent of the Seer of Lublin, once asked the Seer: How is it that so many flock to you? I am much more learned than you, yet they do not throng to me.

The Tzaddik answered: I too am astonished that so many should come to one as insignificant as I, to hear God's word, instead of looking for it to you whose learning moves mountains. Perhaps this is the reason: they come to me because I am astonished that they come, and they do not come to you, because you are astonished that they do not come.

Thursday

⁛

When someone speaks of being humble, O God, remind me to smile—but only inwardly. Why hurt his or her feelings? As for me, I have seen some humble people, and they all seem to have one thing in common—they don't know they're humble. Teach me to be humble enough, at least, not to boast of my humility.

Chasidic *Honor flees the one who pursues it, and pursues the one who flees it* (Talmud Erubin 13b). We know from the Talmud, a man said to Simcha Bunam, that honor runs after the one who flees honor. Well, I have always run away from honors, yet none have come after me!

The sage replied: Stop looking over your shoulder.

Chasidic Why did God give us two eyes? One eye is for observing our neighbor's virtues, and the other for detecting our own failings.

Michel de Montaigne To say less of yourself than is true is stupidity, not modesty. To pay yourself less than you are worth is cowardice and pusillanimity, according to Aristotle. . . . To say more of yourself than is true is not always presumption; it too is often stupidity. To be immoderately pleased with what you are, to fall therefore into an undiscerning self-love, is in my opinion the substance of this vice.

The Rabbi of Kobrin said: However high your position, never think you got there because of your greatness. If a king chose to hang his crown on a wooden peg in the wall, would the peg boast that the king chose it for its beauty?

Chasidic

⁘

Friday

I sometimes think I know better than those who came before me, and perhaps I do, once in a while. Help me, though, to keep in mind that others will come after me, and they, too, will think they know better than those who came before them. They, too, will be right, sometimes.

In the Creation Story we are told that humankind was created last, and it was for the following reason: if we become arrogant, we are reminded that the gnat was created before us.

Talmud

One would suppose that intelligent human beings living on this wandering island in the sky, on the outskirts of a universe where the nearest fixed star is millions of light-years away, would in the nature of things be humble when they try to formulate the truth about life as they see it.

Harry Emerson Fosdick

Surgeons must be very careful
When they take the knife!
Underneath their fine incisions
stirs the culprit,— Life!

Emily Dickinson

The pride that is proud of its lack of pride is the most intolerable of all.

Marcus Aurelius

⁘

Shabbat

It is said: *Yet You made us little lower than the angels.* If ever I feel like that, it must be when I am at peace on Shabbat. So teach me to find my Shabbat. Don't let me imagine, however, that *little lower* is not lower, yet help me realize that little lower is not always a lot lower. My prayer is to see and feel the middle ground solid under my feet.

Talmud Rabbi Joseph said: One should ever learn from the wise ways of the Creator. For the Holy One ignored all the high mountains and hills, and settled the Divine Presence on Mount Sinai [to reveal the Torah], and ignored all the goodly trees, and settled the Divine Presence on the [lowly] thornbush.

Chasidic The Gerer Rebbe asked a young man if he had learned Torah. He answered: Just a little. The Rebbe then said: That is all anyone has ever learned of the Torah.

Midrash The Holy One said to Israel: What do I seek of you? All I ask is that you love one another, and honor one another, and respect one another, and that there be found in you neither transgression nor theft nor anything ugly, so that you do not become tainted. As it is said: . . . *walk humbly with your God* (Micah 6:8). Read it this way: *Walk humbly, and your God will be with you.*

∴ *Terms and Abbreviations*

Avot de Rabbi Natan. An early commentary and expansion upon *Pirké Avot*. Many readings cited as "Period of Mishnah" are from this work.

B.C.E. Before the Common Era.

C.E. Common Era.

Chasidic. A tale or teaching from the literature of Chasidism (also spelled Hasidism), the religious/spiritual movement in Judaism that arose in Eastern Europe during the eighteenth century.

cs. Chaim Stern, editor and compiler of *Day by Day*.

Dhammapada, The. Buddhist Sacred Texts.

Forms of Prayer. The prayer book of the Reform Synagogues of Great Britain, whose full title is *Forms of Prayer for Jewish Worship*, ed. Assembly of Rabbis of the Reform Synagogues of Great Britain, 1977.

Gates of Prayer. The prayer book of the Reform Movement in North America, ed. Chaim Stern.

Gates of Repentance. The prayer book of the Reform Movement in North America for the Days of Awe, ed. Chaim Stern.

Liberal Jewish Prayer Book. Formerly *The Prayerbook of the Union of Liberal and Progressive Synagogues*, London, ed. Israel I. Mattuck; (see *Siddur Lev Chadash*).

Midrash. A vast collection of ethical, legendary, linguistic, and legal comments on the biblical text, referred to as "Midrash" (uppercase); a single comment from the collection is referred to as "a midrash" (lowercase).

Mishnah. The law-code compiled at the end of the second century C.E. by Rabbi Judah the Prince. *Pirké Avot* was subsequently added.

Period of Mishnah. Roughly, the first two to three centuries of the Common Era. Here used mainly to refer to *Avot de Rabbi Natan* (see above), or to the Tosefta, a compilation from this period that was excluded from the Mishnah (see above), but which is often quoted in the Talmud.

On the Doorposts of Your House, the New Union Home Prayerbook. The prayer book of the Reform Movement in North America for the home, ed. Chaim Stern. Contains many readings and meditations found here.

Pirké Avot. A tractate of the Mishnah dating from 250 C.E. and containing selected teachings of individual sages on a variety of subjects.

Proverbs. When it appears without modification, this refers to the biblical Book of Proverbs.

Psalm. From the biblical Book of Psalms.

Siddur Lev Chadash. The prayer book of the Union of Liberal and Progressive Synagogues, London, ed. John D. Rayner and Chaim Stern. It replaced *Service of the Heart*, also ed. John D. Rayner and Chaim Stern.

Sidra. The portion of the Torah assigned to be read for a particular week.

Sufi. A religious movement in Islam. Like Chasidism and Zen, one of its distinguishing characteristics is the "teaching story."

Talmud. The immense body of law and lore using the Mishnah as a starting point and compiled some centuries later. There are two "Talmudim": the Babylonian Talmud is the better known of the two; the other is called the Jerusalem or Palestinian Talmud.

Tao/cs. The *Tao Te Ching*, of Lao-Tzu (sixth to fifth century B.C.E.), in a free version by Chaim Stern.

Upanishad. Sacred texts of Hinduism.

∴ Further Reading

I have always enjoyed reading "Commonplace Books," collections of tales, and anthologies. Here is a very small sampling of books, some of whose contents have inspired me; you may find them helpful for additional readings and meditations.

J. Donald Adams. *The Treasure Chest.* E. P. Dutton & Co., 1946.

Mortimer J. Adler and Charles Van Doren. *Great Treasury of Western Thought.* R. R. Bowker Company, 1977.

W. H. Auden. *A Certain World: A Commonplace Book.* The Viking Press, 1970.

W. H. Auden and Louis Kronenberger. *The Faber Book of Aphorisms.* Faber and Faber, 1962.

Joseph L. Baron. *A Treasury of Jewish Quotations.* Crown Publishers, 1956.

Lewis Browne. *The Wisdom of Israel: An Anthology. Modern Library,* 1945.

Martin Buber. *Tales of the Hasidim* (2 vols.), trans. Olga Marx. Schocken Books, 1947, 1975.

———. *Ten Rungs: Hasidic Sayings,* trans. Olga Marx. Schocken Books, 1962.

Charles P. Curtis. *A Commonplace Book.* Simon and Schuster, 1957.

Charles P. Curtis and Ferris Greenslet. *The Practical Cogitator.* Houghton Mifflin Company, 1953.

Nahum N. Glatzer. *The Judaic Tradition: Jewish Writings from Antiquity to the Modern Age.* Beacon Press, 1968.

Victor Gollancz. *A Year of Grace.* Penguin Books, 1950, 1955.

Elizabeth Goudge. *A Book of Faith.* Coward, McCann & Geoghegan, 1976.

Sidney Greenberg. *A Treasury of Comfort.* Crown Publishers, 1954.

———. *A Treasury of Modern Jewish Thoughts.* Thomas Yoseloff, 1960.

———. *A Treasury of the Art of Living.* Hartmore House, 1963.

John Gross, ed., *The Oxford Book of Aphorisms.* Oxford University Press, 1983.

Dag Hammarskjöld. *Markings.* Trans. Leif Sjöberg and W. H. Auden. Faber and Faber, 1964.

Joseph H. Hertz. *A Book of Jewish Thoughts*. Oxford University Press, 1921.

Halford E. Luccock and Frances Brentano. *The Questing Spirit*. Coward-McCann, 1947.

Bernard Mandelbaum. *Choose Life*. Random House, 1968.

Michel de Montaigne. *Essays*. Trans. Donald M. Frame. Stanford University Press, 1948, 1957.

Claude G. Montefiore and Herbert Loewe, *A Rabbinic Anthology*. Schocken Books, 1974 (1938).

Louis I. Newman and Samuel Spitz. *The Hasidic Anthology: Tales and Teachings of the Hasidim*. Bloch Publishing Company, 1944.

———. *The Talmudic Anthology*. Behrman House, 1947.

———. *Maggidim & Hasidim: Their Wisdom*. Bloch Publishing Company, 1962.

Blaise Pascal. *Pensées*. Trans. W. F. Trotter. Modern Library, 1941.

Bernard S. Raskas. *Living Thoughts*. Hartmore House, 1976.

François de La Rochefoucauld. *The Maxims*. Trans. Louis Kronenberger. Stackpole Sons, 1936.

George Seldes, comp. *The Great Quotations*. Lyle Stuart, 1960.

Chaim Stern, *Gates of Prayer: The New Union Prayerbook*. Central Conference of American Rabbis, 1975.

———. *On the Doorposts of Your House*. Central Conference of American Rabbis, 1994.

———. *Pirké Avot: Wisdom of the Jewish Sages*. KTAV Publishing House, 1997.

Isidore Twersky, ed. *A Maimonides Reader*. Behrman House, 1972.

Carl Hermann Voss, ed. *The Universal God*. Beacon Press, 1953.

∴ Credits

Grateful acknowledgment is made for pemission to reprint the following previously published material:

Ruth F. Brin: "Discovery" from *Harvest: Collected Poems and Prayers* by Ruth F. Brin (Reconstructionist Press, 1986). Reprinted by permission of Ruth F. Brin.

Carcanet Press Ltd.: "I saw how rows of white raindrops. . . ." by Andrew Young from *Selected Poems*. Reprinted by permission of Carcanet Press Ltd., Manchester, U.K.

Irving Greenberg: Excerpt from "Cloud of Smoke, Pillar of Fire: Judaism, Christianity and Modernity after the Holocaust" by Irving Greenberg. First published in *Auschwitz: Beginning a New Era?* (Ktav, 1977). Reprinted by permission of Irving (Yitzchak) Greenberg.

Harcourt Brace & Company, Inc.: "What the Bird Said Early in the Year" from *Poems* by C. S. Lewis, edited by Walter Hooper. Copyright © 1964 by the Executors of the Estate of C. S. Lewis and renewed by C. S. Lewis Pte. Ltd. and Walter Hooper. Reprinted by permission of Harcourt Brace & Company and in the U.K. by HarperCollins Publishers.

Henry Holt and Company, Inc.: "The Secret Sits" from *The Poetry of Robert Frost* edited by Edward Connery Lathem. Copyright 1942 by Robert Frost, copyright 1970 by Lesley Frost Ballantine, copyright 1969 by Henry Holt and Company, Inc. Reprinted by permission of Henry Holt and Company, Inc.

James Kirkup: "There Is a New Morning" and "On Not Understanding, Which Is Zen" from *Collected Shorter Poems* and *Collected Longer Poems* by James Kirkup (University of Salzburg Press). Reprinted by permission of James Kirkup.

Alfred A. Knopf, Inc.: "Sonnet vi" by Robert Nathan from *A Winter Tide*. Copyright 1940 and renewed 1968 by Robert Nathan. Reprinted by permission of Alfred A. Knopf, Inc., a division of Random House. "Let No Charitable Hope" by Elinor Wylie from *Collected Poems*. Copyright 1932 by Alfred A. Knopf, Inc. and renewed 1960 by Edwina C. Rubenstein. Reprinted by permission of the publisher.

EDNA ST. VINCENT MILLAY SOCIETY: "What lips my lips have kissed" by Edna St. Vincent Millay from *Collected Poems* (HarperCollins). Copyright © 1923, 1951 by Edna St. Vincent Millay and Norma Millay Ellis. All rights reserved. Reprinted by permission of Elizabeth Barnett, literary executor.

NEW DIRECTIONS: "The Thread" (excerpt) by Denise Levertov from *Poems 1960–1967*, copyright © 1966 by Denise Levertov. Reprinted by permission of New Directions Publishing Corporation. "Variation on a Theme by Rilke (The Book of Hours, Book 1, Poem 1, Stanza 1)" by Denise Levertov from *Breathing the Water*. Copyright © 1987 by Denise Levertov. Reprinted by permission of New Directions Publishing Corporation. Published by Bloodaxe Books in the U. K. and reprinted by permission of Laurence Pollinger Ltd.

GRACE PALEY: Preface to *The Shalom Seders* (Adama Books, 1984). Reprinted by permission of Grace Paley.

RANDOM HOUSE, INC.: "I think continually of those who were truly great" by Stephen Spender from *Selected Poems*. Copyright 1934 and renewed 1962 by Stephen Spender. Reprinted by permission of Random House, Inc., and in the U.K. by Faber & Faber Ltd.

SCHOCKEN BOOKS, INC.: Excerpts from *Tales of the Hasidim: The Early Masters* and *Tales of the Hasidim: The Later Masters* (2 vols.) by Martin Buber, trans. Olga Marx. Copyright © 1947, 1948 and renewed 1975 by Schocken Books, Inc. Reprinted by permission of Schocken Books, distributed by Pantheon Books, a division of Random House, Inc.

SCRIBNER: Excerpts from the following poems by William Butler Yeats: "When You Are Old," "Adam's Curse," and "Among School Children" from *The Collected Works of W. B. Yeats, Volume I: The Poems*, revised and edited by Richard J. Finneran. Copyright © 1928 by Macmillan Publishing Company; copyright renewed © 1956 by Georgie Yeats. Reprinted by permission of Scribner, a Division of Simon & Schuster and in the U.K. by A. P. Watt Ltd. on behalf of Michael Yeats.

DANNY SIEGEL: "Psalm 17" from *The Lord Is a Whisper at Midnight: Psalms and Prayers* by Danny Siegel (Town House Press, Pittsboro, N.C., 1985). Copyright © 1985 by Danny Siegel. Reprinted by permission of Danny Siegel.

STAINER AND BELL LTD.: "My Believing Bones" from *The Two-Way Clock* by Sydney Carter. Copyright © 1971 by Stainer & Bell Ltd., London, England. Reprinted by permission of Stainer & Bell Ltd.

THROUGH THE FLOWER ART PUBLICATIONS: "Merger Poem" by Judy Chicago. Copyright © 1979 by Judy Chicago. Reprinted by permission of Through the Flower Art Publications.

∴ Index of Names

IN HONOR OF THE SPECIAL BIRTHDAY OF
BETTY GAINSLEY
FROM
BARBARA & LLOYD SIGEL